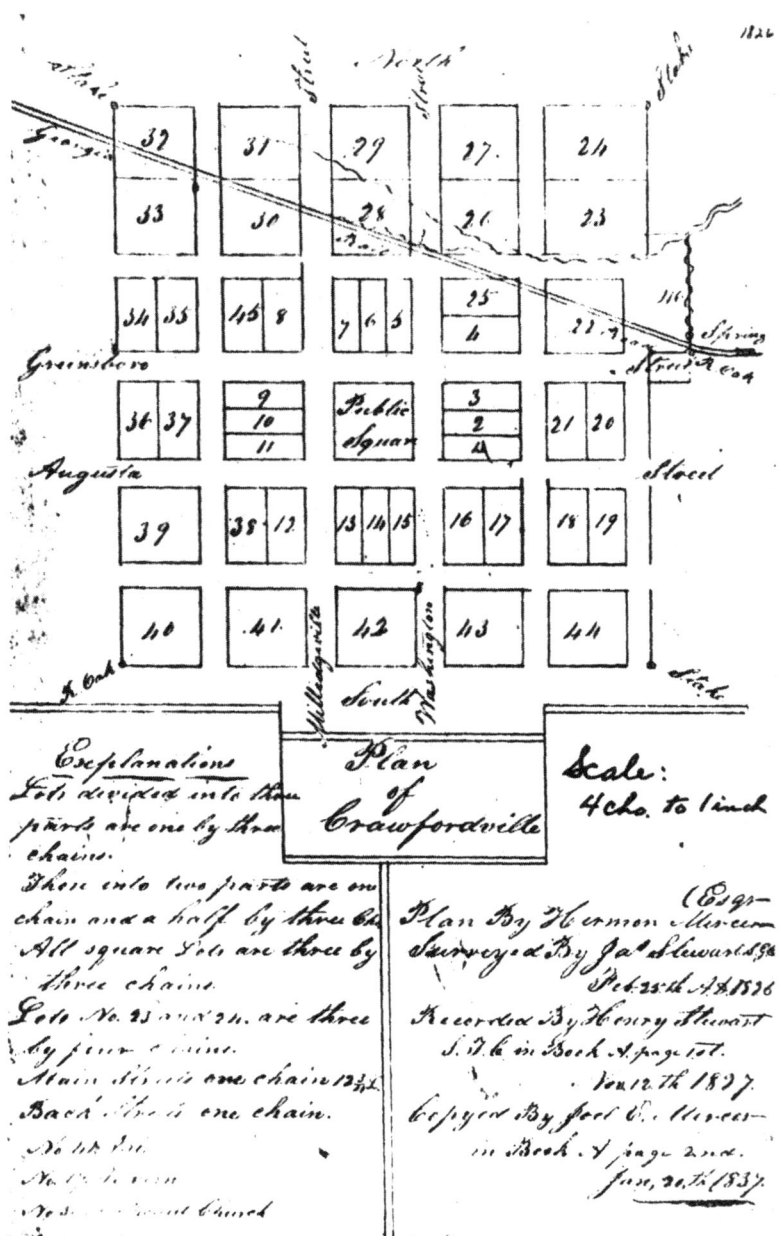

CRAWFORDVILLE, TALIAFERRO COUNTY, GEORGIA.
Founded 1826. Plan by Hermon Mercer; survey by James Stewart. "New Purchase" of 1773.

THE FIRST ONE HUNDRED YEARS OF TOWN PLANNING IN GEORGIA

By

Joan Niles Sears

ATLANTA
CHEROKEE PUBLISHING COMPANY

Sears, Joan Niles.
  The first one hundred years of town planning in Georgia / by Joan Niles Sears. — Atlanta : Cherokee Pub. Co., 1979.
    xiii, 220 p. : ill. ; 24 cm.
    Based on the author's thesis, Emory University, 1977.
    Bibliography: p. 196-208.
    Includes index.
    ISBN 0-87797-046-7

  1. Cities and towns—Georgia—History—18th century. 2. City planning—Georgia—History—18th century. I. Title.
  HT123.5.G4S4   309.2'62'09758   78-74091
                                                    MARC

  Library of Congress   79[7909]

All rights reserved. No part of this work may be reproduced or transmitted in any form, by any means, electronic or mechanical, including photocopying and recording, or by any storage or retrieval system, excepting brief quotes used in connection with reviews, without the permission in writing from the publisher.

This book is printed on acid-free paper which conforms to the American National Standard Z39.48-1984 *Permanence of Paper for Printed Library Materials*. Paper that conforms to this standard's requirements for pH, alkaline reserve and freedom from groundwood is anticipated to last several hundred years without significant deterioration under normal library use and storage conditions.

Manufactured in the United States of America

ISBN: 978-0-87797-046-0 Hardcover
ISBN: 978-0-87797-367-6 Paper

Copyright 1979 by Joan Niles Sears

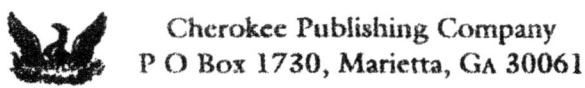

Cherokee Publishing Company
P O Box 1730, Marietta, GA 30061

Whoever is a lover of mankind will join his wishes to the success of a design so plainly calculated for their good: undertaken and conducted with so much disinterestedness . . .

"Reasons for the Establishment
of the Colony of Georgia."
London 1733

Table of Contents

	Page
LIST OF ILLUSTRATIONS	vii
INTRODUCTION	xi

CHAPTER

		Page
I.	THE LAND AND ITS HISTORY	1
II.	TOWN TYPOLOGY IN GEORGIA	11
III.	TOWN PLANNING IN COLONIAL GEORGIA, 1733–1776	33
IV.	COURTHOUSE TOWNS IN THE HEADRIGHT REGION 1777–1802	55
V.	COURTHOUSE TOWNS IN THE LOTTERY LAND	94
VI.	FIVE TOWNS PLANNED BY THE STATE	157
VII.	A VALUABLE LEGACY	184
NOTES ON THE ILLUSTRATIONS		188
BIBLIOGRAPHY		196
INDEX		209

List of Illustrations

Notes on the illustrations begin on page 188

Figure		Page
Frontispiece	Plan of Crawfordville, Georgia 1826	v
1	Map of Georgia Rivers	3
2	Map of Indian Cessions	5
3	Treaty and Lottery Dates	9
4	"Washington" Plan	15
5	"Augusta" Plan	17
6	"Sparta" Plan	18
7	"Savannah" Plan	19
8	Contour Map of Monticello, 1972	20
9	Contour Map of Sparta, 1972	21
10	Contour Map of Dublin, 1972	22
11	Contour Map of Cuthbert, 1972	23
12	Plan of Petersburg, 1965	25
13	Plan of Indian Springs, *ca.* 1827	26
14	Plan of Athens, *ca.* 1825	28
15	Plan of Oxford, 1827	30
16	Map of Towns in Colonial Georgia	33
17	Plan of Savannah, 1757	37
18	Plan of Savannah, 1818	39
19	Plan of New Ebenezer, Georgia	40
20	Plan of Darien, 1767	42
21	Plan of Darien, 1806	43
22	Plan of Hardwick, 1794	45
23	Plan of Brunswick, 1829	48
24	Plan of Wrightsborough, 1807	49
25	Map of Georgia Courthouse Towns Before 1790	58
26	Plan of Washington, 1805	59
27	Plan of Waynesborough, 1857	61
28	Plan of Greensborough, 1812	63

Figure		Page
29	Plan of St. Marys, 1788	64
30	Map of Courthouse Towns After 1790	66
31	Plan of Elberton, 1791	68
32	Plan of Warrenton, 1974	69
33	Plan of Lexington, 1897	73
34	Plan of Sandersville, 1974	74
35	Plan of Sparta, 1960	76
36	Plan of Lincolnton, 1854	78
37	Map of Courthouse Towns After 1790	80
38	Plan of Statesborough, 1806	82
39	Plan of Springfield, 1821	84
40	Plan of Riceborough, 1796	86
41	Plan of Mount Vernon, ca. 1813	87
42	Plan of Williamsburg, 1793	88
43	Map of 1802-1805 Indian Cessions and Courthouse Towns	94
44	Map of Madison, ca. 1809	100
45	Plan of Dublin, ca. 1735	102
46	Plan of Marion, 1814	103
47	Map of 1817-1818 and 1819 Indian Cessions and Courthouse Towns	105
48	Plan of Gainesville, 1820	110
49	Plan of Clarkesville, ca. 1970	112
50	Map of 1821 Indian Cession and Courthouse Towns	113
51	Plan of Decatur, 1866	119
52	Plan of Forsyth, 1955	120
53	Plan of Perry, 1925	122
54	Map 1826 Indian Cession and Courthouse Towns	123
55	Plan of Talbotton, 1828	127
56	Plan of LaGrange, 1860	128
57	Plan of Greenville, 1828	129
58	Plan of Carrollton, 1971	130
59	Plan of Americus, 1869	132
60	Plan of Cuthbert, 1962	133
61	Map of 1814 Indian Cession and Courthouse Towns	134
62	Plan of Bainbridge, ca. 1974	137
63	Plan of Newton, 1832	138
64	Plan of Blakely, 1906	139
65	Plan of Irwinville, ca. 1845	140
66	Map of 1835 Indian Cession and Courthouse Towns	141
67	Plan of Dahlonega, 1832	147
68	Plan of Rome, 1864	149
69	Plan of Rome, 1890	150

Figure		Page
70	Plan of Marietta, 1911	152
71	Map of Towns Planned by the State	158
72	Plan of Augusta, 1783	163
73	Plan of Augusta, 1937	164
74	Plan of Louisville, 1938	167
75	Plan of Milledgeville, 1808	169
76	Plan of Macon, 1828	173
77	Plan of Macon, 1831	174
78	View of Macon, 1855	176
79	Plan of Columbus, 1830	179

Introduction

The time span which I have covered begins with the founding of the colony in 1733 and ends when Georgia finally obtained control over all the lands within her borders in 1835. After Independence and until 1835, the state was in her greatest town-founding period as Indian cession after Indian cession had to be organized into counties, with each county requiring a courthouse town as the local government center. The period ended just before the railroads were built and before Atlanta was founded.

My view of the colonial, courthouse and state town plans is basically two-dimensional. When a third dimension was considered it was usually that of the topography and not the architecture. Relatively few pre-1835 buildings are left. Most existing courthouses, usually the main building in a town, were not constructed until the late nineteenth century. There was little tradition in the county seats for fine commercial buildings, and few had been built by the end of the period which I have covered. A number of handsome Greek Revival houses remain and date from these early years. When their location made an important impact on the town plan, they have usually been mentioned.

I have visited all of the Georgia colonial, courthouse and state-planned towns which were in existence in 1835. I have also visited the sites, when they could be found, of towns which today no longer exist. My travels and search of long-lost town plats were certainly the most entertaining part of producing this work. The greatest loss of old maps resulted from fires which destroyed courthouses and county records, although frequently these early maps simply disappeared. Some plats thought to be lost probably still exist, forgotten, in one of the dozens of deed books in which each county keeps its records. When no early map was available I made a sketch of the town from visual survey or I used a plan published by the state highway department or local chamber of commerce.

Some county clerks' offices, where the older town plats were usually to be found, were well organized and the early plans instantly available with copying machines standing ready to enlarge, reduce or simply copy whatever I needed. Not infrequently, however, the courthouse had no copying facilities. I soon learned never to set out without pencils, tracing paper and triangles, and a number of illustrations used here are the result of tracings made from county deed books. My Ph.D. thesis from which this book developed contains illustrations of every town which is mentioned, but it has seemed desirable to eliminate some of them prior to publication.

Most southern historians and town planners are distressingly mum on the subject of town planning in Georgia. Among the few dealing with it are John W. Reps, who discusses in *The Making of Urban America* several Georgia colonial towns and land-use patterns. E. Merton Coulter, in *Old Petersburg and the Broad River Valley* and in *Auraria, The Story of a Georgia Gold Mining Town*, as well as in various articles, tells the history of particular towns but his interest does not lie in their plans. James C. Bonner in *The Georgia Story* includes a map of Milledgeville but writes little concerning it. There are other sources, but only Milton S. Heath in *Constructive Liberalism, the Role of the State in the Economic Development in Georgia* devotes any real thought to the philosophy behind the history of Georgia's town planning. Local histories may include a map or a few legislative acts pertaining to the county seat, but these have to be ferreted out and put together rather like a jigsaw puzzle. From time to time someone has taken the trouble to list all legislative acts concerning a town. These works tend to be found in typescript in the local library's vertical file. I found one such typescript in the excellent Hall County Library and others done under the WPA in the University of Georgia library and the Georgia State Archives. The most extensive and useful information is to be found in the acts of the colonial government and the General Assembly concerning colony and state lands and towns. These are published in the *Colonial Records of the State of Georgia* and in the well-indexed compilations, digests and acts and resolutions of the General Assembly.

My thanks and appreciation are expressed to Professor James Rabun of Emory University for his unfailing encouragement over what became an inordinately long period of time. Professor John W. Reps of Cornell University has offered helpful suggestions and patiently read certain chapters in various unfinished states. The staffs of the Georgia Collections at the University of Georgia Library, the Special Collections at Emory University Library, the Georgia Department of Archives and History and the Georgia Surveyor General's office have been most generous with their time and knowledge. I am also indebted to Virginia Cobey who painstaking helped in the preparation of the manuscript and to Miss Anna Lane who did the final typing with unusual care.

Joan Niles Sears

Ithaca, New York
October 3, 1978

THE FIRST ONE HUNDRED YEARS OF TOWN PLANNING IN GEORGIA

Chapter I
The Land and Its History

Physical Geography

Towns in an agricultural society depend strongly for their success on the geology of the surrounding regions. In Georgia the fertility of the soil was as important to the history of town planning as any other single factor.

The state can be divided into fairly well-defined geological groups. The Coastal Plain includes more than half the state and is bounded by the Fall Line, the Chattahoochee and Savannah rivers, Florida and the Atlantic Ocean. Originally this plain was covered by ocean and the Fall Line, delineating the coast of a past geological age, is marked by river rapids and water falls and by a change in topography from the flat Coastal Plain to the rolling Piedmont. The Tidewater part of the Coastal Plain was the birthplace of the Georgia colony. The coast of this low-lying, often swampy country, is broken by four major rivers which form wide deltas at their mouths. The region proved valuable for rice and indigo culture and as a source of naval stores. It was also to prove excellent for growing the superior long-staple cotton. The Tidewater was, however, swampy, malarial and prone to flooding. It was not always everything that the colonists had hoped it would be. The Pine Barren-Wire Grass regions characterized the south-eastern section of the Coastal Plain. The Pine Barrens were considered worthless until the end of the nineteenth century when lumber companies discovered their rich potential. The Wire Grass region was used for cattle range, mainly by North Carolinians who settled there in the early nineteenth century. These two regions were the most sparsely inhabited in the state. The counties were large and the courthouse towns few and far between. Descriptions by the few travelers who ventured there tell of endless pine forests, little water, non-existent roads and sparse settlement. Nearer the Fall Line were the Sand Hills and the more fertile Red Hills. Certain parts of the southwest Coastal Plain proved to be some of the richest land in the state, if also the most isolated. Indians occupying the regions to the north were effective in keeping immigration into the southwest to a minimum until the middle 1820s. Many Virginians and Georgians from the coast then settled there and it became, in the decades before the Civil War, a region of large and profitable cotton plantations.

Above the Fall Line and north approximately to the Chattahoochee River was the Piedmont, the second main geological division. Here was the most consistently fertile land, the largest population concentrations, and the greatest prosperity. After Independence the eastern part of the Piedmont was settled by Virginians and Carolinians. In that era tobacco, grains and livestock were the main products of this region. The farms were small and owned by yeoman farmers. By 1830, however, all of the Piedmont to the Chattahoochee had come under the aegis of the state, and a monoculture of cotton had taken over. The farms had become plantations, the people richer and the slaves more numerous.

In North Georgia, the third main geological division, the Appalachian mountain chain enters Georgia as the Blue Ridge in the east and as the Cumberland Mountains in the west. Because of navigable rivers and wide valleys the western half of North Georgia was the more prosperous and became an important trade route for produce from the Ohio Valley.

The main Georgia rivers (*Fig. 1*) which flow southeast into the Atlantic are the Savannah and Ogeechee, the Oconee and Ocmulgee which join to form the Altamaha, and the St. Marys at the Florida border. Flowing into the Gulf of Mexico is the Appalachicola, which is formed by the confluence of the Flint and the Chattahoochee south of Bainbridge. With the exception of the main seaport—Savannah—it was along the Fall Line of these rivers that the important towns were located: Augusta, Milledgeville, Macon and Columbus. The Savannah and Chattahooche rivers proved the most valuable for transportation to the sea and for industry at their falls. The Ogeechee, Oconee, Ocmulgee and Flint were used primarily to float cotton barges to the ocean ports. In western North Georgia the city of Rome was located at the confluence of the navigable Oostanaula and Etowah rivers, which flow from there into Alabama. They were extensively used by Rome for transportation of produce and for water power.

Fig. 1. GEORGIA RIVER SYSTEMS.

Georgia was unusual among the states in having widely varying topography, soils, climates and river systems. The location and siting of towns were as dependent on these naturel features as their prosperity would be after founding.

Land Acquisitions

Georgia, now the largest state east of the Mississippi, at the end of the Revolution had control of about one quarter of what would become her territory; the Creek and Cherokee Indians occupied the rest. The state's land consisted of a strip along the coast from St. Marys in the south to the northern boundary of the "New Purchase" (or Wilkes County, as it would become after 1777). At the beginning of Independence Georgia was the only original state faced with the problem of having some three-fourths of its areas occupied by Indians.

The British had acquired the colony's land in three treaties. It was on the first small grant, made by the Creek Indians in 1733, that the colony was founded. Thirty years later additional land was ceded by the Creeks to the north and south of the original grant. The last cession made under the Crown was the "New Purchase" which gave the colony the most productive land she had so far acquired. (*Fig. 2*)

The state's fight to gain control over her questioned territory was one of the main activities of the legislature from 1783 until 1835. After 1789 the federal government became the sole authority over Indian affairs, and it was to this authority that Georgia had to turn for the removal of the Indians. Until Indian land was ceded to the state, no settlers were allowed beyond the state's then-recognized boundaries. The first cession after statehood consisted of a large area containing land in both the Piedmont and the Coastal Plain. Georgia was always just a little ahead of true legality in occupying a cession. In the 1780s many whites had moved into the area west of the Ogeechee after a series of meetings between state representatives and Creeks. These Indians apparently did not

TOWN PLANNING IN GEORGIA

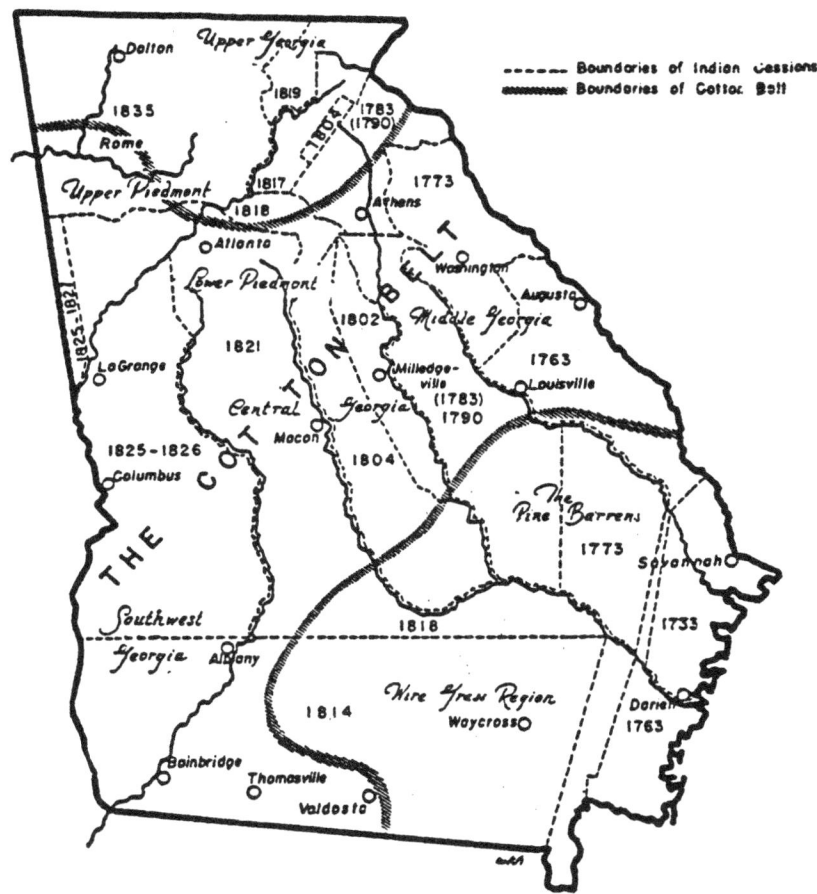

Fig. 2. INDIAN CESSIONS.

represent a majority, and after the state had laid out the counties of Washington, Greene and Franklin and founded Greensborough, the town was promptly burned in an Indian raid. The 1790 Treaty of New York, made by the federal government, gave Georgia approximately the same land she herself had already negotiated, but it satisfied the Indians. Thereafter, these frontier counties became safer for the many settlers waiting to take up land.

Treaties in 1802, 1804 and 1805 extended the state's land to the Ocmulgee River. This area included some of the fertile Piedmont, and was settled in remarkably short time. No more land was acquired by Georgia for almost a decade. Then, after the War of 1812, indemnities forced the Creeks to cede an enormous area running across the southern part of the state. This area consisted mainly of Pine Barren-Wire Grass lands (the fertile section in the west would not be discovered until the mid-1820s), but the state did nothing to encourage settlement, nor did immigrants hurry to settle there. A series of treaties with the Cherokees in 1817, 1818 and 1819 ended with Georgia receiving approximately a third of what is known as North Georgia. This mountainous land of narrow valleys and swift rivers did little to assuage the land-hungry Georgians. In this period the legislature passed acts to have this cession, as well as the 1814 cession, surveyed and laid off into counties. Neither area was popular with immigrants, however, and both were slow to be settled.

The United States government was finally needled by the state legislators into arranging for another cession of the valuable Piedmont. In the Treaty of Indian Springs in 1821 Georgia received land which pushed her frontier west to the Flint River and which added more of the much-desired Piedmont to her area. Of all the cessions this was the most quickly settled. Immigrants moving from the eastern counties had only to cross the Flint River to be in virgin land. Poor farming practices, which wore out the land in five to ten years, was the principal reason for the eager western migration.

In the 1826 and 1827 cessions the Creeks gave up the last of their Georgia lands and the state expanded her western border to the Chattahoochee. For ten more years the Cherokees clung to their North Georgia fastness. In 1836 they, too, were dispossessed of their territory and the state finally gained control of her disputed lands.

The Public Domain

For fifty years after Independence, land was the first business of the Georgia government. Some of the legislature's problems were to define the state's boundaries, to extinguish Indian titles and to dispose of the public domain. The colonial government had also made land its first business, but then land business had been limited to the disposal of the public domain. Under the Georgia Trustees[1] fifty acres were granted settlers sent over from England at the Trustees' expense. More acreage was given those who paid their way. Large land grants were not allowed and a complicated system of land ownership was enforced. Under these rules, which had idealistically been made to aid the yeoman farmer, the colony languished. Only the intervention of the Crown kept Georgia from disappearing entirely. By the simple expedient of allowing large land grants and ownership in fee simple the Crown gave the colony a new lease on life, if not the same idealistic government.

The history of the state's public land business can be divided into two periods: the first from the Revolution until the land acts of 1803 and the second from 1803 until 1836. The difference between the two periods could not have been more absolute.

Before 1802 a method similar to that which had been used by the Crown was employed. It was called headright and allowed a maximum of 1,000 acres to the head of a family. Under this system land grants and surveys were made and registered with county officials. The decentralized policy of acquiring ownership enabled grants of many more than the legal 1,000 acres to be transferred and an extraordinary number of fraudulent land deals to be made. The manner of surveying in the headright lands aided dishonest transactions and added to the confused condition of land disposal. Any acreage not taken up could be acquired by a prospective landowner. Irregular-shaped tracts dotted the counties, leaving small areas which no one wanted and over which there was no control.

The *dénouement* came, not in the counties, although dishonest land dealings were frequent enough at that level, but at the state, national and even international level. Problems implicit to the headright method were compounded by Georgia's isolation from the rest of the country and her enormous public domain. These factors allowed state officials to sell, through various land companies, more land than the state actually had. The most famous of the land frauds was that of the Yazoo Land Company. When the bubble finally broke, the state found herself faced with numerous lawsuits and submerged far above her head in debts. Unable to handle finance on this scale, the state turned to the central government for help. With the land companies doing a booming business in the sale of mostly-mythical lands, Georgia, alone among the original states, had refused to turn over to the federal government her western lands. But now the United States was in a position to bargain. She would, in return for the western lands, pay Georgia $1,250,000, and assume the obligation of settling the claims of the land companies. Further negotiations resulted in the state boundaries being permanently located and the government declaring the Indians would be removed from the state's now-recognized land demarkation.

A political upheaval was to be expected after the degrading discovery of the state's land frauds. It is seldom that any government has made such an about-face as now took place in Georgia and which resulted in the 1803 land acts.

> The social philosophy of the new land policy was predominantly the radical liberalism of the Revolution. The essence of the latter in Georgia was that individual freedom rested upon the inalienable rights to equal access to nature's productive powers and to the full product of one's labor.[2]

In the constitution of 1798 James Jackson declared that "monopolies of the land by individuals is . . . contrary to the spirit of free government."[3] Until the last of her public domain had been brought under her control, the state's philosophy after 1803 was to be based on these principles and on the full development of the land by the small farmer.

To bring the ideals of the 1803 land acts into reality the General Assembly prescribed a new policy for disposing of the public domain. Any new land was, before habitation, to be surveyed into sections and then into land lots. These land lots were usually 202½ acres. In the less desirable areas they were 250 acres or 490 acres. After the survey a lottery was to be held for them. The eligibility of participants was carefully defined, but the terms were extremely liberal. Figure 3 gives a list of the cessions and the lotteries which followed them.

The 1803 land laws gave the General Assembly control over the organization and disposal of the public land. The legislature continued its custom of appointing commissioners or justices of the county inferior court to lay out towns. Formerly county surveyors had been locally hired but now they, too, were brought under state control. This resulted from abuses during the headright period when, for a consideration to the surveyor, it was easy for a prospective landowner to have his acreage doubled in size, but

Indian cession treaty	Ceded territory	Date of lottery
Fort Wilkinson, 1802	Trans-Oconee region; Tellassee region south of Altamaha River	1804
Flint River, 1804 and Washington, 1805	All remaining Creek lands between Oconee and Ocmulgee rivers	1806
Cherokee Agency, 1814	Wafford's Settlement in northeast Georgia	
Fort Jackson, 1814	All remaining Creek lands in south Georgia	
Cherokee Agency, 1817	Tract in northeast Georgia	
Creek Agency, 1818	Tract in north-central Georgia; tract south of Altamaha and Ocmulgee rivers	
Cherokee Agency, 1819	Tract in northeast Georgia	1820
Indian Springs, 1821	All remaining Creek lands east of Flint River	1821
Indian Springs, 1825, 1826, and 1828	All remaining Creek lands in Georgia	1827
New Echota, 1835	All remaining Cherokee lands in Georgia	1832 (gold)1832

Fig. 3. DATES OF INDIAN CESSIONS AND LAND LOTTERIES.

filed and paid for as a smaller tract. After the land acts became the law, stringent rules were set up for surveyors. They were employed only through the state and the survey of a cession was detailed by the legislature as to the length of time allowed, the size of the sections and lots, the land to be reserved for the state, how many and what persons the surveyor could have as helpers and the size of the bond which was required of him.

The purpose of the survey and the lottery was to encourage homesteading, to discourage large land holdings and to keep speculation to a minimum. It turned out to be a surprisingly successful scheme and the system was followed after each cession until 1835 when the last Indian land was turned over to the state. The influence which these two methods of land disposal, headright and lottery, had on town founding and planning are discussed in Chapters IV and V.

Notes

1. The Trustees for the Georgia colony were a group of aristocratic British philanthropists who were attempting to found a utopian colony for the deserving poor, in particular those released from debtors' prison. Chapter III contains an explanation of the beginning and early years of the colony.

2. Milton S. Heath, *Constructive Liberalsim—The Role of the State in the Economic Development in Georgia to 1860* (Cambridge, 1954), p. 158.

3. *Ibid.*, p. 142.

Chapter II
Town Typology in Georgia

Town Founding

Although colonial land policy differed drastically from the state land policy concerning town founding, throughout the period being considered the state retained a number of colonial town-founding traditions. The benevolent social philosophy of the Trustees for the Georgia Colony was never, either under the Crown or in the early decades of statehood, completely extinguished. More often than not, the liberalism which had been introduced by the Trustees was continued in the state's urban legislative acts.

The social philosophy which permeated the founding, the plan and the early laws of Savannah offered the supreme example of the Trustees' desire to produce a situation allowing healthful urban living and an equal right to property. After statehood there was the same concern for the health and welfare of town dwellers as well as increased safeguards against speculation and land inflation. In the many General Assembly acts concerning courthouse and state towns, there is evidence of the state's philosophy of an idealistic liberalism which took into account the well-being of all Georgians.

As to the practical reasons for town founding, the state's path led sometimes in the same, sometimes in different directions from those of the colony. Georgia towns were located in population centers, and after the Revolution these were in the Piedmont and not on the coast as they had been in colonial times. The state laid out towns as market centers, as the British had, but also, as the British had not, as local government centers for court trials, county business, voting and land registration. With a relatively small territory and population to control, the colonial government needed a minimum of legislation to approve and advise new towns. Authorization from the governor and his council for a land grant and approval of a town site (although the government from time to time might refuse such requests) was relatively easy to obtain. After statehood there was a manifold increase in the size and population of the state and legislation concerning new towns became more complex.

In the early years of statehood it was imperative that Georgia achieve solutions for settling and controlling her large public domain of wilderness territory. During British rule there had probably been less local self-government in Georgia than in any other colony. The all-powerful British government was centered in Savannah, while the parishes, mainly a method of land division and representation in the Council, were responsible only for keeping up the parish church and for looking after the poor. The concept of local county rule had few precedents in colonial Georgia. The state, deciding on the county unit as a method of land division and local government, took some years to perfect laws which would allow this system to function properly.

There were two main factors which encouraged the organization of new counties and the founding of county seats. One was the upstate settlers' determination to have equal representation with the Tidewater counties in the affairs of government. By securing legislation encouraging the formation of new counties, these politically liberal upstaters hoped to keep the conservative coastal population a minority in the legislature. In the 1789 state constitution, representation from the original eight counties and from the new counties was equalized and carefully spelled out. The document provided that when population growth indicated such action the General Assembly was to alter county boundaries, lay off new ones, and decide on a fair representation. The other equally important reasons for creating counties, in a state left devastated by war, were the restoration of law and order, regularizing methods for legalizing land deeds and promoting education. The legislature planned to use the newly-formed county governments to help achieve these goals.

It was necessary to organize a county seat for every county established by the state. These courthouse towns were legislated into existence by specific acts of the General Assembly. After the naming of a new county and the fixing of its boundaries, commissioners were appointed to acquire land for it. The amount of land to be acquired and the location were regulated by the legislature. Also, frequently, the size of the lots and the methods of selling them, the construction of the courthouse and jail, and the designation of lots to be reserved for public buildings were directed by the legislature. The directives were carried into effect by the appointed commissioners or justices of the Inferior Court. After the town was laid out by the commissioners or justices and the lots sold, the justices took over the county business, but the state-appointed commissioners continued to be responsible for the town and often for the local academy. The orderly growth and business of both town and academy were close to the heart of the General Assembly and it kept, through its commissioners, a close tab on the town's progress and character.

Town Typology

The colonial towns can be categorized into three types. There were the public towns:[1] Savannah, Hardwick and Brunswick, which were ports of entry with customs and other accoutrements of government; towns for ethnic or religious groups, such as Sunbury and Ebenezer; and forts and trading posts such as Augusta. All colonial towns except the forts and trading posts were modelled on Savannah, which featured broad streets and a number of open squares. The two trading towns planned by the state, Macon and Columbus, could be classed with the colonial public towns, and the three state capitals—Augusta, Louisville and Milledgeville—served the same purpose as had English Savannah. However, by far the largest type of state town, for which there was no colonial equivalent, was that of the county seat.

After Independence the county seats and the state towns were the focus of town planning in Georgia. The courthouse towns, which form the largest group, are presented here chronologically as to Indian cession, then geographically within the particular cession, and finally according to the type of plan they followed. There were four types of plans which were followed by all courthouse towns with two exceptions, Perry in Houston County and Rome in Floyd County. The four types have been labelled "Washington," "Augusta," "Sparta," and "Savannah" after the first town laid out in that particular design.[2]

The four prototypes differ in origin. The genesis of the "Washington" and "Sparta" types of courthouse plans cannot be exactly identified. It may be significant, however, that these two prototypes apply to towns settled by immigrants from Virginia and the Carolinas. Towns with a central square, the outstanding feature of the "Washington" and "Sparta" plans, were a distinctive feature of courthouse seats in Virginia and the Carolinas. Thus, it is likely that these plans were imported from these regions. The "Augusta" plan derives from a practical solution of adding a courthouse and an academy to an already-existing community, the "Savannah" plan, using only one square and of which there were only a few, seems to have been influenced by that colonial town.

With the exception of more knowledgeable handling of the siting and of the features of the particular plan, no new development occurred in these types of plans in the years covered by the present study. The only evolution to be found in town plans was a tendency to change from the public square as the central nucleus of the street grid to a linear plan featuring long, wide streets. A town layout is one of the most conservative of all designs and does not change rapidly. A particular layout symbolized a community to the inhabitants. In the wilderness, far from the civilization the settlers had known, it was important to cling to past experiences and memories.

The "Washington" type plan was first used in Washington, Wilkes County. Figure 4 shows three variations, all based on a central square designed for the courthouse. Variation "A" is the sim-

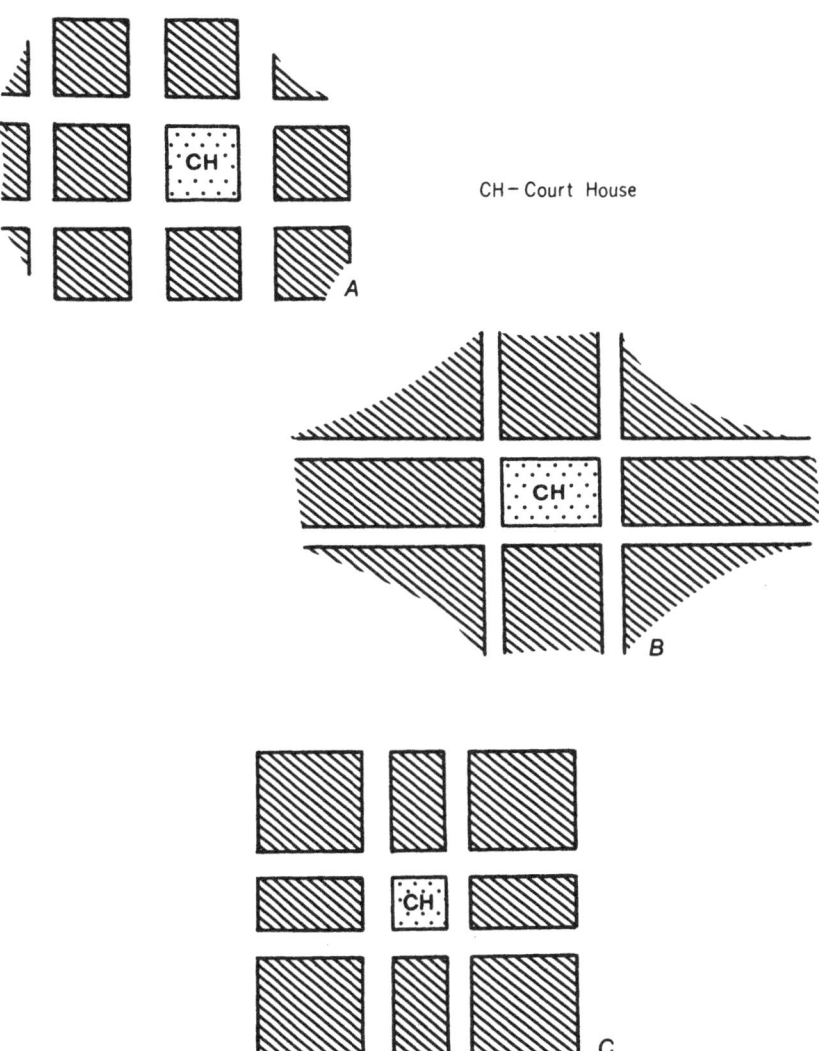

Fig. 4. SCHEMATIC DRAWING OF "WASHINGTON" TYPE PLAN.

plest, with one size for both blocks and square. Because in most towns blocks consisted of four acres, a large courthouse square resulted. Crawfordville (*Frontispiece*) is an example of the "A" variation. Washington (*Fig. 26*) followed the "B" pattern in which all blocks are of similar size except the range which contains the square. This arrangement made for an oblong but smaller square. The most complex of the "Washington"-type courthouse town plans is "C." In this plan two ranges of lots of smaller dimensions than the other town lots are laid out at right angles which form the courthouse square at their crossing. This resulted in a smaller square, shorter blocks surrounding the square, and in smaller commercial lots being laid out in this central area. Gainesville (*Fig. 51*) is a fine example of this type.

Figure 5 gives four variations of the "Augusta" plan. The plan was dependent on a wide important street, typically a hold-over from an earlier settlement. Augusta (*Fig. 76*) followed "A" variation in which the courthouse was located to face down a short street toward the main thoroughfare. In variation "B" the courthouse was placed in a corner lot in what was usually a small park. Waynesborough (*Fig. 27*) is an example of variation "B." In "C" the courthouse is placed in a lot within the block. "D" is similar but the courthouse park becomes a square of sorts surrounded on the sides and rear by narrow streets. Statesborough, Bulloch County (*Fig. 38*) is an example of "C" and Warrenton, Warren County (*Fig. 32*), an example of "D."

The "Sparta"-type plan (*Fig. 6*) usually resulted in the most interesting layout. In the "A" variation, four streets run to the center of the courthouse square rather than to the sides as in the "Washington" type. Sparta (*Fig. 35*) is the prototype for the classification and follows the "A" variation. "Sparta"-type courthouse towns in North Georgia typically used the "B" variation in which only two main streets enter the square at the center of two sides; the other streets enter at the corners of the square. Clarkesville (*Fig. 49*), and Dahlonega (*Fig. 67*), are two of the North Georgia towns following this pattern.

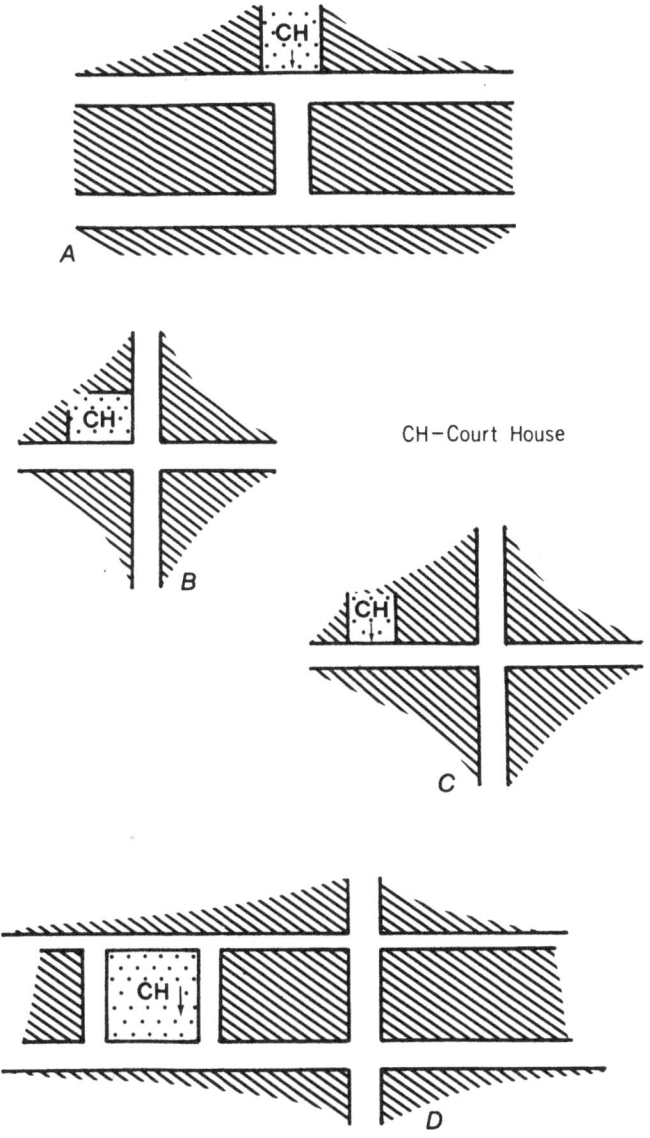

Fig. 5. SCHEMATIC DRAWING OF "AUGUSTA" TYPE PLAN.

The "Savannah"-type plan (*Fig. 7*) had either two main streets running to the center of the courthouse square and three streets on the other two sides or three streets with double blocks on all four sides. This seldom-used plan was followed in the now-vanished town of Marion in Twiggs County (*Fig. 46*) and in Marietta (*Fig. 70*).

Which type of layout was followed depended to a large extent on the location and topography of the site. If located at an existing settlement on a trading path or on an important road, the "Augusta" plan was usually laid out. If sited in flat-to-rolling topo-

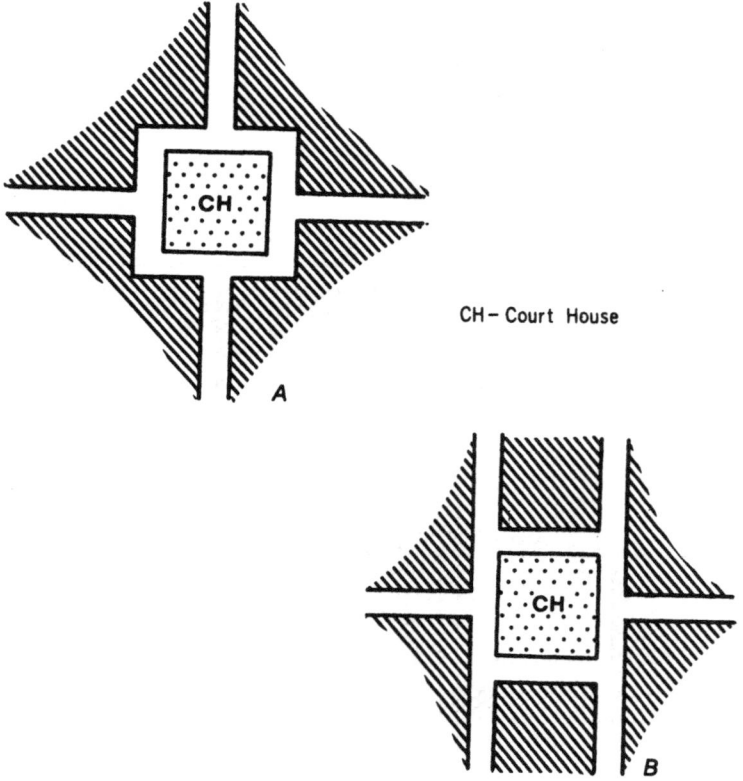

Fig. 6. SCHEMATIC DRAWING OF "SPARTA" TYPE PLAN.

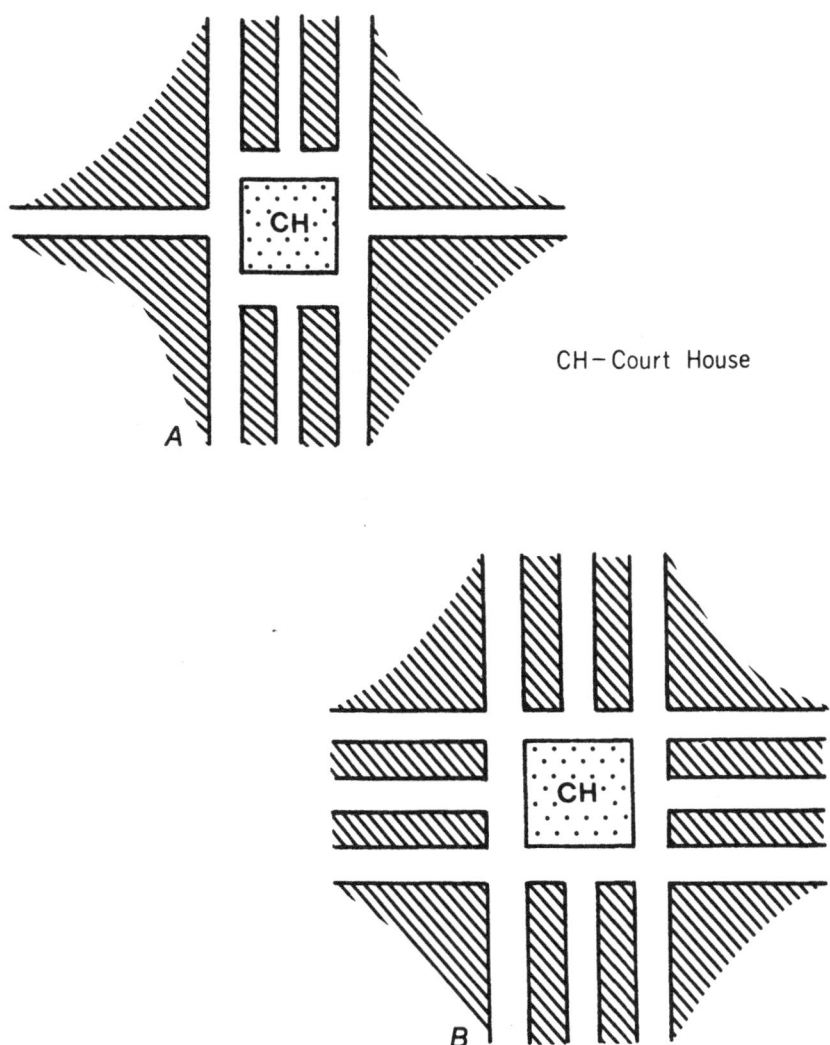

Fig. 7. SCHEMATIC DRAWING OF "SAVANNAH" TYPE PLAN.

graphy, which was typical of the Piedmont, the "Washington" plan was most often used; if in more mountainous country, the "Sparta" plan; and if in level topography, the "Savannah" plan. In all types the courthouse was, if at all possible, located on the highest eminence available in the particular locality where the town was to be laid out. Figure 8 shows the siting of the "Washington"-

Fig. 8. MONTICELLO, JASPER COUNTY, 1972.

TOWN PLANNING IN GEORGIA   21

Fig. 9. SPARTA, HANOCK COUNTY, 1972.

type plan of Monticello. The circled bench marks make clear the elevation of the courthouse square. The "Sparta"-type plan depended to a great extent on one or more steep inclines to the square. Figure 9 shows the shorter and steeper approach to central Sparta. Dublin (*Fig. 10*) follows the "Sparta"-type plan and the

Fig. 10. DUBLIN, LAURENS COUNTY, 1972.

steep approach to the square is made, rather dramatically, directly from the river. In Cuthbert (*Fig. 11*), the "Sparta" plan is also followed and the square is approached from valleys on all four sides. It is particularly in these handsome "Sparta" planned county seats that the care and knowledge of the surveyors in siting a town is most noticeable.

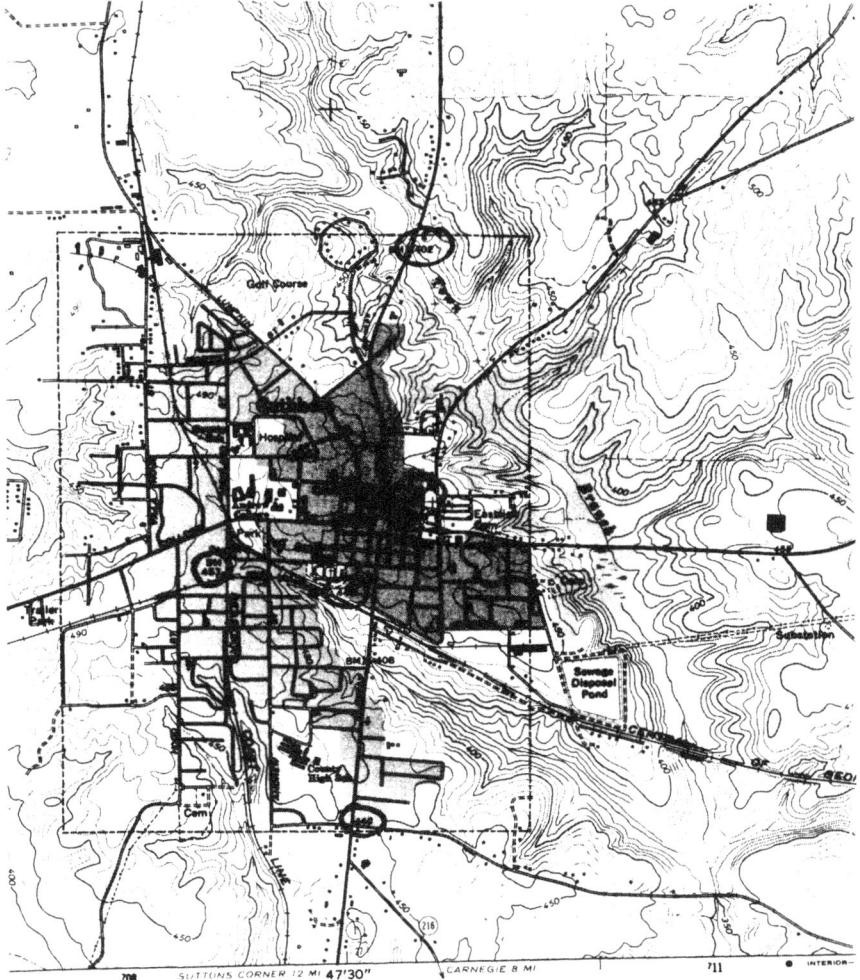

Fig. 11. CUTHBERT, RANDOLPH COUNTY, 1972.

A brief resumé of other Georgia town typology is in order to round out the picture of the state's urban settlements. Various types of small communities, besides county government centers, existed throughout the state. They had come into being because of a crossroads, a particularly suitable location on a trade route such as the presence of a good spring, at a ford on a river, or at a spot consisting of a trading post, which might serve as a sort of inn, and perhaps a few houses. A more organized plan was followed by the forts, which were constructed at a number of strategic locations throughout the Indian territory. These consisted generally of a stockade and barracks with an area outside the stockade set aside for Indians. A number of county seats and some state-planned towns were sited at or near these settlements because of their advantageous situations. A few examples are Macon and Bainbridge which were located near forts, Elberton at a settlement which had grown up around a spring, and Dublin at an important ford on the Oconee River. After the 1826 cession, commissioners appointed to site county towns were sometimes advised to designate other places in the county, the house of a well known citizen or a cross-roads settlement, where the nearby residents might vote. These satellite voting centers often grew into small communities. None of these settlements followed a formal plan.

There was little industry in agricultural Georgia. Columbus, Augusta and Rome eventually grew into industrial centers, but their industrial development in the mid-1830s was not particularly advanced. So it is no surprise that in these first decades of statehood, towns devoted solely to commerce or industry were practically nonexistent. E. Merton Coulter, in *Petersburg and the Broad River Valley*,[3] has pieced together from deeds the plan of the commercial and trading town of Petersburg (*Fig. 12*). Located on the Savannah and Broad rivers, its main reason for existence was for the storing and inspection of tobacco, the main crop in the eastern Georgia Piedmont in the late eighteenth and early nineteenth centuries. The grid plan of one-half acre lots was laid out by a developer. So long as tobacco was the main crop, the town flourished and speculation was rampant, the owners and buyers considering it a second Augusta.[4] Declining after the 1830s, however, Petersburg eventually became a ghost town. Today the site is under a lake formed by a Savannah river dam.

Of greater interest were academy, college and resort towns which sometimes were planned with the care of a courthouse seat. Resort towns began to appear in the late 1820s and became quite

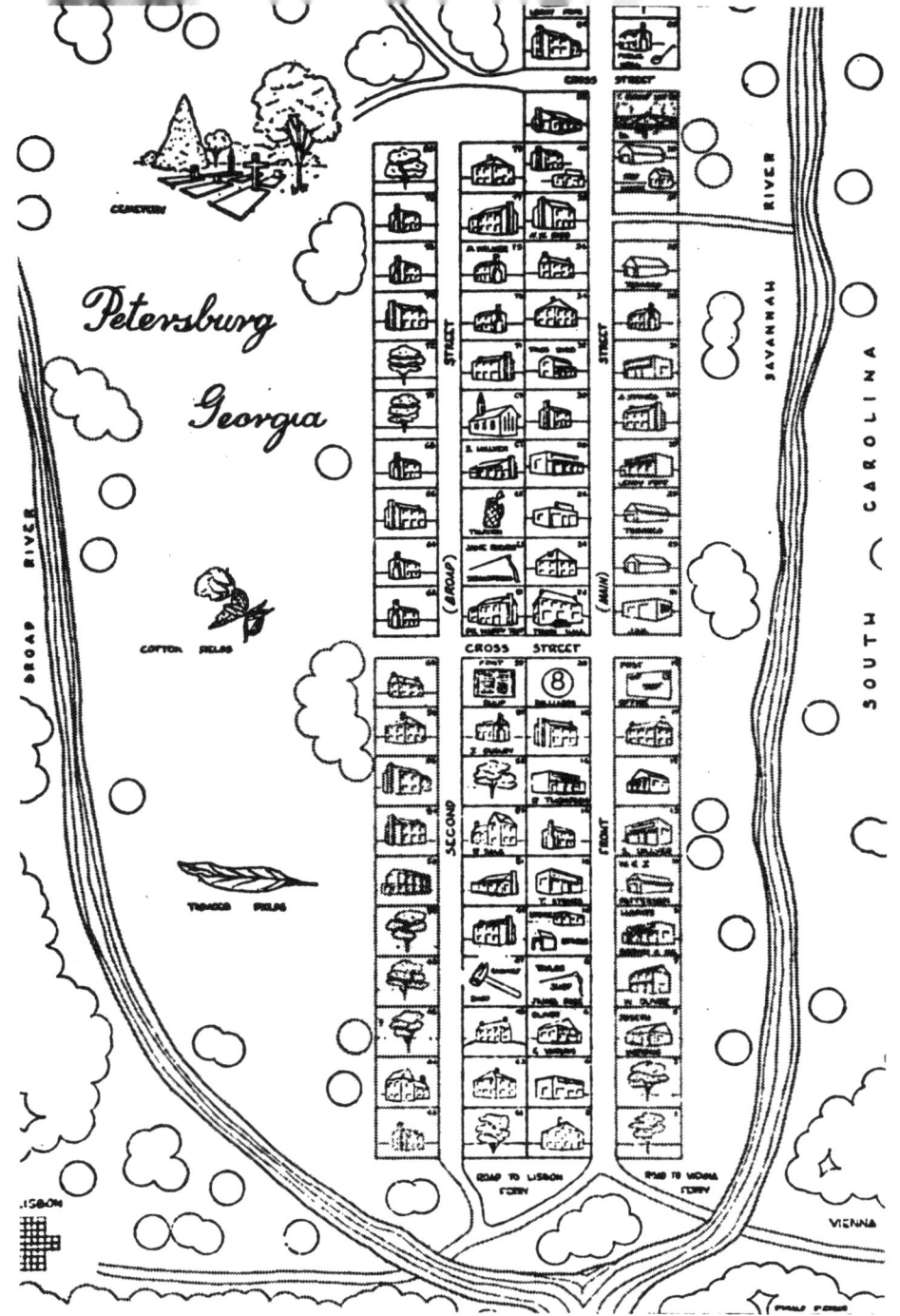

Fig. 12. **PETERSBURG, ELBERT COUNTY**
Created from deeds in the courthouse for E. Merton Coulter's *Old Petersburg and the Broad River Valley of Georgia* (1965). Used here by permission of the University of Georgia Press.

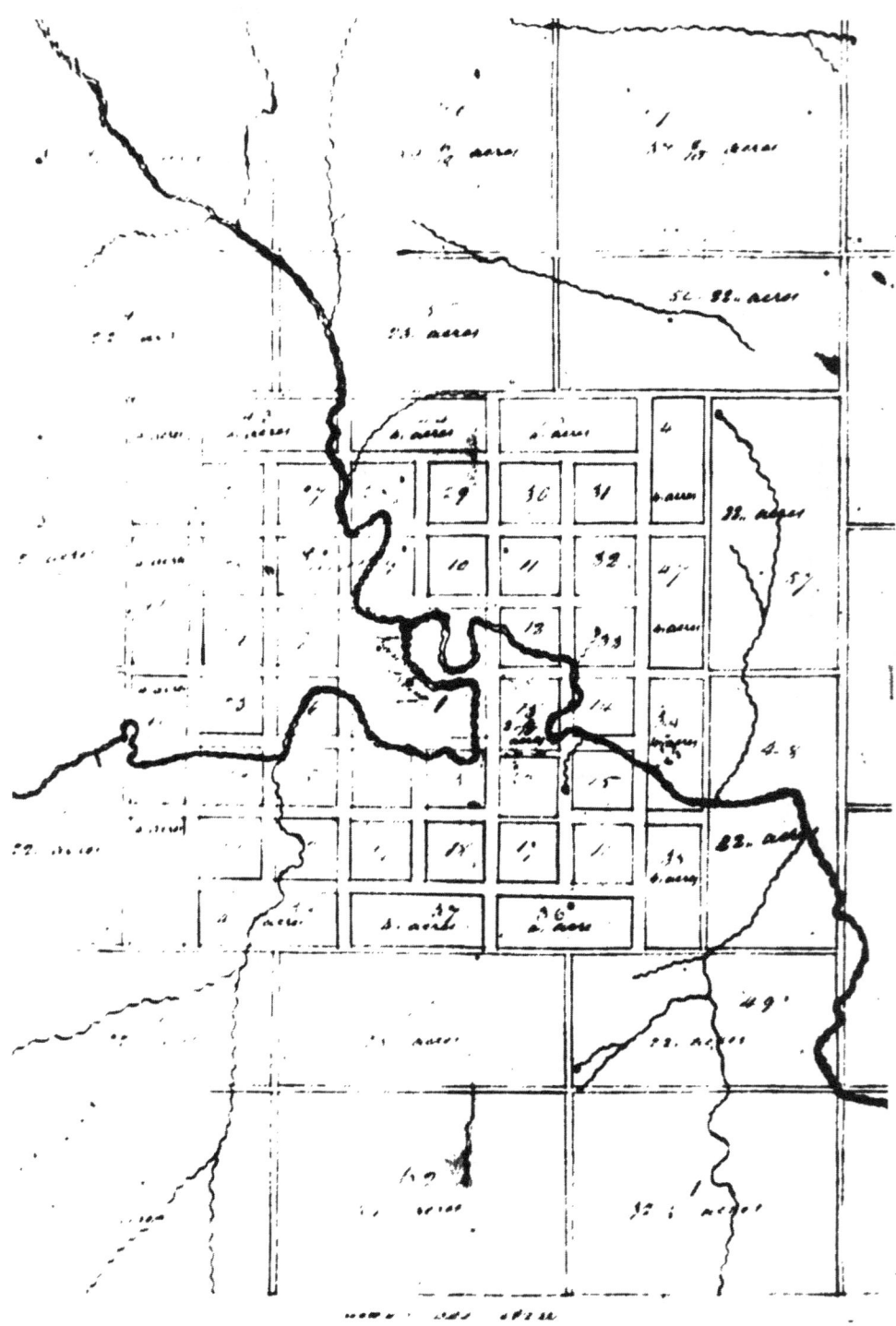

Fig. 13. INDIAN SPRINGS, BUTTS COUNTY, *circa* 1827.

numerous by 1840, particularly in North Georgia. Indian Springs (*Fig. 13*) was laid out on land reserved by the state in the 1826 cession. The General Assembly was almost as exact in its instructions for the plan of this resort as it had been for Columbus, the state-planned trading town created at the same cession.[5] The legislature directed the commissioners to center the spring (which was famous throughout the state) in a ten-acre park and to lay out two-acre lots around it. The size of the lots was to increase the further they were located from the spring and park. After the lots were laid out, the legislature ordered that they were to be sold at auction. The park and the spring are today a state park. There are only few remains left of the surrounding town.

The patterns which the college and academy towns followed were similar to each other. The procedure was for a citizen, a church, or the state to give a certain amount of land, usually between 300 and 400 acres, for a scholastic institution. This tract was then laid out into lots, with a certain acreage reserved for the school. The lots were sold and the funds thus generated were used to build the college or academy. It was the fashion in the 1830s and 1840s to isolate these educational facilities from existing communities. Incorporated into the new town laws were many clauses prohibiting alcoholic beverages, gambling, and other activities thought to be detrimental to Georgia's youth. It was felt that students would be less tempted by worldly vices in an isolated and socially-controlled atmosphere. Two examples are Franklin College (now the University of Georgia) and Mercer Institute (now Mercer University and long relocated to a new campus in Macon). Athens (*Fig. 14*), founded as the site for the state college, was laid out on a tract of 633 acres donated to the state by Governor Milledge. Thirty-seven acres were set aside for the college and the rest laid out into town and farm lots to be sold to help build the school. Penfield, near Greensborough, was founded for the new college started by the Rev. Jesse Mercer. Land had been given to the Baptist church (private education was handled almost exclusively by various religious sects), which was then laid out into a town and school on 450 acres. Again the sale of lots was expected

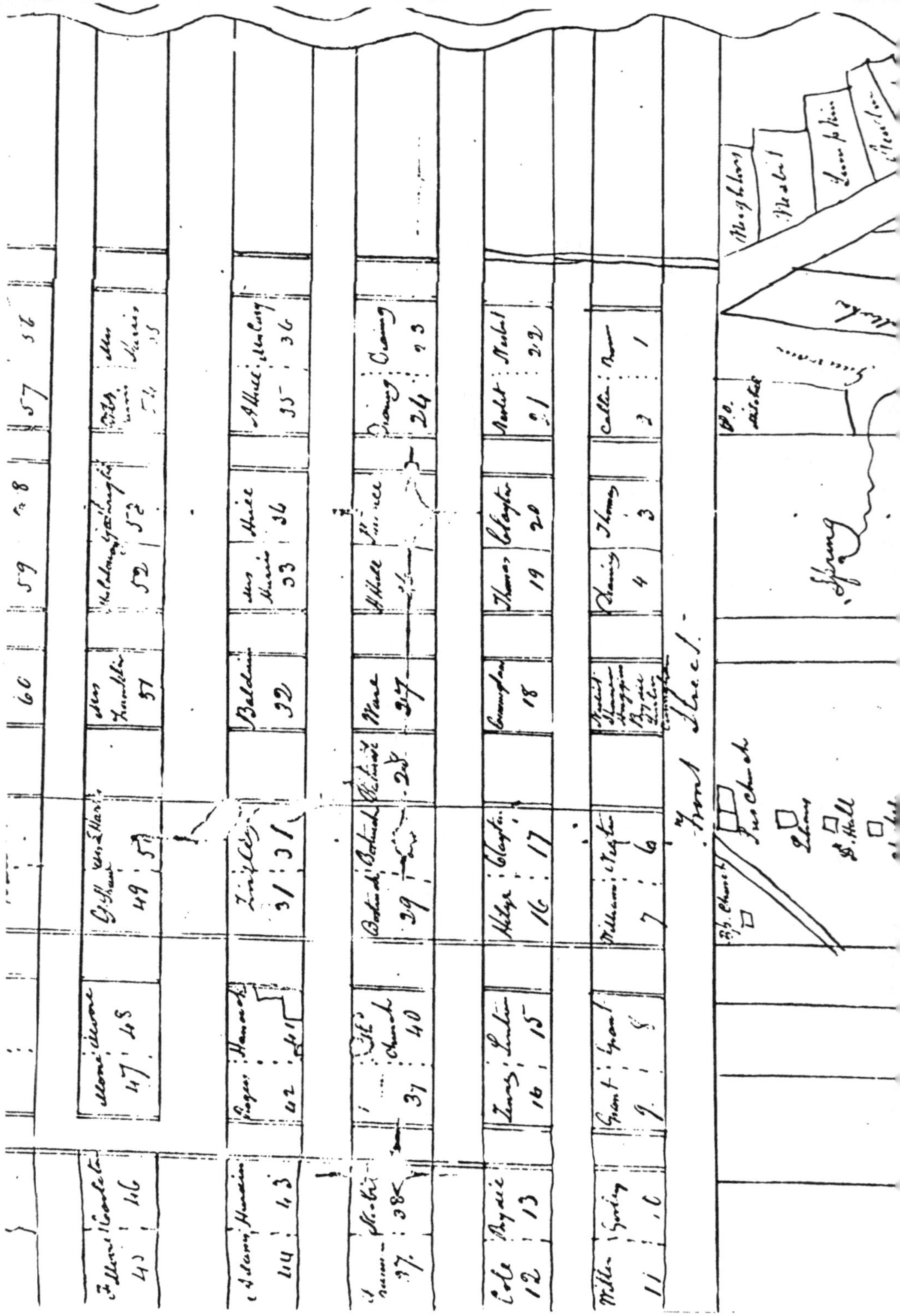

Fig. 14. ATHENS, CLARKE COUNTY, circa 1825.

to pay for the school buildings. Neither the plan of Athens nor that of Penfield is exceptional. Both were laid out in a grid of blocks containing usually one-half acre lots with the institution sited on a reserved section located always on one side of the town.

By far the most imaginative of the academy and college towns is Oxford, where Emory University was first located. In 1817 the Methodist Church bought a large tract of land near Covington and laid out a college, with a town attached, on 330 acres (*Fig. 15*). Edward Lloyd Thomas, the surveyor for the state-planned town of Columbus, was the planner for Oxford and the college. He laid out the main streets in a radiating pattern which converged on the college square.[6] Such a plan is entirely without precedent in grid-oriented Georgia. Fortunately, although the main university was later moved to Atlanta, one of its liberal arts colleges remains in Oxford, and this extraordinary plan has been kept intact.

Not only were many colleges with attached towns founded in Georgia, but also academies. The county academy, which was coeval with the organization of a county and a county town, was located at the courthouse seat and was liberally endowed by the state. An example of a private academy and town—and there were many in pre-Civil War Georgia—was Culloden in Monroe County. The lots laid out in Culloden were purchased mainly by planters from the region in search of a nearby community where their children might be educated. According to one authority, the town was brimming with cultural advantages offered by the academy and the Methodist church. It was also said that a spring was located in the public square and that the lots were laid out in blocks surrounding it. These academy towns were not noted for their longevity. The heyday of Culloden lasted about twelve years, and today only a few buildings remain of the once-thriving village.[7]

Both as a colony and as a state, Georgia saw town planning as a necessary part of her duties to her citizens. After statehood, towns were needed in the lands as they became available after each Indian cession. The state did not hesitate to found them. And excellent towns they were, with careful thought given to wide streets, parks, squares, reserved lots for churches, academies, and ceme-

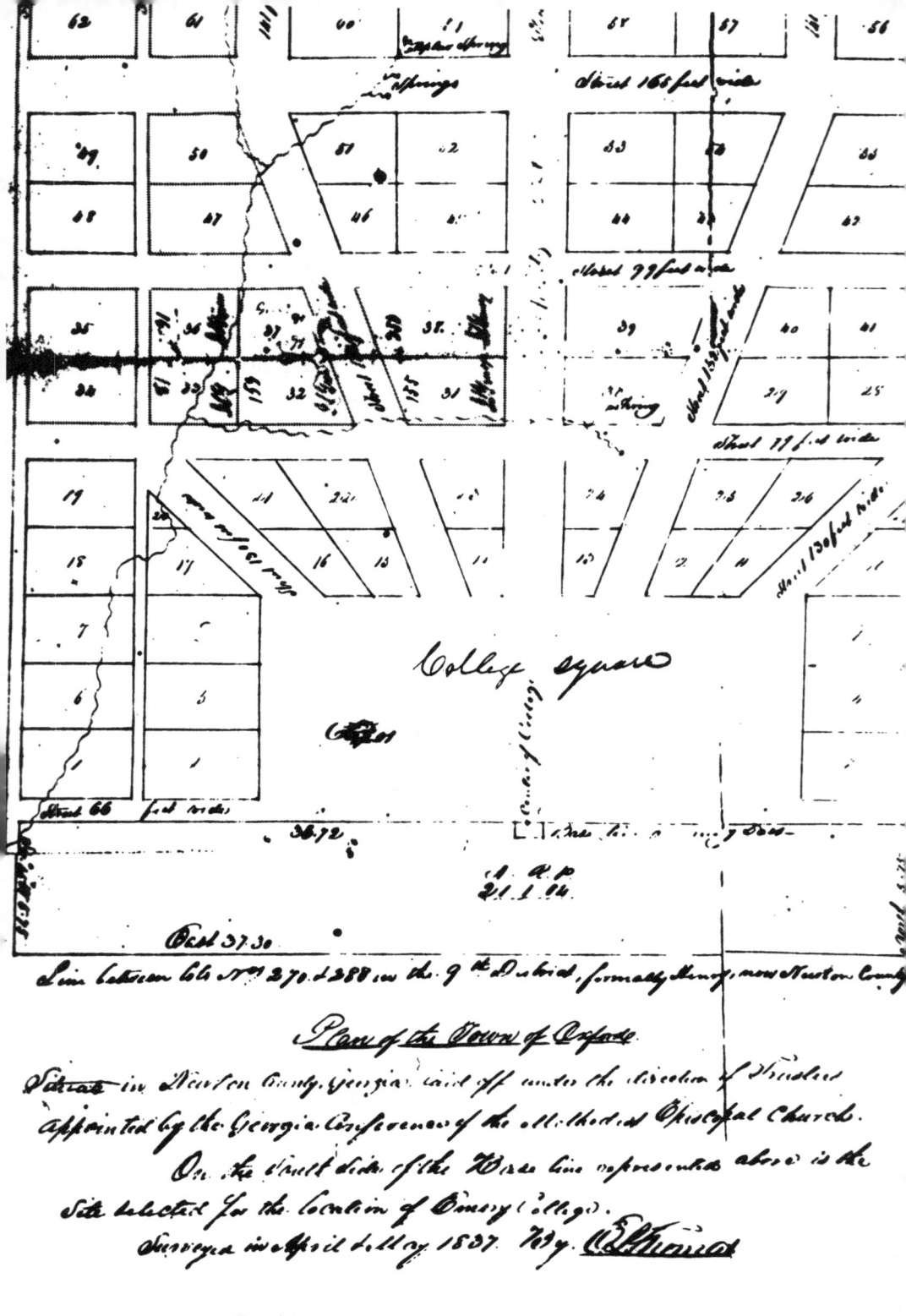

Fig. 15. OXFORD, NEWTON COUNTY, 1827.

teries, and great consideration given to choosing a healthy location. Most important of all, perhaps, was the care the General Assembly took in reducing speculation. A careful study of the town acts reveals its concern with this all-important issue. It seems safe to say that the influence of the social liberalism of the Trustees and the philosophy behind the plan of Savannah was kept alive in these first decades of statehood by the legislature's careful monitoring of the new towns.

A note of caution should be sounded concerning this perhaps overly-glowing account of Georgia towns. No matter how good the intentions of the state, commissioners or surveyors, a new Georgia town was a frontier town. And as such, and as travelers so often mentioned, it was frequently a place of violence, dirt and squalor. The state was well aware of these deficiencies and numerous acts were passed concerning the cleaning of springs, straightening of roads which had become crooked, filling holes in the streets, cleaning trash from the public square, and making other health and structural improvements. However, as civilization caught up with the frontier, a well planned town was there, available for adornment with the amenities of urban living.

Notes

1. The term "public town" was used by the British and reference to this term may be found in *The Colonial Records of the State of Georgia*. A public town, as referred to in *The Colonial Records*, meant a town planned by the government to be used by the whole colony for government, trade and shipping. From this definition Darien (during the Trust period), Ebenezer, Wrightsborough and Sunbury were not public towns. The public towns in the colony were Savannah, Hardwick and Brunswick and perhaps Darien after the Crown took control. Allen D. Candler comp. *The Colonial Records of the State of Georgia* (Atlanta, 1907). Hereafter abbreviated as C.R.G., IV, 423.

2. Edward Price in his article "The Central Courthouse Square in the American County Seat," followed a division of courthouse town typology similar to those which I have devised. (*The Geographical Review*, LVIII [1968]: 29-60.) From his article, it appears that some of the prototypes used in the present work may apply to courthouse town plans outside of Georgia.

3. E. Merton Coulter, *Old Petersburg and the Broad River Valley of Georgia* (Athens, 1965), frontispiece.

4. The reason for the state's regulations for the sale of county and state town lots is clear when the speculation of a privately developed town, such as Petersburg, is considered.

5. William C. Dawson, *A Compilation of the Laws of the State of Georgia, 1819-1829* (Milledgeville, 1831), pp. 263-264.

6. The L'Enfant plan of the national capital had been published early in the century and printed copies of the city's layout were easily available. There is little doubt that Thomas was influenced by Washington's radiating streets.

7. Compiled from Thomas M. Norwood, *The Story of Culloden, A Famous Village in Middle Georgia* (Savannah, 1909).

Chapter III
Town Planning in Colonial Georgia, 1733–1776

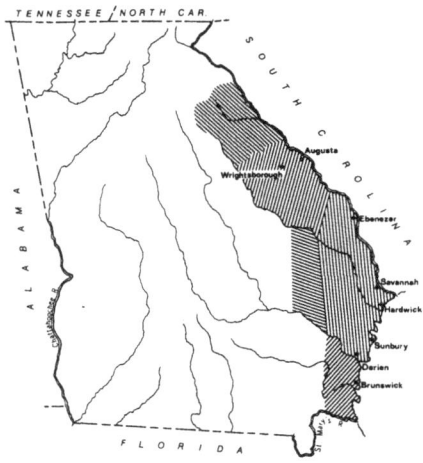

Fig. 16. TOWNS FOUNDED IN COLONIAL GEORGIA, 1733–1776.

Town Planning Under the Trustees, 1733–1752

Communities
 Savannah
 Ebenezer
 Darien

The romanticised idealism of the eighteenth century found one outlet in utopian communities located or planned to be located in North America. Among others, Sir Robert Montgomery's visionary scheme, the Margravate of Azilia, was to be located between the Savannah and Altamaha rivers. Jean Pierre Purry intended to bring Europeans to South Carolina to engage in the pursuit of that mythical panacea, the culture of silk. Christian Priber had plans for a "Kingdom of Paradise" among the Cherokee Indians. The Georgia Trustees infused their colony with this same breed of idealism. The elaborate utopian plans for Georgia differed, however, from the others in that they were actually carried out; they resembled the others in that they ultimately failed. Their plans resulted, nonetheless, in the founding of Georgia.

General James Oglethorpe had headed Parliament's investigation of English prisons and the publicity given to the horrifying condition he described inspired some philanthropists, with Oglethorpe at the head, to form a committee to found a colony for imprisoned debtors. The commitee was drawn mainly from Oglethorpe's prison inquiry group. After some months of negotiation with the Crown they were given a trusteeship and land south of Charleston for a colony, to be called Georgia, consisting mainly of deserving debtors.

If the Trustees' plans for the Georgia colony fulfilled the idealistic leanings of the aristocracy, the Crown's interest in the colony as a military and trading base fulfilled the practical needs of England. Florida was in possession of Spain and the area between South Carolina and Florida was a no-man's land—a prize waiting to be seized by the most industrious. With a colony located on the Savannah river, England could hope to check the Spaniards in Florida. An extra toehold in North America also meant for England increased trading with the Indians and an important new source of scarce naval stores. The plan and site of the first town in Georgia, Savannah, were influenced by these factors and by the idealistic tenets of the Trustees and their representative in the colony, General James Oglethorpe.

Town planning under the twenty-year Trust period was limited to those towns founded and apparently planned by Oglethorpe. Five main communities were laid out under his direction:[1] Savannah, Ebenezer, Darien, Frederica and Augusta (*Fig. 16*). Frederica was a garrison and fort and Augusta a garrison and trading post. As it was a fort and not a town, Frederica's plans will not be considered in this work. Augusta's plan will be described in a later chapter.[2] There are numerous theories concerning the sources of the unusual plan of Savannah. Gardens of ancient villas, the parterre pattern of French gardens, the new British towns in Ireland, and even the city of Peking have been suggested as possible influences. Certainly the eighteenth century London grid pattern interrupted by open squares was an important influence. Although it has never been conclusively proved that Oglethorpe designed Savannah, his background more than equipped him to lay out such a plan. He had served on the water board of London and knew city problems. He knew the plans of the British towns in Ireland, he had helped financially with the publication of Castell's *Villas of the Ancients*, and he had lived in France.[3]

Oglethorpe and the original settlers first landed in America at Charleston. Colonel William Bull, the Royal governor of South Carolina, accompanied the group when they sailed south in search of a location for their new settlement. It seems likely that it was Bull, an experienced surveyor, who settled on the location for Savannah. His choice of a site on a high bluff, some eighteen miles inland from the sea, on a deep-water harbor and on the main Georgia river flowing into the Atlantic was about as good as the coast of Georgia had to offer. Ebenezer and Darien, while similar in plan to Savannah, show wide divergencies from it in their siting. Ebenezer was placed in such a poor location that within a year it had to be moved. Oglethorpe's main objective at Darien was to locate a town which could serve as protection against the Spaniards. That the site was low, swampy and unhealthy seems not to have been considered. Thus it is probable that though Oglethorpe could well have planned Savannah, he did not choose the site for it.

The first and foremost of Oglethorpe's towns was Savannah, the public town of the colony. The Savannah plan which was to become the prototype of all colonial Georgia towns, both Trustee and Crown, was closely interwoven with the Trustees' utopian land-use and land-grant systems. The maximum land grant was 500 acres but for the majority of settlers, the charity immigrants, fifty acres was the maximum. Savannah was planned to give each of the town's freeholders this area of land; the town and garden lot equalled five acres, and the farm lot forty-five acres. In Oglethorpe's other main towns, Darien and Ebenezer, the same town, garden and farm lot system was followed. The Savannah town plan had a political base for its ward and tithing system. A block of ten lots divided by a narrow lane plus eight Trust lots and a large open square made up a ward from which representatives could be appointed. The design continued to be adhered to in the other Trustee and Crown towns, though many of the original reasons for these elements of the Savannah plan became lost. The specific arrangement of a nucleus of streets, square and blocks used in the Savannah ward plan, in part for governmental reasons, became in other Georgia colonial towns simply a copy of the street and block pattern with the political implications ignored. In addition to being philanthropists, Oglethorpe and the Trustees were Londoners and were influenced in their New World planning by the unsanitary conditions which resulted from overcrowding.[4] Wide streets and large open public squares featured in Savannah were a method of keeping light and air in a new community. These characteristics were copied in the other Georgia colonial towns, apparently for the same reason. In Savannah, fortifications made a compact town a necessity. The rectangular exactly-defined grid with right-angled streets and symetrically arranged squares for sheltering outsiders in case of war gave the desired containment. However, even after fortifications became unnecessary, this element of the plan was carefully followed both in Savannah and in other colonial towns. The common surrounding Savannah was planned for defense, for general use and for an experimental garden (the latter was specifically demanded by the Trustees). The common continued to be planned as a part of the other colonial towns, but came to be considered mainly as an area for lumbering, for grazing and later for expansion of the town.

A map by Surveyor General William DeBrahm (*Fig. 17*) shows the original four wards and the repeat pattern of the streets, blocks, lots and squares. It reveals that by 1757 the town had grown to six wards, the new wards repeating the original design. DeBrahm states that at this time the town was 2115 feet by 1425 feet in area; there were 240 freeholders, each with a town lot sixty feet by ninety feet; and the streets dividing the wards were seventy-five feet wide.[5] For every tithing or ten lots there was a square mile of land laid out beyond the garden lots. This area was divided

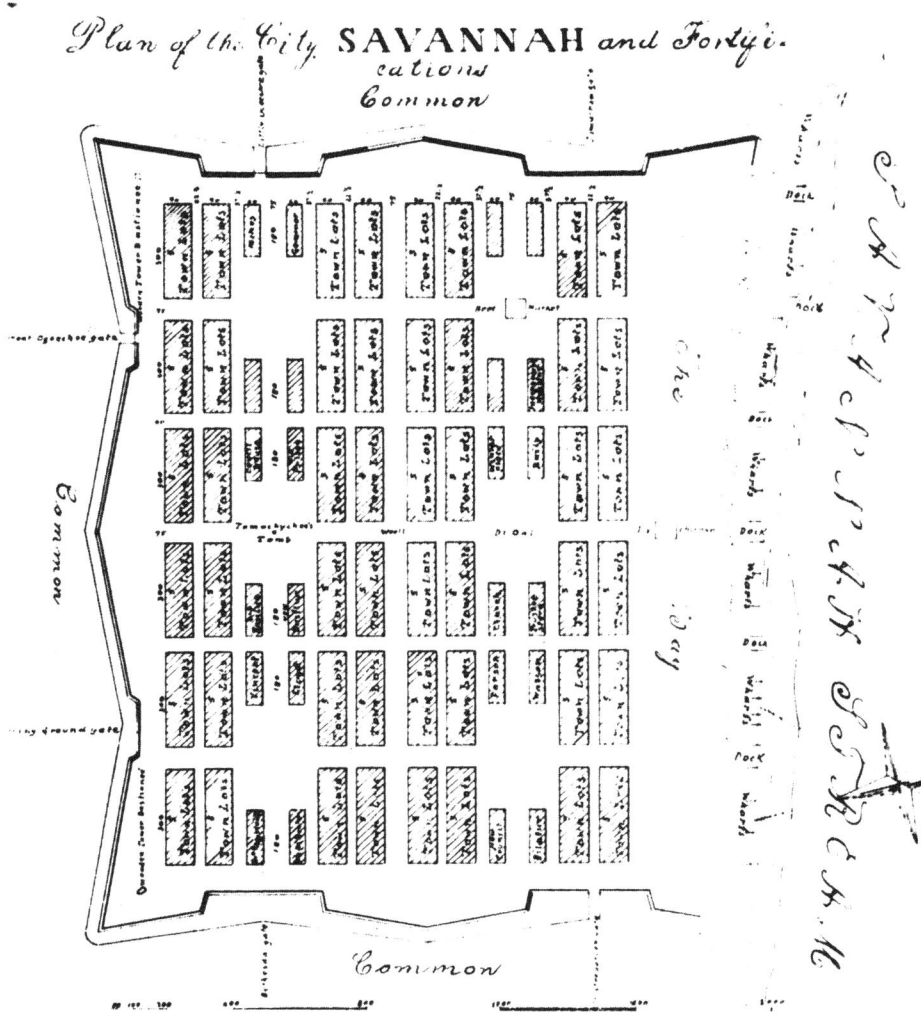

Fig. 17. SAVANNAH, CHRIST CHURCH PARISH (CHATHAM COUNTY). Founded 1733. Surveyor: General James Oglethorpe. 1733 Grant.

into twelve lots, ten for freeholders and two for the Trustees "in order to defray the charge of the public."[6] In this square mile the freeholder had his farm lot of forty-five acres, completing the fifty acres which the Trustees had decided were adequate to sustain an immigrant family.[7]

Beyond the twenty-five square miles which Savannah needed were other villages, an integral part of the Trustees' land grant system, which had farms radiating from a community nucleus. Four of these small communities constituted a ward. In time of war these communities were assigned to a Savannah ward and it was planned that their people camp in the ward's public square. Because of the complicated landowning rules imposed on the colony by the Trustees these communities were seldom successful and most died within a few years.

The 1818 map (*Fig. 18*) shows through the continued repetition of the ward system the subsequent history and success of the Savannah plan. Using the common for expansion, the town had grown to the east and west. Two wide east-west boulevards were important additions to the early nineteenth century town. After the colonial period the basic Savannah unit was seldom used in Georgia town plans; however, the Savannah type of wide boulevard with a central tree-lined park became an important element in the state-planned towns and in some county seats.[8]

For the first hundred years after its founding travelers to Savannah all agreed on certain points. One, and President Washington was particularly vociferous on this subject, was that the sandy streets made walking disagreeable or impossible and that in windy weather even houses became insufferable and full of blowing sand.[9] William Makepeace Thackeray, an inveterate traveler and lecturer, grumbled "We now arrive in the land of the unpaved." Another reaction by visitors was more favorable. The plan was unfailingly praised for being laid out in an elegant manner. Philadelphia itself, it was said, was not more perfect in its symmetry. It was noted that water pumps were conveniently placed in the center of the tree-planted squares and trees planted on each side gave shade to the wide, hot streets. The broader streets were described as being shaded by avenues of trees running down the center.[10]

TOWN PLANNING IN GEORGIA

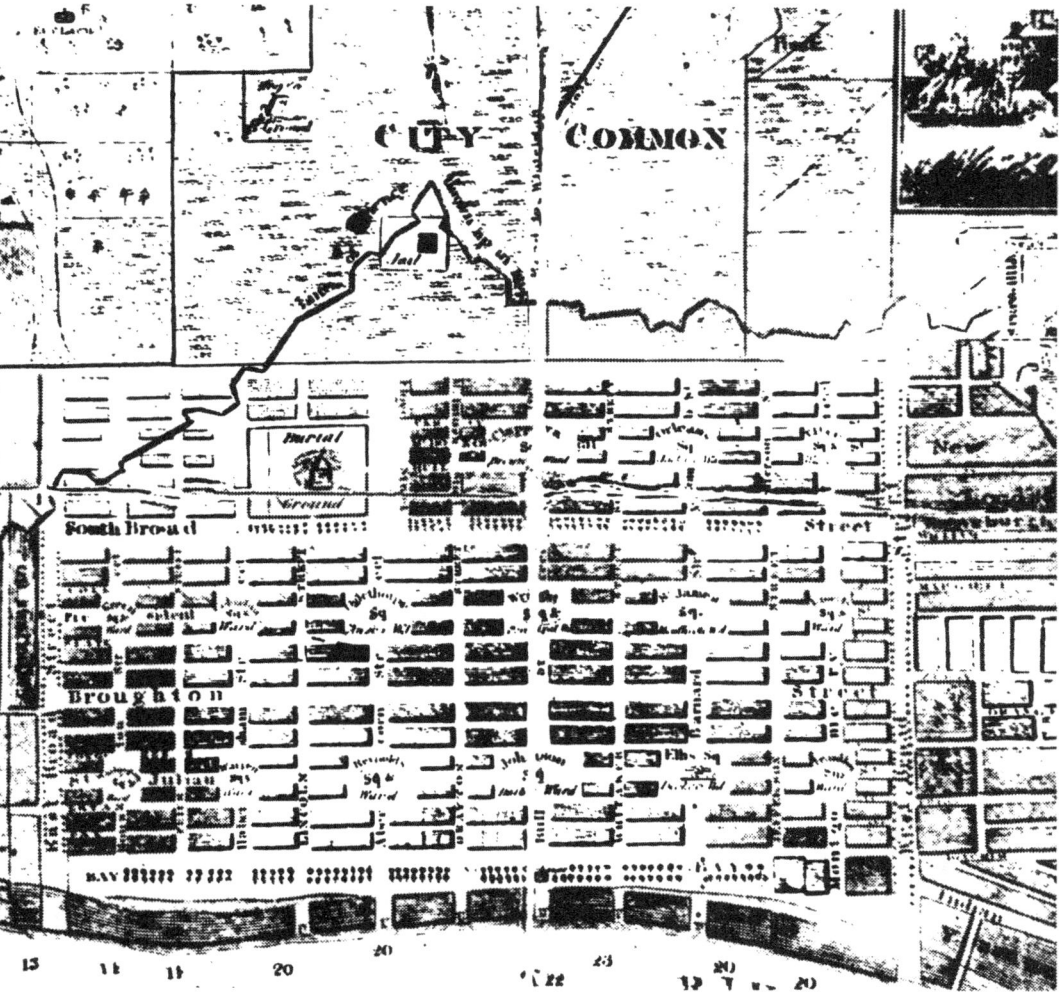

Fig. 18. SAVANNAH, CHATHAM COUNTY. 1733 grant.

Oglethorpe's two other towns, Ebenezer and Darien, follow with a few variations the Savannah plan and show an equal concern for amenities. In Ebenezer, planned for the German Salzburgers, members of a persecuted religious sect, Oglethorpe followed his Savannah scheme not only in the peculiarities of the town layout but also in the plan of garden and farm lots and com-

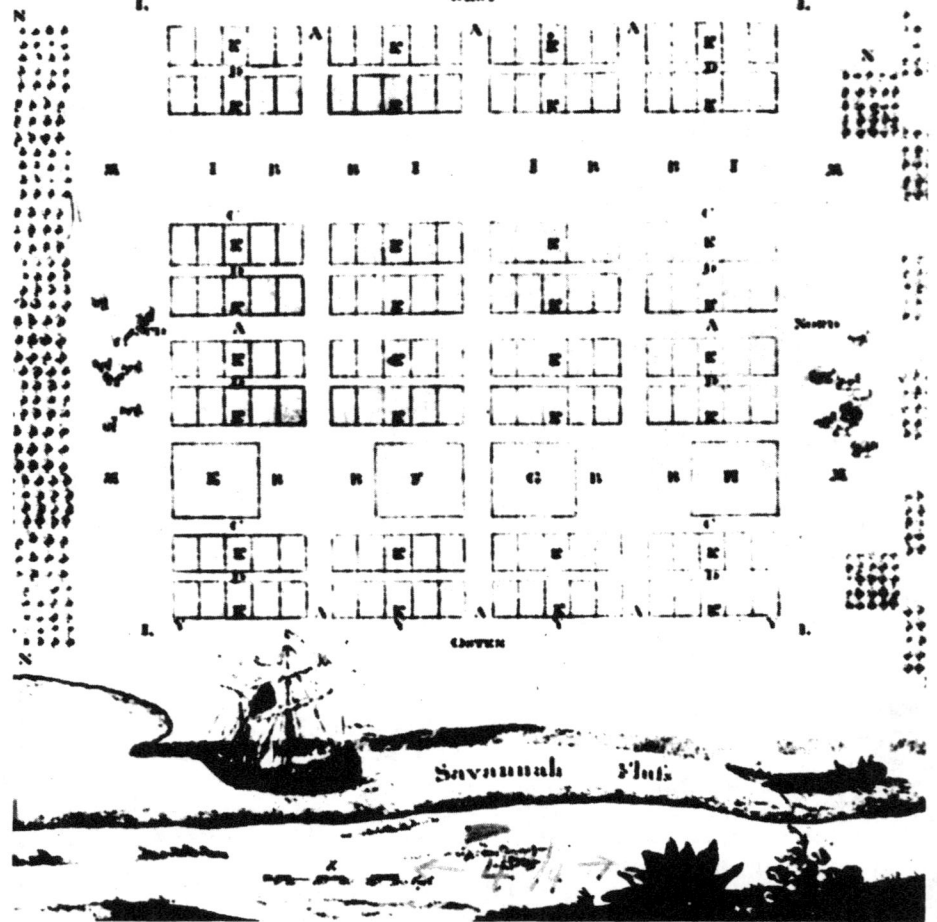

Fig. 19. NEW EBENEZER, ST. MATTHEW PARISH (EFFINGHAM COUNTY). Founded 1736. Surveyor: General James Oglethorpe. 1733 grant.

mon (*Fig. 19*). The Rev. P. A. Strobel, a Salzburger, described Ebenezer as follows:

> *The new town was laid off after the plan of the city of Savannah, and covered an area of a quarter of a mile square. This space was divided into small squares each containing ten building lots and the latter numbered one hundred and sixty. Three wide streets passed through the*

TOWN PLANNING IN GEORGIA

town from east to west, which were intersected at right angles by four others running from north to south; besides which there were a number of narrow lanes, but these extended in only one direction—north and south. Four squares were appropriated to the sale of produce, and called "market-places," and four were reserved as public parks or promenade grounds. Two-thirds of a square was appropriated to the church, parsonage, and academy, and an equal quantity to the orphan asylum and the public storehouse respectively. On the east a short distance from the town, was the cemetery. On the north and east was a large pasture for cattle, and on the south was one for sheep and goats. On the north and south, garden lots were laid out, and still farther south . . . farms were located, each farm consisting of two acres.[11]

Figure 19 does not match this description with much exactitude. Although Strobel is obviously discussing the same town, his directions and the number of streets and squares given by him do not fit the original map.

The Ebenezer plan had the same advantages as the one for Savannah: a compact layout easy to defend, wide streets for better health and air and squares for the people to use for community purposes. The Salzburgers proved to be an excellent addition to the young colony. They were good farmers and for some years produced most of the silk exported from Georgia. Ebenezer was devastated during the Revolution and never recovered. Today it is a ghost town.

Oglethorpe planned Darien (*Fig. 20*) to harbor another group: the Scots Highlanders. These stalwart yeoman settlers fulfilled the rigid idealistic requirements of the Trustees. They also answered the military ones of Oglethorpe, who was charged with defending the colony. Darien, founded in 1736, was sited at the mouth of the Altamaha River as a buffer against the Spaniards in Florida. A few years after the settlement was laid out the Battle of Bloody Marsh, fought between the British and Spaniards, decimated the male population. The town did not recover for several decades. The Crown survey of 1767 explains that the Royal governor had decided on re-founding Darien, and closer adherence to Oglethorpe's plan resulted in an enlargement of the public square. Only a single

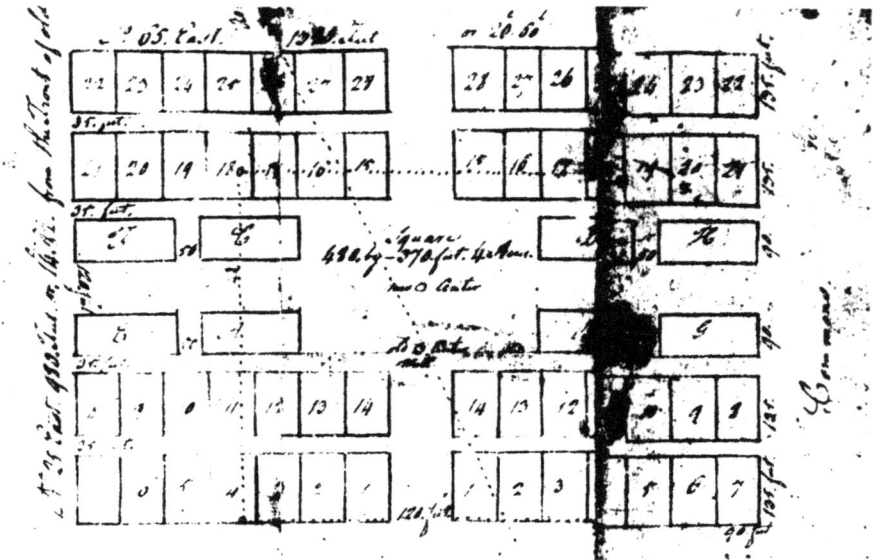

Fig. 20. DARIEN, ST. ANDREWS PARISH (LIBERTY COUNTY). Founded 1736. Surveyor: General James Oglethorpe. 1733 Grant.

unit or ward of the Savannah plan was used in the original and refounded town. Darien was again depopulated during the Revolution. Prosperity returned in the early 1800s when it became the transshipment port for plantations and towns on the Altamaha, Oconee and Ocmulgee rivers. Branches of the Bank of Darien, a relic of the town's past importance, are still to be found in Georgia towns which sent their produce down the rivers to Darien. The 1806 survey (*Fig. 21*) shows this remarkable recovery. From a single square the town had grown to four squares, all repeating Oglethorpe's original Savannah unit of square, block and public lots. Besides these additions more lots were laid out to the west. The colonial prototype was not followed here. Today, owing to the enormous live oaks, sandy streets, early nineteenth century houses and churches and also to the fact that prosperity since the Civil War has bypassed Darien, the town retains a romantic and antiquated atmosphere. Oglethorpe's eighteenth century four-square plan and the first additions to it are still clearly visible, even if bent somewhat askew by time.

TOWN PLANNING IN GEORGIA

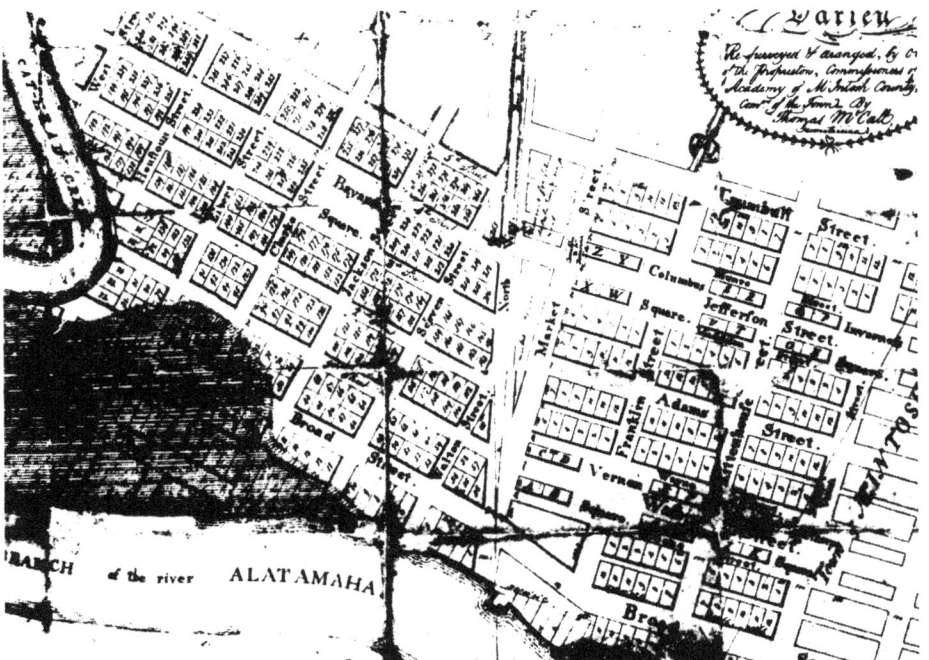

Fig. 21. 1806 SURVEY DEPICTS DARIEN'S GROWTH.

The plans of these three towns founded during the Trust period of the Georgia colony were the results of the idealistic convictions of the Trustees, of the definite ideas which Oglethorpe had concerning the proper layout of a community, and of the necessity for defense against the Spaniards. The basic plan, first tried out in Savannah, and apparently found to be highly satisfactory not only to Oglethorpe but to the Crown, would be followed with only few deviations in the new towns founded after the King took over the colony from the Trustees.

Town Planning Under the Crown, 1753–1776

Hardwick
Brunswick

Wrightsborough
Sunbury

The Trustee period ended in 1752 and the first Royal governor arrived two years later. With this change the last vestiges of an attempted utopia of happy free small farmers disappeared. Slavery and rum, originally forbidden, had become legal in the last years of the Trust regime. Now larger land grants became possible and, as might be expected, though utopian ideals languished, population and economic growth flourished. When the King took over the colony there were 3,000 whites and 2,000 slaves. At the beginning of the Revolution there were 50,000 people, one-half of whom were slaves. This growth took place mainly after 1763 when the French and Indian war ended. For England this meant the acquisition of Florida and more land for her Georgia colony.

Two Indian treaties made during the Crown period more than doubled the area of the colony. In the 1763 treaty the boundary was extended up the Savannah river as far as the Little River and down the coast to the St. Marys River. The later treaty, brought about by Governor Wright in 1773, was in payment of debts the Indians owed white traders. The acquisition extended about sixty miles beyond the Little River and a considerable distance to the west. It added some 2,000,000 acres of rich Piedmont land to the colony.

The Crown laid out two new towns in the twenty years it controlled Georgia: Hardwick in the original land grant territory and Brunswick in the southern part of the 1763 treaty lands. Hardwick was founded in 1754 after a group of landowners had petitioned His Majesty's Council in Savannah to lay out a town on the Ogeechee River on land that "from the first year the colony was settled . . . has been reserved for a public town." Various reasons were given for the need of a new town. One was that a town

> can be no other way effected unless the inhabitants will become purchasers from private hand to carry such needful work into execution . . . more than one public town will certainly be useful and necessary for the inhabitants of so extensive a province as Georgia in all probability will become.

TOWN PLANNING IN GEORGIA

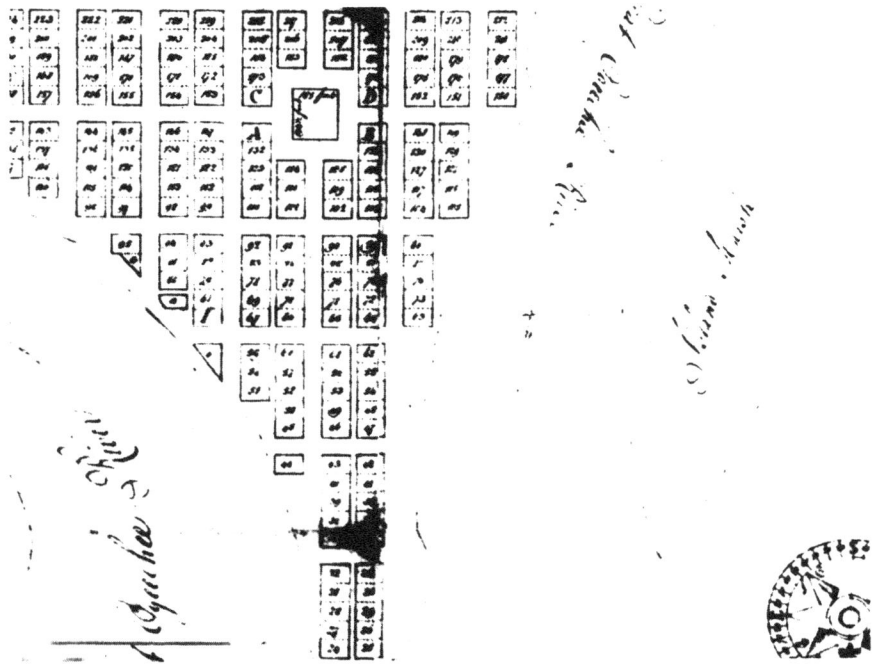

Fig. 22. HARDWICK (GEORGE TOWN), ST. PHILIP PARISH (BRYAN COUNTY). Founded 1754. Surveyor: Henry Younge. 1733 Grant.

From these petitions certain facts can be ascertained: In 1754 Savannah was considered the only public town in Georgia; and the land contemplated for the new town was on one of the tracts originally laid out for a town by the Trustees. Governor Reynolds and his Board declared "The reasons for laying out a town were justly founded." Henry Younge was ordered "to lay a plan of the said land before them [the Council], in order to receive further instructions thereon, in respect to laying out lotts etc.[12] In due course the town was laid out and named by Governor Reynolds first George Town and then Hardwick (*Fig. 22*). Reynolds, much taken with the location—mistakenly considering the Ogeechee a more important river than the Savannah—attempted several times to have the capital moved to the new town.

The plan for Hardwick used the Savannah prototype with some variations. The elaborate ward and tithing system and the fifty-acre total of town, garden and farm lot were omitted. The lack of farm and garden lots in the two Crown towns may have been due to the fact that the men who planned to live there were landowners and the fifty-acre allotment was not necessary or that this amount had been found to be inadequate. The symmetrically arranged squares, wide streets entering at the center of each side of the square, and blocks of ten lots divided by narrow lanes were all similar to those in Savannah. The public squares were not as numerous as they were in Savannah, and the town as a whole was not planned with the care of its prototype. Hardwick had six squares, 600 lots and a rather small common, less than 200 acres. The township contained 500 acres and the town 335 acres. The beginnings of speculation can be found in Hardwick. To encourage settlers, Reynolds granted to various planters, shortly after the town was laid out, 21,000 acres of land in the vicinity. This act bore all the earmarks of later methods of "booming" a town.[13] Even for a Georgia coastal town Hardwick was remarkably unsuccessful, not only during the English period but also after statehood. Following the Revolution the legislature ordered the town re-surveyed on the British plan.[14] The hoped-for resurrection did not materialize and the town continued to revert to waste land. In a last attempt in the 1830s to revive the town the surveyor was instructed to lay it out in any manner he saw fit. Even this did not revitalize the community, and the town is today non-existent.

The third public town in Georgia and the second planned under Crown rule was Brunswick. Laid out in 1771, it was the last town the British were to found in the North American colonies. The location of Brunswick in the southern part of the state may have been influenced by the British attempt to direct American colonists to the south and to the north Atlantic seaboard away from the interior where they were interfering with British-Indian trade. It is interesting to note that although Governor Wright, unlike his predecessor Reynolds, vetoed the plan to move the capital from Savannah to Hardwick, he had hopes of moving it to Brunswick.

TOWN PLANNING IN GEORGIA 47

In 1771 James Habersham, a well-to-do Savannah merchant, wrote to a friend in South Carolina concerning the sale of lots in Brunswick, "I shall put in for a town lot or two at Brunswick, and a water lot for you . . . our governor really thinks at some period that it will be the capital of this fine country."[15]

Brunswick was planned seventeen years after Hardwick, and lessons learned from the several decades of living on the Georgia coast and rivers resulted in an improved town siting. Located on a bluff above the Turtle River some miles inland from the open ocean, the site seemed to acknowledge the advantages of Savannah's similar location. The King's Council at Savannah directed the deputy surveyor, George MacIntosh, to lay out Brunswick in the same pattern as Savannah.[16] Brunswick, like the two other public towns, was planned as a major urban settlement. There were six public squares (Savannah's original plan had four, Hardwick's six), surrounded by blocks of ten lots divided by the usual narrow lanes and public lots (*Fig. 23*). The ward and tithing system and the garden and farm lots were eliminated. As in all Georgia colonial towns, the common was retained and became an important factor in the town's later development. A twin to Savannah, Brunswick was planned with far greater care than Hardwick. A liberal amount of land was set aside for the town and common: 383 acres for the town, 2,024 acres for the common and forty lots for public use. As soon as the town was laid out the Council issued exact instructions concerning the price of lots, public docking and the type of house to be built ("no less than thirty feet in length and eighteen feet in width with a good chimney"[17]).

Most of the inhabitants, being loyalists, fled the country during the Revolution and even after 1783, in spite of state efforts to bring it back to life, Brunswick remained largely deserted. In the 1830s attempts to bring a canal and railroad to Brunswick encouraged the addition of a subdivision in the common. In this new section the streets and lanes of the old town are continued with squares placed at intervals. The squares are, however, simply blocks left empty and do not interrupt the grid pattern as in the old town. The depression at the end of the decade put an end to expansion

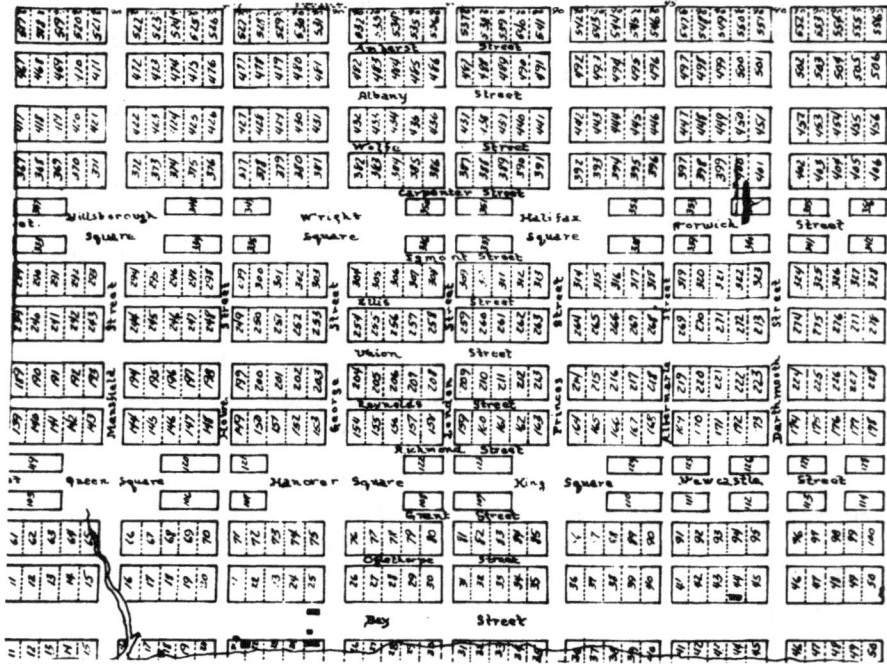

Fig. 23. BRUNSWICK, ST. DAVID PARISH (GLYNN COUNTY). Founded 1771. Surveyor: George McIntosh. 1763 Treaty.

activities and it was only in the twentieth century that the town took on new life. Fortunately a historical society has been active in keeping the old town and the 1830s addition intact.

During the Crown period in Georgia two other towns of importance came into existence, Sunbury, a Puritan town, and Wrightsborough, a Quaker town. Both towns are non-existent today. These were not public towns but were planned by particular sects for others of a like persuasion. In this respect they resembled Ebenezer and Darien. The land on which Wrightsborough (*Fig. 24*) was laid out had originally been granted in 1763 to Edmund Gray, a Quaker from Virginia. Because of Indian raids the territory was not settled. In 1769 Joseph Maddock, a Quaker from North Carolina, thinking the Indian troubles had subsided, petitioned Gov-

TOWN PLANNING IN GEORGIA

ernor Wright to allow a 1,000-acre reserve within the formerly-granted land to be laid out as a township. Within this area a town and common were to be founded which would occupy 194 acres. Governor Wright was interested in protecting the colony on its vulnerable western borders and appears to have been only too pleased to have the settlers lay out a town in that region. He even pampered the Quakers to the extent of allowing them to limit inhabitants to those of their own sect. It was not until after the "New Purchase" of 1773 removed the hostile neighboring Indians that the town prospered. Before the Revolution William Bartram wrote that the town had about sixty families and the township

Fig. 24. WRIGHTSBOROUGH, ST. PAUL PARISH (Later included successively in Richmond, Columbia and McDuffie counties). Founded 1769. Surveyor: Joseph Maddock. 1763 Treaty.

contained 200 families, all Quakers. In 1774 the Quakers freed their slaves. Largely because of the competition of slave labor in the rest of the colony, the sect gradually left the south for the more sympathetic north and at the turn of the century the town had more non-Quakers than Quakers. The gradual decline of Wrightsborough began in 1833 when the citizens voted against allowing a railroad to be built through the town. Today there remains only a Methodist church and a few post-Quaker houses.[18]

Joseph Maddock, the North Carolina Quaker, seems to have been responsible for the plan of Wrightsborough. The layout is as interesting for its differences from English Savannah as for its similarities. The similarities were the compactness of the plan which gave safety to the frontier, the repeated public squares, blocks of ten lots divided by lanes and wide streets running to the center of the squares. The differences from Savannah are the odd "T" shaped plan with squares laid out only at the top of the "T," and in the wide road which surrounds the town. This road allowed access to the common and could be used for defense. In the 1807 re-survey the large common was divided into fifty one-acre lots, perhaps a holdover from the farm lots of the Trustee period.

The Georgia Puritans, founders of Sunbury had originally migrated to South Carolina from Massachusetts. As their land in South Carolina began to lose fertility they acquired in Georgia in the 1750s a tract of 22,500 acres on the Medway River about thirty miles south of Savannah. After settling in this region as rice planters, they bought, in 1758, 300 acres of land on the coast for a port from which to ship their produce. At the time of the Revolution, this port of Sunbury had become the second largest city in Georgia. In 1773 a traveler wrote:

> *This Pretty Town is situated on the sound opposite St. Catherin Island & commands an agreeable prospect of the Inlet 4 or 5 miles from the Barr. There are about one hundred Houses in the Town neatly build of wood frame having pleasant Piases round them. The inhabitants are genteel & wealthy, either Merchants or Planters from the Country who resort here in the Summer & Autumn, to partake of the Salubrious Sea breeze, Bathing & sporting on the Sea Islands. The Bar is a good one.*

Vessells carrying 16 feet water over it. Here is a Custom house and a Naval office for incouragement of Commerce.[19]

Practically destroyed during the Revolution, Sunbury never regained its colonial importance. It is today a ghost town with a few ruins and vague outlines of former streets.

The plan allowed for a large town and a 100-acre common. It was laid out in a grid with 496 lots and three squares: Kings, Church and Meeting. The uniform lots were sixty feet by 130 feet with eight lots to a block. Similar to the Savannah plan were the narrow lanes dividing the lots and the wide streets. Also in the Savannah tradition were the wide streets running to the center of each side of the squares. When this plan is compared with Savannah's, the main differences are to be found in the smaller number of squares and public lots, the placement of the squares, the use of only two street widths, and the smaller common.

During the Trustee period Oglethorpe laid out all the colony's towns; under the Crown, if a group of people applied for permission to lay out a town, the type of plan was left to their discretion. However, both the Quakers in Wrightsborough and the Puritans in Sunbury followed, with certain variations, the basic ideas of the Savannah plan.

The prosperity of these colonial towns depended on their location and site, not on the plan. A successful coastal town (all major Georgia colonial towns except Wrightsborough were on the water) depended on a deep harbor, a navigable river to bring produce from the interior and fertile lands feeding crops into the river highway to the port. Savannah had all three and prospered. Hardwick had a poor harbor and an unreliable river; it never came even near fulfilling its founders' expectations. Darien had a poor harbor but a navigable river and prospered until the mid-nineteenth century when the railroad provided a better means of transportation. Sunbury had a good harbor but no river. It prospered as long as the adjacent land produced adequate crops to ship from the port. Brunswick had an excellent harbor, but was on a small river which drained the Pine Barrens and, unlike Darien, prospered only after the advent of the railroad.

The British laid out large towns in Georgia which they hoped would become important government, trading, and trans-shipment centers. The Crown put much store on having one or more important towns in each of its colonies and though this policy was successful in the northern colonies, in the south there was less success. The plantation system from the beginning, as far back as the early Virginia settlements, discouraged the formation of cities. Over and over the British laid out towns in the south from which they hoped to control the colonists, only to see these towns languish or disappear altogether. Their towns in Georgia, with the striking exception of Augusta and Savannah, followed this history.

After Georgia became a state there would not be until the late nineteenth century any new towns comparable in size to the colonial ones. The three towns planned by the state are exceptions. The citizens of Georgia understood the needs of their society better than the British. Trading, commerce, manufacturing were not of great interest to Georgians. An agricultural society did not demand or require the creation of great centers of distribution. An accessible seaport and, later, towns at the Fall Line of the main rivers were all that the economy needed or could support.

Notes

1. The Trustees' policy was to have areas of several thousand acres laid out into villages with adjacent farms. In this way they hoped to ensure orderly settlement of the land. There were eight of these large tracts ranging from 2,500 to 10,000 acres. The deed for Savannah was for 5,000 acres. The Trustees envisaged little counterparts of Savannah spreading out into the large deed lands. Some small towns did spring up, mostly to disappear within a few years. Highgate, Abercorn, Joseph's Town, and Thunderbolt were some of these villages. When Oglethorpe returned to England in 1734, he claimed to

have settled eleven such communities. Ellis Merton Coulter, *Georgia, A Short History* (Chapel Hill, 1960), pp. 54-55. By permission of UNC Press.

2. Frederica was a military town and the plan had little influence on other towns nor was it influenced by other plans in the colony. Augusta was a garrison for soldiers and a jumping-off place for traders on their way to the Indian country. It had a linear layout which was enlarged after the Revolution when the town was made the state capital. Becoming more American than British, it will be discussed in Chapter VI.

3. Compiled from Amos Aschback Ettinger, *James Edward Oglethorpe, Imperial Idealist* (Oxford, 1936).

4. William Penn, also a Londoner, showed the same interest in opening up a community to light and air in his plan for Philadelphia.

5. Louis DeVorsey, Jr., ed., *DeBrahm's Report of the General Survey in the Southern Districts of North America* (Columbia, South Carolina, 1971), pp. 139-165.

6. Francis Moore, "A Voyage to Georgia Begun in the Year 1735," *Georgia Historical Collections*, I (1840), 97. Also Benjamin Martyn, "The Province of Georgia, An Impartial Inquiry," *Georgia Historical Collections*, I (1840), 177.

7. As the immigrants soon discovered, this was not adequate for a family's farm. The state no doubt had its colonial history in mind when the public domain was divided, after the lottery system was put into effect, into the larger and more practical 202½ acres or more.

8. Dublin, Rome and Augusta are examples of courthouse towns having a wide boulevard with a central park.

9. Archibald Henderson, *Washington's Southern Tour* (Boston, 1923), p. 223.

10. Mills Lane, ed., *The Rambler in Georgia* (Savannah, 1973), pp. 3, 17, 43, 138.

11. Rev. Phillip A. Strobel, *The Salzburgers and Their Descendents* (Baltimore, 1955), pp. 91-92.

12. Chandler, comp., *C.R.G.*, VI, pp. 423-426.

13. Coulter, *Georgia, A Short History*, p. 85. Also Charles C. Jones, "The Dead Towns of Georgia," *Georgia Historical Collections*, IV (1840), pp. 224-232.

14. The state re-surveys of British towns, which had fallen on hard times and needed to be re-founded, always followed the original plan as exactly as possible. This is surprising considering how different the layout was of the towns planned by the state and by the counties.

15. Margaret Davis Cate, *Our Todays and Yesterdays* (Spartanburg, South Carolina, 1972), pp. 162-165.

16. Candler, comp., *C.R.G.*, IX, 385-387.

17. Cate, *Our Todays and Yesterdays*, pp. 162-165.

18. Compiled from: Pearl Baker, *The Story of Wrightsborough* (Thomson, Georgia, 1964). Also Alex M. Hitz, "The Wrightsborough Quaker Town and Township in Georgia," *The Bulletin of the Friends Historical Association*, XLVI (1957), 10-22. Also Candler, comp., *C.R.G.*, X, 690-694.

19. Compiled from Paul McIlwaine, *Dead Town of Sunbury* (Hendersonville, North Carolina, 1971). Also Charles C. Jones, "The Dead Towns of Georgia," *Georgia Historical Collections*, IV (1840), 141-223.

Chapter IV
Courthouse Towns in the Headright Region—1777–1802

The large tract acquired by Governor Wright in 1773 was the most fertile and desirable part of the state open to newcomers. Directly after the Revolution the state turned its attention toward increasing its holdings in this valuable Piedmont region. Land between the Ogeechee and the Oconee rivers was acquired from the Indians in a series of treaties completed in 1790. The cession included a large segment of the rich Piedmont and south of that the almost equally rich Red Hills. The state's liberal land grant laws encouraged the extensive immigration, primarily from the Carolinas and Virginia, which flowed into the Piedmont.[1] Between 1790 and 1800 thirteen new counties were founded mainly in the Piedmont and in the Red Hills which lay north and west of Augusta. In the state's expansion to its western boundary this fertile strip across the middle of Georgia would become the center of activity, growth and political power.

Georgia's legacy of towns from the colonial period was not an impressive inheritance. On the coast, Brunswick, Darien, Sunbury, Hardwick and Savannah had all been partially destroyed during the Revolution. On the Savannah River both Ebenezer and Augusta were in a state of decay and ruin. A few of these would recover; most would expire. From the beginning of statehood Georgia would have trouble founding county towns along the coast. This was mainly because of unproductive land and difficulty of transportation. She had an equally difficult time, for the same reasons, in the Pine Barren-Wire Grass land west of Savannah. There was no question that the Piedmont was where things were happening.

When the 1777 Georgia constitution changed the parishes to counties, only vague political machinery was provided for organizing them or founding their county seats. County commissioners were to be appointed by the General Assembly, and "a courthouse and jail to be erected at public expense in each county, where the present convention or the future legislature shall point out and direct."[3] A more specific act in 1783 concerned Augusta, Washington and Waynesborough. It stipulated that the Augusta reserve land was to be laid out in one-acre lots and that one lot was to be reserved for a church and ten other lots for public use. For Washington, five commissioners were appointed to lay out the town into one-acre lots on land which the state had granted, reserving an adequate number for church and educational purposes. Waynesborough was to be laid out on a reserve of public land (an inheritance from the Crown) into one-acre lots by state-appointed commissioners. This 1783 act concerning Augusta, Washington and Waynesborough neglected to mention the construction of the county buildings. Later legislative acts were to show an all-pervading interest in the building of the courthouse and jail, but the 1783 act only indicated concern in lots for churches[4] and recommended that "a seminary of learning . . . necessary for the instruction of our youth ought to be one of the first objects of attention, after the promotion of religion."[5] The state soon realized the importance of specifying the construction of a courthouse and jail for each county. An act written a year later in 1784 "for fixing and establishing courthouses and jails, and the fixing and regulating elections in the different counties of this state" noted that since no law had ever been passed for erecting courthouses and jails (the act of 1777 seems to have been forgotten), these should be erected in Savannah, Sunbury, at the crossroads in Effingham, in Waynesborough, Augusta and Washington.[6] As evidence of continuing concern, another act stated "no provision hath hitherto been made by law for building a court-house and jail in the county of Greene," and provided that they should be built.[7]

Thus, as a result of methods worked out in the 1780s and in the 1789 constitution, the General Assembly, by 1790, had settled on a workable formula for founding new county seats. The acts after this date varied mainly concerning appointed officials for siting and laying out towns and the amount of land allowed for the

TOWN PLANNING IN GEORGIA 57

county seat. It seemed to be a toss-up whether the justices of the Inferior Court or commissioners appointed by the state legislature were to fix on a convenient site for the public buildings. In Elbert County the justices were to "fix on the most convenient place for building a court-house and jail."[8] In Williamsburg it was the commissioners who were to fix on a site and lay off lots. In one act the legislature appointed commissioners to fix on a place for the courthouse and jail in Warren, Oglethorpe, McIntosh, Bryan and Montgomery, whereas the justices of the Inferior Court were charged with levying taxes and letting the contracts for the buildings.[9] In 1796 an act was passed concerning the overall responsibility of the county justices toward the courthouse and jail.

> *Be it enacted by the Senate and House of Representatives of the state of Georgia in General Assembly met, and by the authority of the same, that from and after the passing of this act, the justices of the inferior courts of every county within the state, in their respective counties, shall cause to be erected and kept in good repair (or where the same shall be already built) shall maintain and keep in good repair, at the charge of such county, one good and convenient court-house of stone, brick or timber, and one sufficient jail, with the necessary apartments for the safe keeping of criminals and debtors, well secured with iron bars, bolts and locks, and shall cause to be erected contiguous thereto, one pillory, whippingpost and stocks.*[10]

By the end of the headright period the justices of the Inferior Court were usually responsible for county business, whereas the commissioners appointed by the legislature were charged with the running of the town.

The General Assembly also vacillated in this period concerning the amount of land to be allowed for the county seat and how this land was to be acquired. Throughout the 1780s the state habitually granted land for new courthouse sites.[11] After 1790 the legislature made an abrupt about-face and not only did not grant any more land but specified the amount the commissioners were allowed to procure.[12] Largely because of the random surveys made under the headright method of land grants, these amounts varied widely.[13]

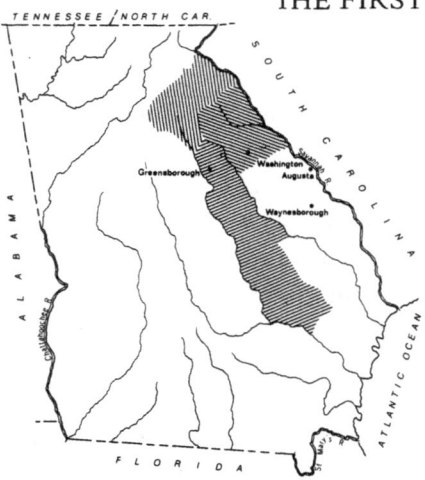

Fig. 25. COURTHOUSE TOWNS IN THE HEADRIGHT REGION BEFORE 1790.

Courthouse Towns Before 1790

Washington
Augusta (*reviewed in Chapter VI*)
Greensborough
Waynesborough
St. Marys

The five towns laid out in the first years after Independence were Augusta, Washington, Waynesborough, Greensborough and St. Marys. With the exception of St. Marys, all were carefully controlled by the legislature as to location, lot size, and lots to be reserved for courthouse, academy and churches.

That body did not specify, however, even in these early years of detailed instructions, how the lots were to be laid out. Washington featured a central courthouse square surrounded by a network of streets laid out at right angles, and was the plan which would be most copied in later Piedmont towns. The layout which evolved in Augusta would be typical of towns located on a tract where a settlement already existed. Greensborough and Waynesborough

TOWN PLANNING IN GEORGIA 59

both followed this plan. St. Mary's plan is nearer to that of colonial Savannah. In keeping with the British tradition, Greensborough, Waynesborough and St. Marys were planned as sizable urban centers. Greensborough had 217 lots, Waynesborough 200 and St. Marys eighty-eight. A more realistic estimate of town size in early Georgia was Washington, with forty-eight lots, and Augusta, with forty lots.

Washington came into existence in 1783 when the legislature appointed commissioners to lay out a 100-acre grant into a common and a town of one-acre lots (*Fig. 26*). It was specified that money derived from the sale of the lots was to be used for a court-

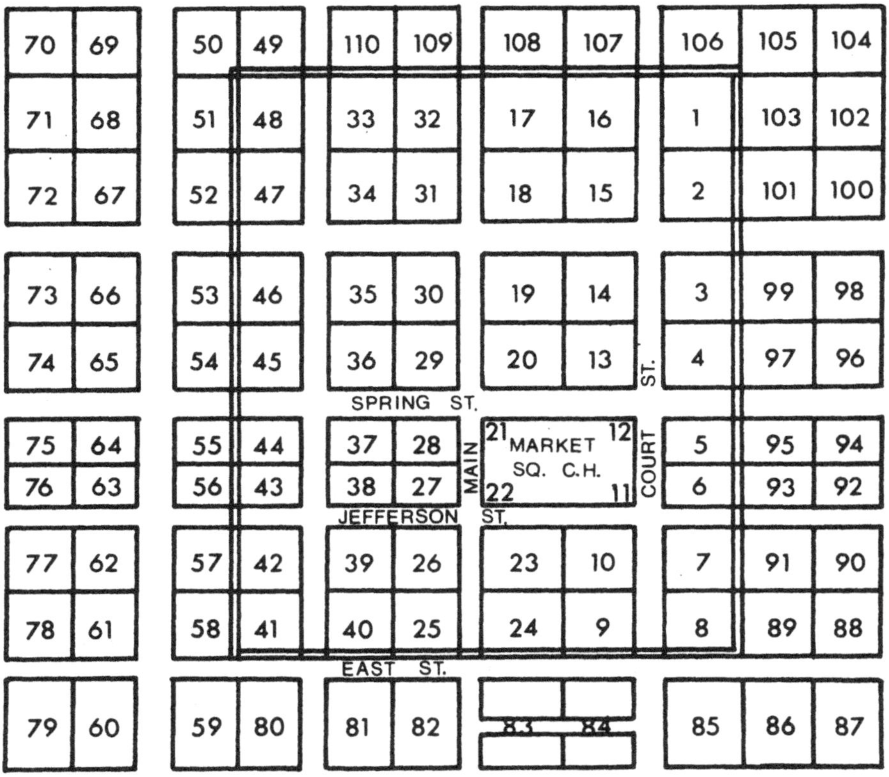

Fig. 26. WASHINGTON, WILKES COUNTY. Founded 1783. Surveyor: Commissioners. "New Purchase" of 1773.

house, a jail, a school, and a cemetery. Later that year the legislature, finding that the first commissioners had failed to comply with certain restrictions, declared that the town grant should revert to the state.[14] Shortly thereafter, in another act, that body seems to have repented and regranted the town land, which subsequently was divided into forty-eight lots forming a rectangle with a surrounding common. In 1793, when the legislature allowed Washington to divide the common into sixty-eight new lots, the original streets and lot sizes were continued. This enlargement took in the remainder of the original state grant of 100 acres.[15] Each block, with the exception of the range of blocks containing the market square, is four acres divided into one-acre lots. The courthouse was originally sited in the center of the market square. Washington, on a stage route leading northwest from Augusta, was a successful town and needed relatively little prodding from the legislature to build and increase her population.

Waynesborough

In 1783 when the legislature authorized the laying out of Waynesborough (*Fig. 27*), it instructed the commissioners to site it on a "reserve of public land" which was south of Augusta. This reserve was an inheritance from colonial days when the British government typically reserved lands for future towns. The legislature further directed that the town was to be laid out in 200 one-acre lots and that the commissioners should not dispose of more than 200.[16] The two main streets, Pease and Liberty, cross each other at the center of town. They are ninety-six feet wide; all other streets are sixty feet wide. Lots A, B, C, D were public lots set within a block with the courthouse located on one. The main street seems originally to have been a highway with a settlement built along it. With an earlier settlement located where the new town was laid out, and with the courthouse sited on a lot located within a block, the Waynesborough plan can be placed in the "Augusta" group of courthouse town plans. For a Georgia

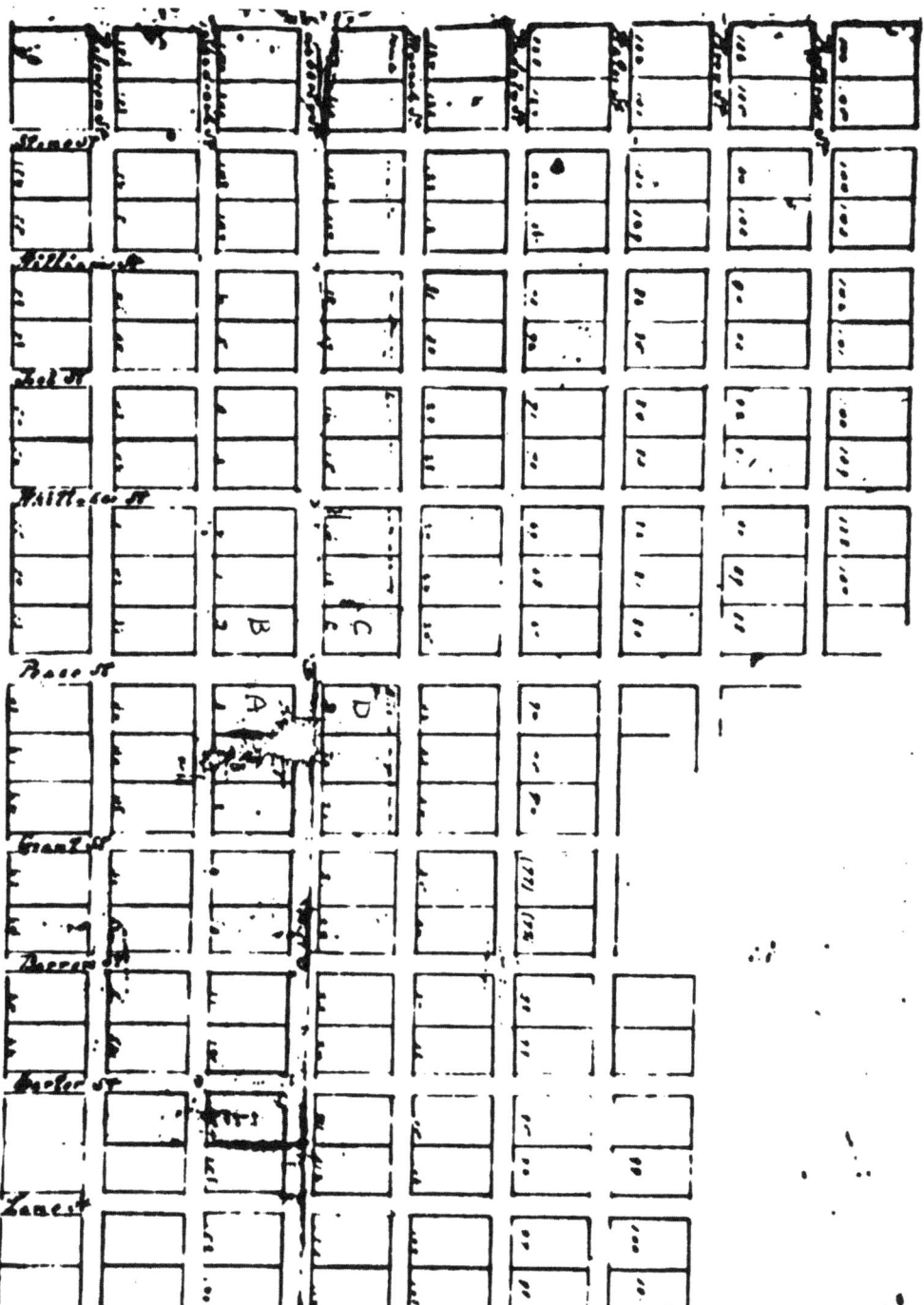

Fig. 27. WAYNESBOROUGH, BURKE COUNTY. Founded 1783. Surveyor: Commissioners. 1763 Treaty.

town the Waynesborough plan was surprisingly large. It took many decades before the original layout was fully occupied.

Although Waynesborough had its academy and race course, each a "must" for a southern town, it was some time before a church was built. In these early years of rugged frontier living preachers were not welcome. Francis Asbury wrote "Let neither preacher or people catch me in Waynesborough again until things are altered and bettered. . . ."[17] In 1791 George Washington on his southern tour noted

> lodged at Waynesborough . . . a small place, but the seat of the court of Burke County . . . six or eight small houses is all it contains, an attempt is making (without much apparent effect) to establish an academy as is the case in all the counties.[18]

Greensborough

In 1786 the legislature ordered eight tracts surveyed and sold for the support of the state university. The university site was to be on the Richmond Survey in Greene County, located in the 1790 cession. With this in mind the Assembly passed an act in which Greensborough (*Fig. 28*) was to be laid out on part of the 1020 acres set aside for town and common. The act stated that the trustees of the university were "to lay out a town which shall be known by the name of Greensborough . . . and after reserving a number of lots sufficient for public buildings, to sell and convey the remaining lots."[19] The land adjacent to the town was to be divided into 202½-acre lots and was to include the remainder of the Richmond Survey.[20] It was hoped that the sale of town and farm lots would bring in funds with which to start the university. Protesting their treaties with Georgia, the Creek Indians burned Greensborough in 1787. It was some time before the border quieted down and it was not until the early nineteenth century that Greensborough recovered and gained in population. The university site, in the meantime, was moved to Athens. In Greensborough, the town center from which the boundaries were meas-

Fig. 28. GREENSBOROUGH, GREENE COUNTY. Founded 1787. Surveyor: William Greer. 1790 Cession.

ured was the market place. This suggests that the town was not primarily a county seat, for usually when measurements were taken for a county town the courthouse was used as the center. Although Greensborough was not located at the site of an already-existing settlement, it follows the "Augusta"-type plan, with the courthouse built on a lot which is part of a block and faces the main street. The alleys used in the plan may possibly be a holdover from the lanes laid out in Savannah and other colonial towns. They are a feature found in several later towns such as Sandersville, Monroe, Bainbridge and Newton.

St. Marys

For a headright town, the founding of St. Marys (*Fig. 29*) followed an unusual pattern. According to James T. Vocelle, an historian of the town, settlers on Cumberland Island, needing a port from which to export produce, in 1787 bought 1,672 acres from Jacob Weed for that purpose. The agreement for founding the town allowed each subscriber four one-acre lots. It stipulated that

Fig. 29. ST. MARY'S, CAMDEN COUNTY. Founded 1788. Surveyor: James Findley. 1763 Grant.

within six months the owner must build a frame or brick house not less than sixteen by twenty-four feet or forfeit his lots. James Findley, the county surveyor, laid out the town.[21] In 1792, the legislature made St. Marys the county seat and appointed commissioners to transmit to the surveyor general the plan of the town and to build a courthouse and jail.[22]

Findley's plan had eighty-eight one-acre lots and two four-acre public squares. As in Savannah, these squares were not built upon and were aligned with the main street running to their center. The still-existing Presbyterian church (1808) is located at the side of one of these squares.

One of the few travelers to get to this out-of-the-way town noted in 1811 that it was built about one-half mile up the river from the bay. "The site of the town is an extensive square. The streets are broad and laid off intersecting each other at right angles." As other travelers would note of Georgia towns, this author wrote that few lots were built upon and the forest encroaching on the houses gave the town an appearance of being buried in the woods. He further commented that "on account of its proximity to the Spanish settlements and its remoteness from Courts of Justice [St. Marys] is the resort of all the Blackguards of the Western World."[23]

Courthouse Towns After 1790—in the Piedmont and Red Hills

"Augusta" Plan Towns
  Elberton
  Warrenton
  Carnesville

"Washington" Plan Towns
  Lexington
  Sandersville
  Crawfordville

66 THE FIRST 100 YEARS OF

"Sparta" Plan Towns
  Sparta
  Lincolnton
  Jefferson
  Danielsville

Other
  Louisville (*reviewed in Chapter VI*)
  Appling
  Watkinsville

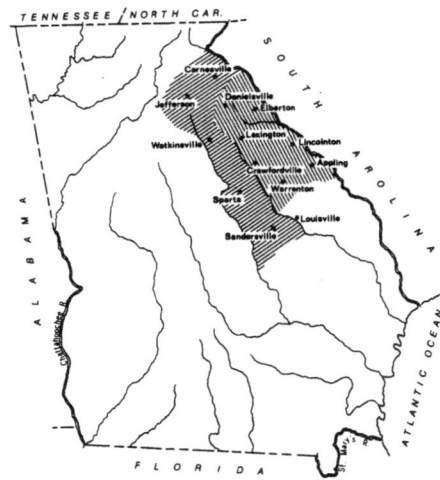

Fig. 30. COURTHOUSE TOWNS IN THE HEADRIGHT REGION AFTER 1790.

Georgia's population increased rapidly after 1790 and, in line with new legislation, counties and county towns were formed to keep up with the burgeoning growth (*Fig. 30*).[24] While the legislature was systematizing the acts for founding county seats, the state-appointed commissioners or justices were systematizing the forms which the county towns took.

"Augusta" Plan Towns

White traders and settlers had penetrated into the region of the 1773 and 1790 cessions long before the Indians gave up these lands. Numerous trading paths had been cut through the wilderness, and the active trading carried on with the Cherokees and the Creeks kept them open and encouraged small trading posts along the routes. Elberton, Warrenton and Carnesville were sited at the location of such settlements. In planning for the public buildings of these new county seats, the commissioners had an existing village and a main road to take into consideration. As was usual in such planning situations, the "Augusta"-type court town plan was followed. All three towns have an important main street, the original route through the region, and a strip development along it. In Carnesville and Warrenton the courthouse is placed in a park at one side of the main road, and Elberton's courthouse is located a block away, as in Augusta.

According to a local historian, a settlement existed at Elberton (*Fig. 31*) as early as 1769, growing up around a spring.[25] In 1792 the state appointed commissioners and charged them with locating a county seat for the newly-formed Elbert County. They purchased from John Baker fifty acres of land adjoining the spring where a settlement and a main trading route already existed, and laid out, to the south of this settlement, a grid with a square in the center. It is a layout such as would be expected from a courthouse town planned on the site of an earlier settlement. College is the main street and Oliver the secondary one. At one time the jail was located at the intersection of these two streets. The courthouse square, located at the crest of a hill, is one block south of the main east-west thoroughfare, College Street. The square is approached from the south by a short street which dead-ends at the center of one side. However, the square is also bounded by Oliver Street and three other small streets, giving the town something of the appearance of the "Washington"-type plan. In many towns planned between 1790 and 1805 certain characteristics of

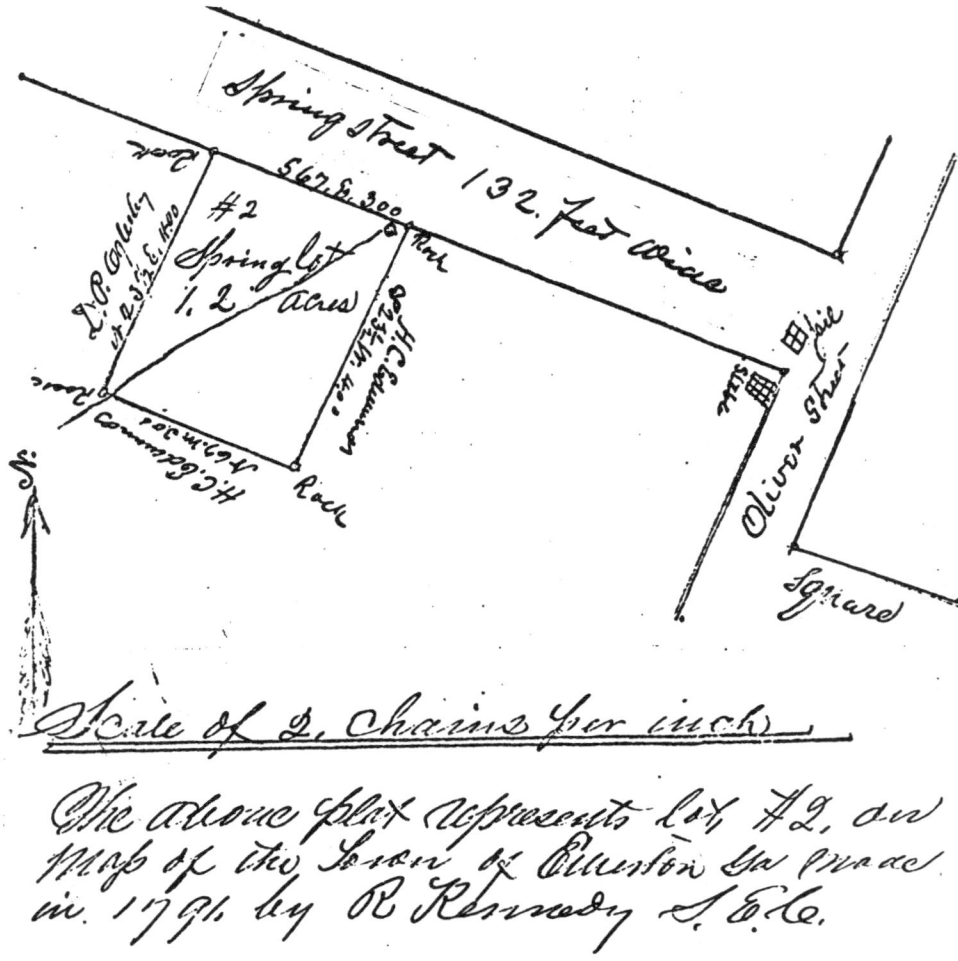

Fig. 31. ELBERTON, ELBERT COUNTY. Founded 1791. Surveyor: R. Kennedy. "New Purchase" of 1773.

the three types of town plans might be used by the planner. After 1805 this would seldom be the case.

Since all records concerning the original plan of Warrenton (*Fig. 32*) have been lost, it is not possible to reconstruct, with certainty, the town as it was first laid out. However, from some facts and from visual survey certain assumptions can be made. It seems likely that it was laid out on a trading route. The courthouse square was

TOWN PLANNING IN GEORGIA

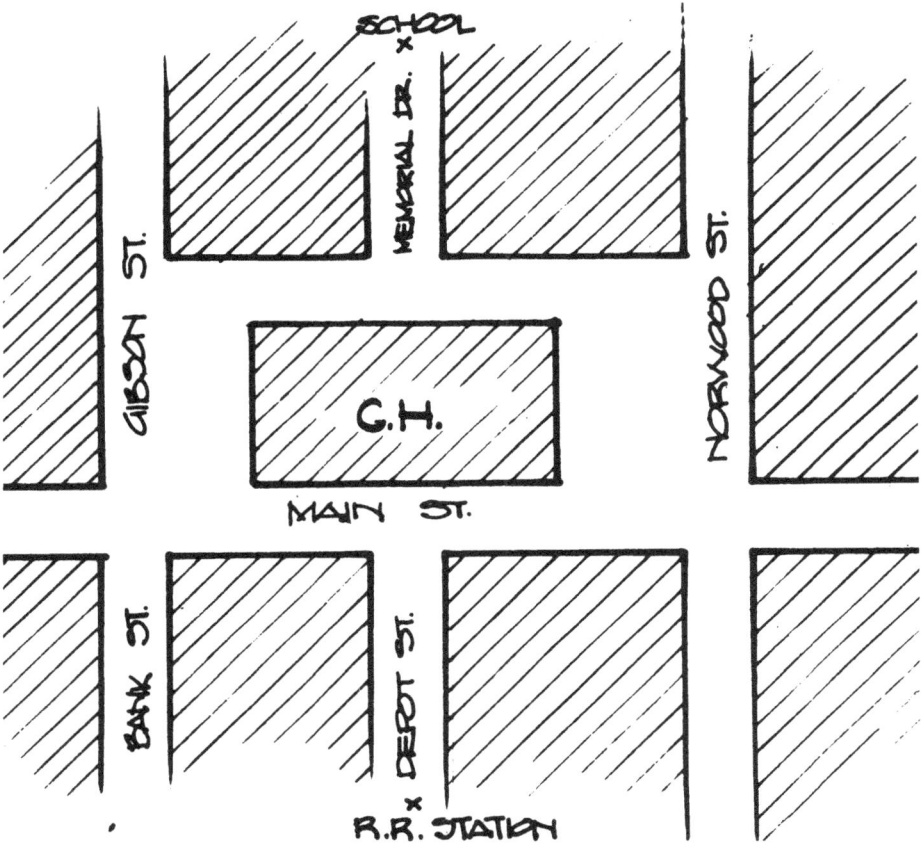

Fig. 32. WARRENTON, WARREN COUNTY, GEORGIA. Founded 1797. Surveyor: Commissioners. 1763 grant.

placed on this main road, making it a variation of the "Augusta"-type plan. Influences of the other types of plans are also evident. Instead of the square being part of a block, it is surrounded by streets as in a "Washington"-type plan. The square, however, is oblong in shape and smaller than is usual and the surrounding streets, with the exception of the main road, are narrow and used for traffic circulation rather than for stores. The town was built and expanded in a linear arrangement along the main thoroughfare and not around the square. Two streets were added at a later date which nicely complemented the early plan. One of these, Depot Street, runs up from the railroad station to the center of one side of the square; the other, Memorial Drive, leads from the opposite side of the square to a school. Lots on both sides of the latter street are used for parks and public buildings. Although this street arrangement resembled the "Sparta"-type plan, the predominant structure of the town plan followed the "Augusta" type.

A landowner who happened to own acreage in the center of the county, where the legislature usually insisted that the county town be built, influenced the siting of Warrenton by donating some of his land for the courthouse square. This, of course, had the effect of raising the price of the remainder of his land.

The following Act is quoted in full and is typical of such a situation:

> 1. That the permanent seat for the court-house and jail in the county of Warren shall, and is hereby declared to be, on a lot or parcel of land, on the plantation whereon Sterling Gardner now resides, which was pointed out and agreed upon by the late commissioners appointed for that purpose. Provided, That said Sterling Gardner shall, within three months after the passing of this act, well and truly execute and deliver a deed in fee simple, for seven acres of land, to be conveyed to the said commissioners, herein after named and their successors in office, to, and for the use of the said county, to be laid out in lots, and appropriated as the said commissioners may direct, so as to carry into full effect a contract heretofore made between the commissioners of the said county and the said Sterling Gardner.
>
> 2. And be it further enacted, That the justices of the inferior court of the said county and their successors in office, are hereby declared to be commissioners of the court house and jail of the county aforesaid, and they or a majority of them are hereby authorized and fully empowered to let the same to the lowest bidder, after giving thirty days' notice in three or more public places in the said county, on such plan as they may think proper, any law to the contrary notwithstanding.[26]

The third town in the "Augusta" group is Carnesville, which also shows influences of the "Washington" and the "Sparta" plans. Franklin County, located in the northern part of the 1790-treaty land, had been organized in 1784 before the cession was made

TOWN PLANNING IN GEORGIA 71

legal. Because of its isolated situation, the legislature was unable to bring a county town into existence until almost ten years later. A strip development had (probably) grown up along a main east-west route from the Carolinas into Georgia along which Carnesville was located. In laying out the town, the commissioners planned a large freestanding square with one side on Lavonia Street, the old trading route. In siting the public land and buildings in this location the planners had to deal with the steeply sloping ground of the square. This necessitated placing the courthouse directly on the main street rather than in the middle of the square. It is this siting of the courthouse and the strip development which gives the town its "Augusta" appearance. Elements of the "Washington" plan are seen in the free-standing square surrounded by buildings, and of the "Sparta" plan in Royston Street which runs up from the valley near to the center of the south side of the square. Carnesville was located not only in an isolated but also in a poor section of the state. It was many years after siting the town before the legislature could get the appointed commissioners to build a courthouse and jail. Once the town was laid out and the courthouse built, the legislators had to constantly admonish the commissioners to keep the town tidy, to clean out the spring, to remove obstructions from the square, and to control their rowdy citizens.[27]

"Washington"-Plan Towns

Most towns in the headright region were laid out before 1805, the date of the succeeding Indian cession. Virgin land held a great fascination for Georgians, and after each cession many would leave their worn-out farms and plantations and move to the new territory. Practice in laying out towns in the western lands resulted in more knowledgeable treatment of the plan and competent siting of the later towns. Three towns in the headright land followed the "Washington"-type courthouse plan: Lexington and Sandersville, laid out in the 1790s, and Crawfordville, which was not laid out until 1826. Compared with the other two, Crawfordville shows the finesse which had developed as a result of some thirty years of handling the popular "Washington" plan in the Piedmont region.

Oglethorpe County, in the upper reaches of the Piedmont, was cut off from Wilkes in 1793 to take care of the great influx of Virginians who had settled in the Broad River Valley. Commissioners appointed by the legislature to site a county town laid out a grid around a central square. Lexington was a nucleated plan with the courthouse square the center of activity, and shops and stores surrounding it on four sides. An announcement in the *Augusta Chronicle* in 1797 bears this out. John Lumpkin, a Lexington citizen, hoped to sell some lots in Lexington by pointing out that they were beautifully situated and quite convenient to the public square.[28]

The state had passed liberal acts by which land was given to the counties to sell for the support of their academies. These academies frequently became an important element in the life of the county town as well as in the town plan. In this respect, Lexington is a particularly striking example. When Francis Meson, a successful Lexington merchant, died in 1806, he left both money and land for an academy. Meson Academy became, after Augusta's famed Richmond Academy, probably the best known school in the Piedmont. Although it gave great prestige to the town, it also had a detrimental effect on Lexington's growth. Because of Meson's will the land could not be sold and the town could not expand in that direction, nor could the railroad be built to the town since the route would have been through the academy land.[29] Figure 33 shows Church Street and a survey of part of the school property made when a new building was being constructed.

Lexington was not as well sited as later "Washington" plan towns would be when it would become customary to place the courthouse on the highest available lot in the town plat. In Lexington a considerably higher ridge to the north had the effect of placing the square in a depression. Some years after the town was

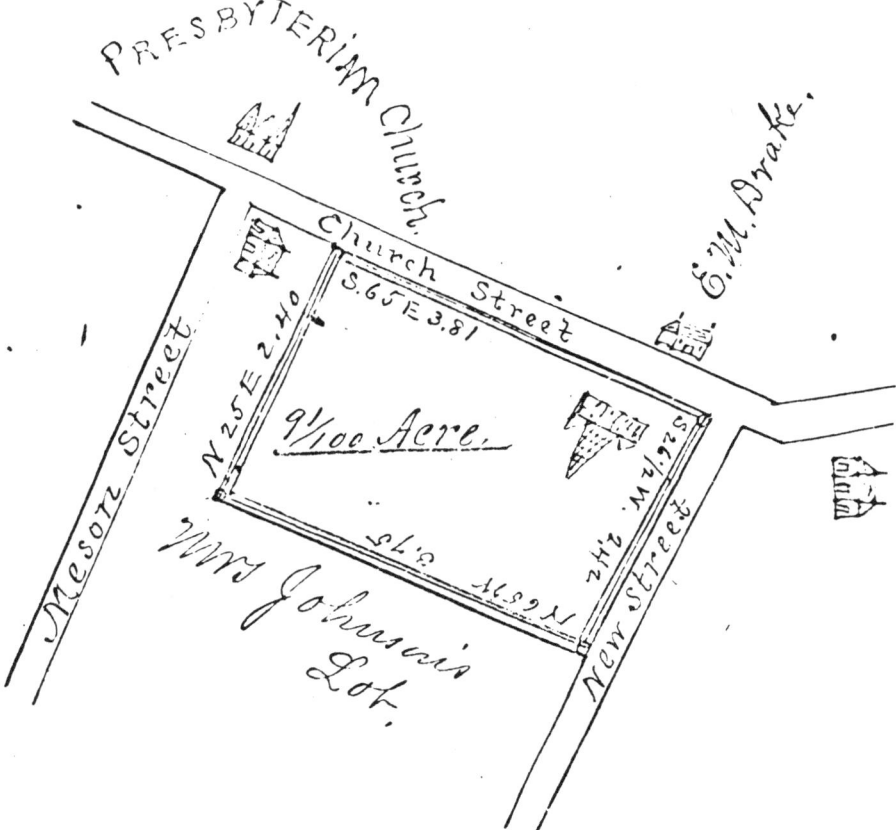

Fig. 33. LEXINGTON, OGLETHORPE COUNTY. Founded 1793. Surveyor: Dr. George Phillips. "New Purchase" of 1773.

laid out, this ridge developed as Church Street where the finest houses and churches were built.[30]

The 1790 cession was originally divided into two counties, Franklin and Washington. The first courthouse town for Washington County was Warthen. Tradition has it that a Mr. Sanders, who owned a store at a place called Sanders' Crossroads, gave a tract of land to the county with the stipulation that the county seat be moved to this site. His gift was accepted and the new courthouse town was named Sandersville (*Fig. 34*). A large square

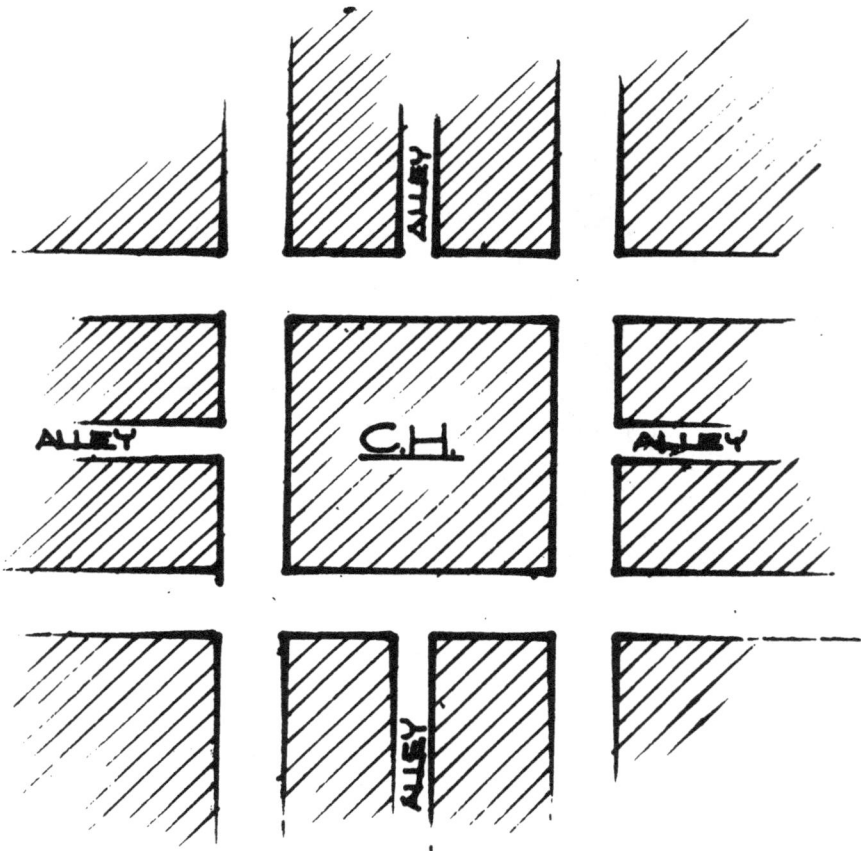

Fig. 34. SANDERSVILLE, WASHINGTON COUNTY. Founded 1796. Surveyors: John Watts and Daniel McCord. 1790 cession.

contains a handsome courthouse and bandstand. Equally fine buildings surround the square, including a particularly interesting Greek Revival library. An unusual feature of the plan is the alleys, in the middle of the blocks surrounding the square, which give access to the rear of the buildings. This feature was used in several later Georgia towns.

Crawfordville (*Frontispiece*) was not laid out until 1826, when Taliaferro County was formed. It is the perfect example of the

TOWN PLANNING IN GEORGIA

"Washington" type of county seat. Drawn by a knowledgeable surveyor (surveyors with some technical training were more numerous in the 1820s than they had been in the 1780s and 1790s), the plan is meticulously oriented to the central focal point, the public square. The large lots are 198 feet by 198 feet, the smaller lots sixty-six feet by 198 feet. The farther away from the public square, the larger were the lot sizes. The main streets are seventy-four feet wide and the side streets sixty-six feet wide. Hermon Mercer, the planner, allotted public lots for the town spring, a tavern, a church and a jail. The public square, where the courthouse stands, is 198 feet by 198 feet or just under an acre. Alexander H. Stephens' home and farm lie to the north of the town.

"Sparta" Plan Towns

The "Sparta" designation is given to those courthouse towns which were, ideally, sited in an acropolis location and had entering streets running up to the center of the square. Four towns followed the "Sparta" plan in the headright era: Sparta, Jefferson, Lincolnton and Danielsville. The surveyor for Jefferson and Lincolnton, though following the "Sparta" plan, did not seem to understand the importance of the acropolis siting. In Jefferson one approach is downhill to the square and in Lincolnton the topography is flat. However, a decade later in Danielsville, the surveyor carefully sited the town on an eminence in order that the four approaches would form a grade up to the courthouse square.

The founding of Sparta (*Fig. 35*) had the ring of land speculation and followed the method frequently used after the state had ceased granting land to the counties. Major Charles Abercrombie, a Revolutionary soldier from North Carolina, received state bounty land in an area which would become Hancock County. His land was centrally located when the new county was formed, and he apparently thought his grant could best be put to use if he founded a town and sold the lots. In 1795 he laid out a town into one-half acre lots and named it Sparta. Commissioners had been appointed by the state to locate a courthouse near the center of the new county. When Abercrombie deeded to the county four lots in his town, the commissioners selected the Sparta site as their county seat. These four lots form the two-acre public square containing the courthouse.[31]

Abercrombie oriented his town north and south, making the main entrance from the north where Greensborough had already been founded. The approach to the town is masterfully handled. A broad street follows a rather steep rise which today affords a dramatic view of the handsome late-nineteenth century courthouse. There is another, though later, fine element in the plan. Where East Broad Street divides, a triangle of land was left. A library was built here which visually brings the town to an end. Often, as here, the original town plan was put to good use in relating a later important building to the existing street pattern. The library in Dublin was built in a similar situation in relation to the town plan and with equally good results.

Never more than a small village, Lincolnton is today bereft of its courthouse square which is remembered only by a widening in the highway and a market. Although the original courthouse is gone, three houses shown in the plan (*Fig. 36*), to the south and right and left of the courthouse, remain. The plan is a variation of the "Sparta" prototype with two streets, instead of four, entering the center of the square. The main road through Lincolnton was oriented east-west, the route of most immigrants. The courthouse faced this road. The plan shows a narrow road running from the east which broadens to the west of the square into a wide avenue planted with trees. The north-south road, apparently a former trail, comes into the town at an angle, is straightened out at the courthouse, and leaves at an angle.

Jefferson follows Lincolnton in having two main streets entering the center of the square. Unusual for a "Sparta"-type plan, the entrance to the town from the north is downhill. The low swampy land chosen for the courthouse necessitated relocating it some years later to a hilltop. It was not often that a Georgia county seat

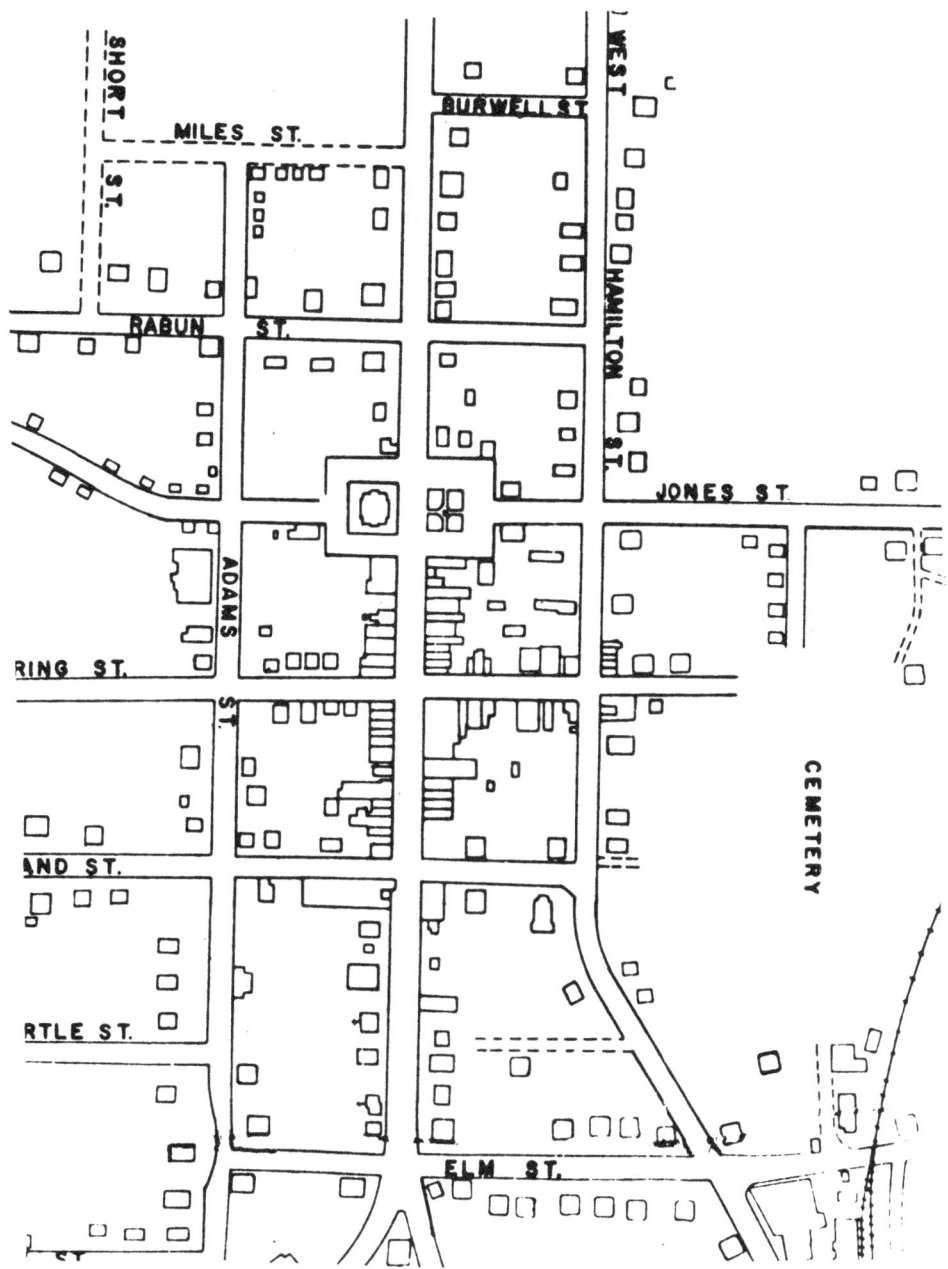

Fig. 35. SPARTA, HANCOCK COUNTY. Founded 1795. Surveyor: Major Charles Abercrombie. 1790 Cession.

was so poorly sited. As in many Upper Piedmont towns the main road through Jefferson was originally east-west, the route of the settlers. The public square and courthouse were centered on this road. The other roads came in at the sides of the square. Although the courthouse has been moved, the square has been retained in the present-day town.

Similar to Carnesville in the predominant poverty of the village and surrounding farms, Danielsville, laid out in 1814, has as sensitive a handling of its plan in relation to the topography as any town in this group. The planners brought the four main streets into the center of each side of the square. The square was located on an eminence, and the courthouse rises grandly from each of the four approaches. There has been no strip or linear development in this town and the few stores in it face the square. Although the siting is typical of the "Sparta" plan, narrow streets which run into the east-west corners of the square make it somewhat reminscent of a "Savannah"-type plan.

Other

The first county seat of Clarke County, Watkinsville, shows today little of the original plan. It seems likely from visual survey that the plan was of the "Washington" type. After Athens became the courthouse town, Watkinsville declined and today its interest lies mainly in an early nineteenth century tavern which was restored by the Georgia Historical Commission.

William Appling gave five acres in 1792 for the Columbia County courthouse site. It is the only courthouse town in Georgia which seems to have had no plan. The only visible evidence today that any plan might have existed is a slight widening in the road opposite the courthouse and jail. In keeping with its non-existent plan it was referred to until the middle of the nineteenth century simply as Columbia Courthouse. By 1816, however, it had been incorporated and the legislature recognized the limits of the town to be 300 yards to the north of the courthouse and "the same dis-

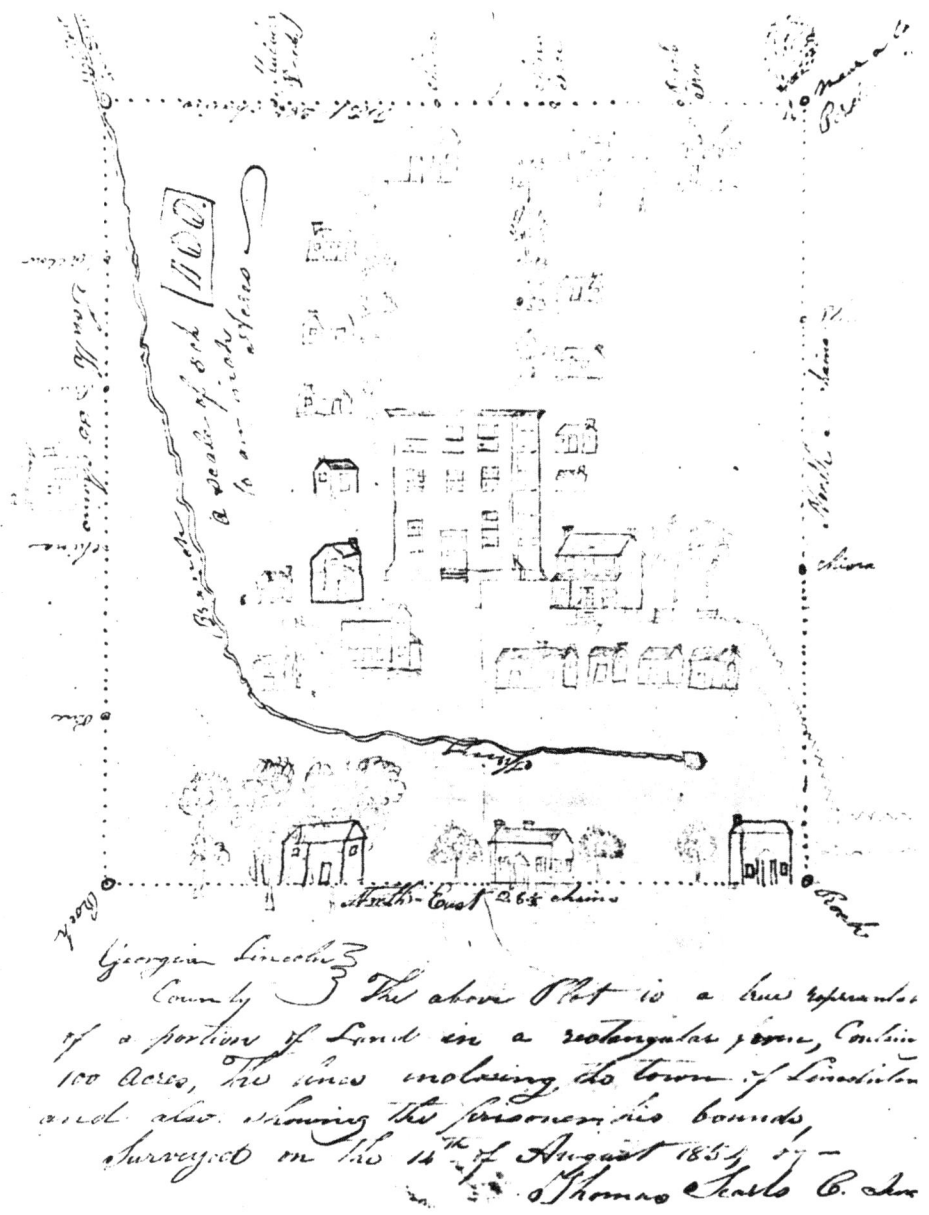

Fig. 36. **LINCOLNTON, LINCOLN COUNTY, GEORGIA.** Founded 1798. Surveyor: Commissioners. "New Purchase" of 1773.

tance east south and west of the same forming a square as near as may be, around the said court-house."[32] The difficulty of surveying in the headright district is again evident both in this act and in the irregular plan which Appling filed with the county clerk in 1792. In spite of the poverty of the town the region surrounding it was fertile and inhabited by prosperous Virginians. The uninteresting small village may be the result of the Virginians' generally preferring to live on their plantations rather than in their towns. There was a tendency, on the other hand, for rich Georgians to leave their plantations in the hands of overseers and to build their fine houses in a town. This obviously affected not only the town plan but its appearance as well.

COURTHOUSE TOWNS AFTER 1790—IN THE COLONIAL LANDS AND THE PINE BARREN-WIRE GRASS REGION

"Augusta" Plan Towns
    Statesborough
    Swainsborough
    Springfield

"Washington" Plan Towns
    Riceborough (dead town)
    Mount Vernon

Other
    Williamsburg (dead town)
    Jacksonborough (dead town)

TOWN PLANNING IN GEORGIA 81

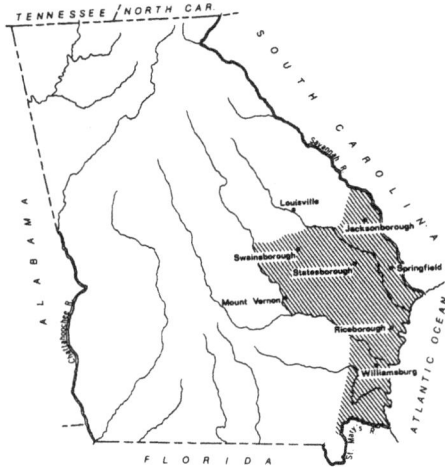

Fig. 37. COURTHOUSE TOWNS IN THE HEADRIGHT REGION AFTER 1790—in the Colonial Lands and the Pine Barren-Wire Grass

"Augusta" Plan Towns

Towns in the region to the south and west of Savannah (*Fig. 37*) were not successful. The land was poor, the transportation difficult and the population sparse. Bulloch County was no exception. Ever since it had been laid out in 1796 the General Assembly had regularly appointed commissioners to decide on a site for the courthouse. Finally in 1801 George Sibbald, who owned over half a million acres in this Pine Barren district, gave the county 200 acres for the courthouse town. Even after this generous gift (so different from the seven acres given for Warrenton and five for Appling) it took three years for Statesborough to be laid out. Growth was not rapid. In 1880 there were only twenty-five inhabitants.[33] It was a foregone conclusion that poor soil, large landholdings and few people would not produce urban development.

Statesborough (*Fig. 38*) was a simple grid with two sixty-six feet-wide streets and four smaller thirty-three feet-wide streets.

Lots measured one acre and one-half acre. The square was taken out of a block and was a minimum one-quarter of an acre.[34] The town seems to have been laid out at a crossroads and it follows the "Augusta" plan in the placement of the public buildings.

It was two years after Emanuel County was organized that the county seat, Swainsborough, was located. In 1813 the legislature appointed five commissioners to purchase a tract of land not less than fifty nor more than 100 acres. They were to lay off lots for a courthouse town and reserve a sufficient number for the county. The act continues with an unusual statement: "In case the commissioners cannot agree on a site the justices may appoint a proper person to ascertain the center of the county."[35] Apparently this was the case, as Jesse Mezzle, the county surveyor, was hired to find the center of the county. A year later the site was decided on, and Mezzle laid out the town into forty-eight lots ranging in size from one-half to three-fourths acre. The two main streets are sixty feet wide, the others fifty feet wide. The courthouse and jail were given two one-half acre lots contiguous with four other lots in the block. Considering that the town was laid out in what apparently was a complete wilderness, it was unusual, especially at this late date, not to have a grid plan oriented to a central square. Instead the town had a typical "Augusta" plan with a linear development.

In Springfield (*Fig. 39*) the "public" road, which was the main thoroughfare between Savannah and Augusta, became Washington Street. Along this road, before Springfield was laid out, a linear settlement typical of the early highway communities had developed. When Springfield was made the county seat the surveyor appropriated the old main road, straightened it out and made it the town's main street. The courthouse square, as was usual in "Augusta" type plans, was placed one block away from the commercial district. The Rabun Street approach to the center of the square is up a hill from Washington Street. This siting, high above the business district, has helped to give the courthouse an impressive appearance. As in many Georgia county towns, good use was made of the topography to add importance to the building which signified law and order to the community. Another happy develop-

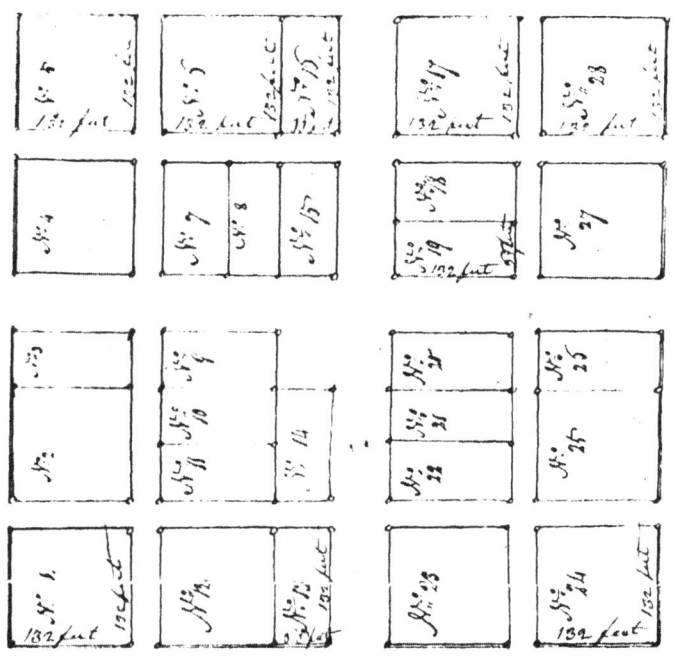

Fig. 38. STATESBOROUGH, BULLOCH COUNTY. Founded 1806. Surveyor: Josiah Everitt. "New Purchase" of 1773.

ment in the Springfield plan is the park south of the courthouse. Located on a ridge which rises east of Washington Street, the park is faced by the courthouse, houses, a school and a church. The use of this open space is a major factor in the plan and has given this small village a distinguished appearance.

Ebenezer had been the main colonial town in this district and it became the court town after Independence. When Effingham, one of the original counties, was formed, Ebenezer was, as the legislature noted, "at an extreme corner thereof." Since 1784 the legislature had been trying to have the courthouse moved to a more convenient location. A typical act in 1797 appointed commissioners to "point out and fix upon the most suitable and convenient place within five miles of the center of the county, for erecting a courthouse and jail thereon."[36] This act produced no more results than the preceding ones. The county would have to wait for a new courthouse town until 1821, when Springfield was finally selected.

"Washington" Plan Towns

Two towns, Riceborough and Mount Vernon, one in the Tidewater region and the other in the Pine Barrens, follow the "Washington"-type plan. Both were minimum towns, one now extinct and the other never more than a small village. Colonial Sunbury, the original Liberty County seat, had been found to be too far from the center of population to be practical. The inhabitants voted to move the courthouse to an existing town, North Newport, and rename it Riceborough (*Fig. 40*). In 1796 Matthew McAllister gave an area measuring 230 feet by 250 feet for the public square, "without any price consideration other than a wish and desire to promote and encourage said town."[37] The act stipulated that the new square was to conform to the plan of the town, apparently meaning that the streets bounding the square should line up with those in the town. Only one thirty-foot-wide street entered the square, which was closed by lots on the opposite side, the other entrances being four lanes only fifteen feet wide. In

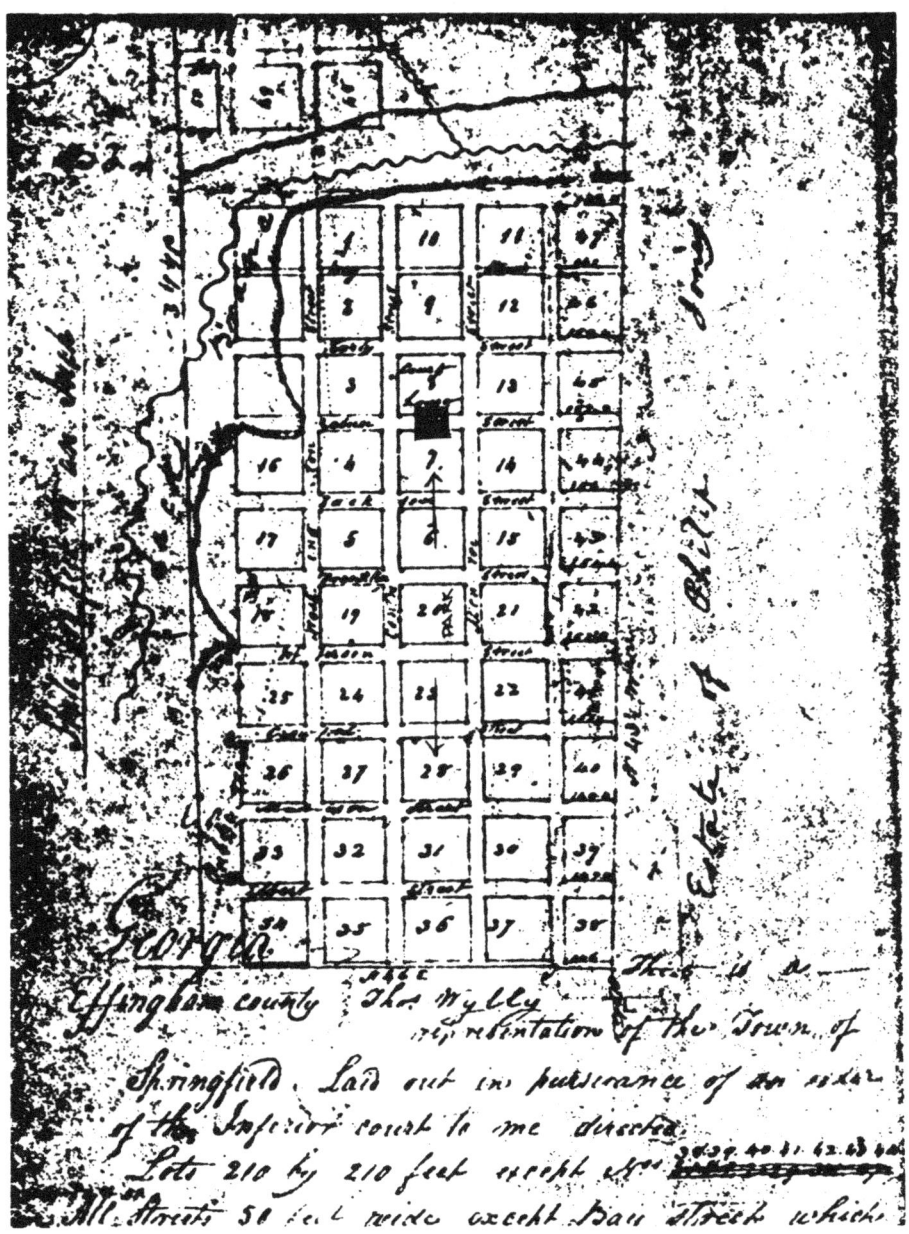

Fig. 39. SPRINGFIELD, EFFINGHAM COUNTY. Founded 1821. Surveyor: Lara(?) Powers. 1763 Grant.

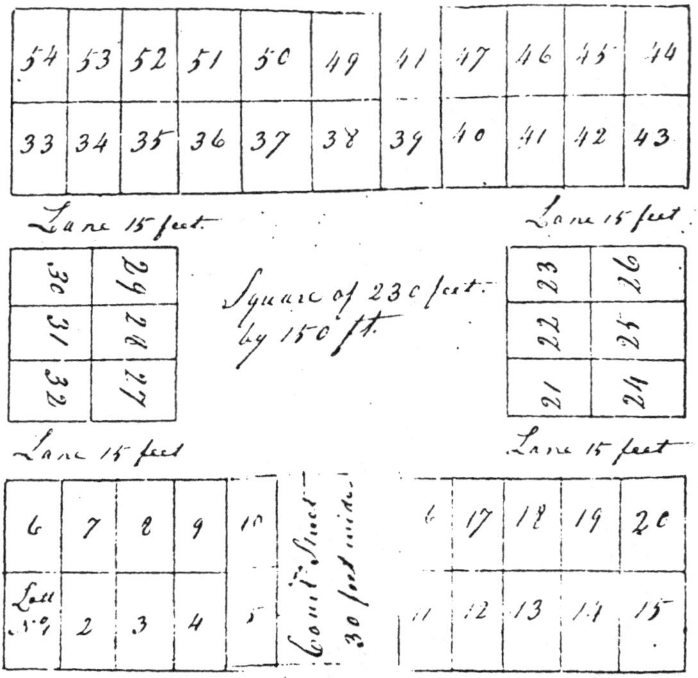

Fig. 40. RICEBOROUGH (NORTH NEWPORT), LIBERTY COUNTY, GEORGIA. Founded 1796. Surveyor: Matthew McAllister. 1733 Grant.

spite of these discrepancies, the plan basically followed the "Washington" type with a central square for public buildings surrounded by lots apparently for stores, houses and inns. In making North Newport a county seat, the commissioners seemed to think that only one change in the town was necessary, and that was to add a square and courthouse. This solution was unique. Usually in such a situation a whole town was newly laid out or the original area considerably expanded. The site of Riceborough is identified today only by a historical marker erected at the side of the road.

The original plan for Mount Vernon described what must be the smallest "Washington" plan county seat in Georgia (*Fig. 41*). Twelve one-half acre lots surrounded the square, and eight streets converged upon it at the corners. Twenty years elapsed after Montgomery County's creation before this miniscule site was fixed upon. The delay was at first partly due to unsettled condi-

TOWN PLANNING IN GEORGIA

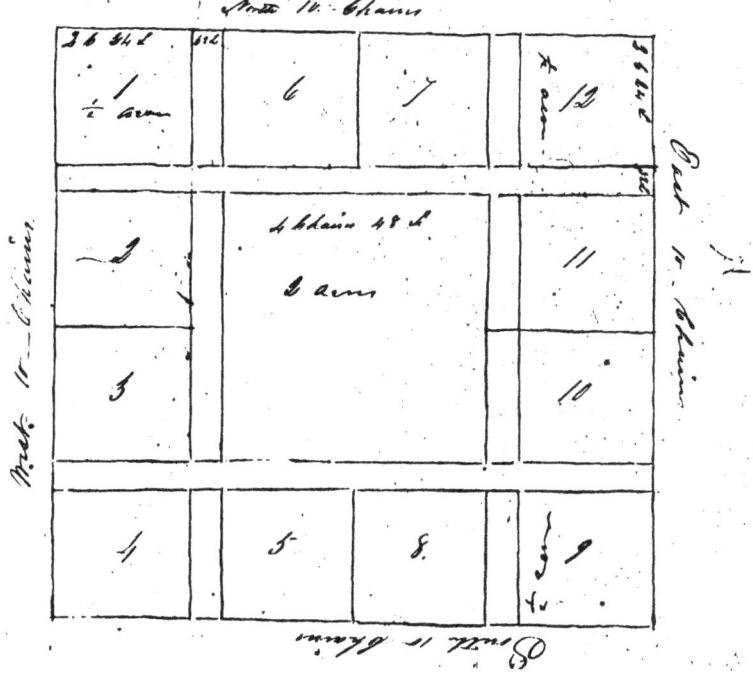

Fig. 41. MOUNT VERNON, MONTGOMERY COUNTY. Founded 1813. Surveyor: Commissioners. 1790 Cession.

tions along the Indian border. By the time Mount Vernon was finally founded, the Georgia border had been moved west and the Creeks were no longer a threat.

Others

Riceborough and Williamsburg were the only towns laid out in the Coastal area before 1790. Both have become extinct. Williamsburg (*Fig. 42*), a port, had an orthogonal plan with two miserly lots for public use and one for public landing. In the handling of the grid and the large number of lots, totaling 123, Williamsburg is nearer to the towns of the 1780s than to those of the 1790s and early eighteen hundreds. The change in the character of the Georgia coast, from the flush times of English rule to the devastated condi-

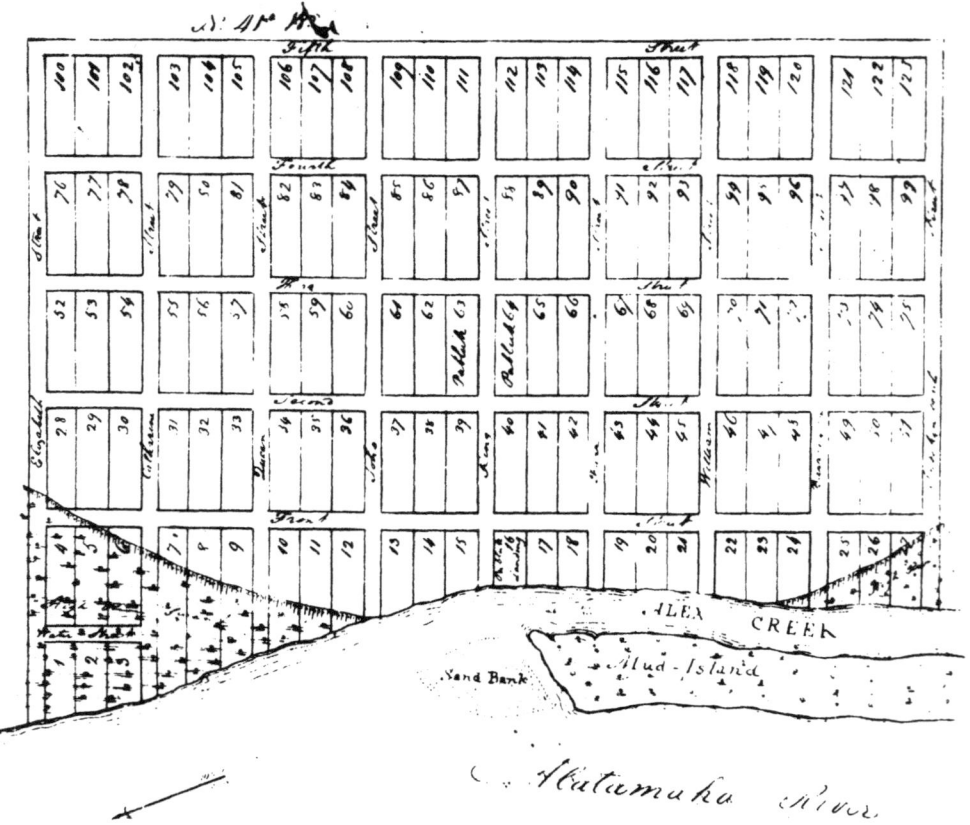

Fig. 42. WILLIAMSBURG, GLYNN COUNTY. Founded 1793. Surveyors: Farr Williams, J. Will Limbert, Roswell King. 1793 Grant.

tion in which it was left after the Revolution, is glaringly evident by comparing the plan of Williamsburg to that of the Crown town of Brunswick which it attempted to replace as the county seat. The location of Williamsburg proved even less satisfactory than Brunswick and the courthouse was returned to its original site.

Only a description exists of Jacksonborough, the first county town in Screven County. An act of the legislature in 1797 appointed five commissioners to locate a site for the county buildings. They were to procure land of not less than five acres nor more than fifty. "All monies which shall be necessary to carry this act into execution shall be provided by the justices of the Inferior Court by exposing such part of the foregoing land as they may think proper."[38] That year fifty acres of land were acquired on Beaver Dam, a site lying on both sides of the Savannah-Augusta road. The land was subdivided into what seems unusually small lots, 150 feet wide and forty-six feet deep, with several reserved for public buildings, churches and a school.[39] It is not clear from the description what type of plan was followed. Tradition has it that Jacksonborough, early in its history, developed an evil reputation for its disreputable citizenry. After the county seat was moved to Sylvania, it soon became extinct.

An evolution of sorts can be traced in both the methods of acquiring county land and in the amounts of land which were acquired during the headright period. Up to 1790 the state granted land for county seats. The loss of population during the Revolution and appropriation of loyalist property and of Crown lands had given the state an embarrassment of public domain. Granting land for a county town was one method of disposal. After 1790 granting acreage for county towns fell into disfavor and the legislature prescribed buying a specified amount of land or accepting a gift from a landowner for a county seat. No explanation is offered in the acts for the wide variation of acreage recommended for different county towns. A clue to this variation may, however, be found in the headright method of land surveying which resulted in irregular land plots.

A development can also be traced in the town plans. Because of legislative regulations, the five towns founded before 1790 were laid out in one-acre lots. No deviation from this rule seems to have been allowed. The number of lots in these towns was also regulated and during these early years the state followed the British Crown precedent of surveying large towns. The number of lots required to be laid out was far more than could be accommodated in the early years of statehood. After 1790, when lot size was specified by the General Assembly, it was usually one-half acre. When the size was left up to the commissioners, lots of one-fourth acre were frequently laid out. After 1790 the number of lots in a town was usually left up to the planner, resulting in an additional shrinkage. The extreme in miniaturization was reached in the courthouse town of Mount Vernon in 1813 which was planned for twelve lots.

From the beginning of statehood the legislature had allowed the commissioners almost complete freedom in the arrangement of blocks, lots, streets and square. Their freedom was modified only by instructions concerning lots to be reserved, lot size and, infrequently, the size of the public square. (The exception, of course, was the state-planned towns.) After 1790 town plans showed a decided break with the sophisticated colonial plans. Crown towns were planned as large urban centers featuring a number of public squares. County towns (again the state-planned towns are the exception) were laid out around one square, or in some cases no square at all. Whereas the colonial towns followed a single plan, the commissioners, in the first decades of state town planning, settled on three types of layouts for county towns: the "Augusta," "Washington," and "Sparta," with the later addition of the "Savannah" type. One or another of these plans would be followed in most Georgia courthouse towns.

Almost all headright towns after 1790 were laid out as small villages. If the population demanded an increase in size, an infrequent occurrence, lots and streets were laid out in the town common. It is interesting to note that after statehood when a colonial town was enlarged, as were Savannah, Darien and Brunswick, the original elaborate British plan was extended and included more British-type squares. In state courthouse towns enlargement never included another square.[40]

Catastrophic land speculations made the headright period in many ways a disastrous era for the state. Nonetheless, during this period a method was successfully evolved for taking care of the rapidly growing population by the organization of new counties and the siting and governing of their county seats.

Notes

1. Virginians of the well-to-do planter class brought to the state their interest in education, in the law, and in whatever culture managed to exist. The Broad River Valley in the "New Purchase," north of Augusta, became a Virginia stronghold. From this center the Virginia-born planters would periodically move west after each land cession, taking their culture with them. They exercised an influence in Georgia education, professions and politics parallel to that of New Englanders moving west in the same era. The Carolina yeoman farmer settling in the Piedmont and Red Hills brought to the state the equally important republican sentiment so frequently evident in the subsequent history of Georgia law. Ellis Merton Coulter, "The Broad River Valley," *Georgia Historical Quarterly*, XVII (1958), 35.

2. Henry Marbury and William H. Crawford, *Digest of the Laws of the State of Georgia, From 1755 to 1800* (Savannah, 1802). Hereafter abbreviated as *D.L.G., 1755-1800*. pp. 14-15.

3. *Ibid.*, p. 13.

4. Although interest in local education continued, it was not until the 1821 cession that legislative acts again ordered lots for churches to be reserved.

5. Marbury and Crawford, *D.L.G., 1755-1800*, p. 132.

6. *Ibid.*, p. 153.

7. *Ibid.*, p. 154.

8. *Ibid.*, p. 164.

9. *Ibid.*, p. 166.

10. *Ibid.*, p. 171.

11. In the 1780s the town of Greensborough was located on more than 1,000 acres granted by the state, Washington was granted 100 acres, Waynesborough a sizable amount and Augusta a large reserve confiscated from loyalists' property.

12. After 1790 the commissioners for Williamsburg were advised to acquire not more than 150 acres nor less than 100 acres. In Bullock County the commissioners were to contract for not more than 100 acres for a county seat. In Screven County the commissioners were authorized to purchase a lot of land of not less than five acres nor more than fifty acres. The legislature gave the commissioners of Elbert County permission to purchase fifty acres and

allowed those for Warren to accept seven acres from a landowner for the county buildings.

13. Flying over Georgia today, one can clearly see the contrast between the disordered landscape east of the Oconee River and the tidy squared-off landscape to the west which resulted from the cadastral type of survey employed by the state after 1805.

14. Marbury and Crawford, *D.L.G., 1755-1800*, pp. 133-134.

15. Compiled from W.P.A., *Story of Washington, Wilkes* (Athens, 1941).

16. Marbury and Crawford, *D.L.G., 1755-1800*, p. 134.

17. Elmer T. Clark (ed.), *The Journal and Letters of Francis Asbury*, 3 vols (London and Nashville, 1958), I, 707.

18. Archibald Henderson, *Washington's Southern Tour, 1791* (New York, 1923), p. 234.

19. Robert Watkins and George Watkins, *A Digest of the Laws of the State of Georgia, From Its Establishment to 1798* (Philadelphia, 1800), p. 322.

20. When measuring in chains, 202½ acres was a convenient size to lay out. This is the first time the legislative acts mention this acreage. It would become in the 1821 and 1826 cessions the unit used for the lottery lots.

21. James T. Vocelle, *Reminiscences of Old St. Mary's* (St. Marys, Georgia, 1913), p. 16.

22. Marbury and Crawford, *D.L.G., 1755-1800*, p. 161.

23. Raymond A. Mohl (ed.), "A Scotsman Visits Georgia, 1811," *Georgia Historical Quarterly*, LV (Summer, 1971), p. 270.

24. 1790 was something of a watershed year in Georgia history. A new constitution passed in 1789 made it easier to take up vacant land and to organize new counties. The 1790 Treaty of New York had the effect of easing Indian troubles. Between 1777 and 1790 only three counties had been laid out, but after 1790 a sudden increase in the population caused thirteen new counties and courthouses to be organized in a period of ten years.

25. Compiled from John H. McIntosh, *Official History of Elbert County* (Atlanta, 1968).

26. Marbury and Crawford, *D.L.G., 1755-1800*, p. 175.

27. Augustin Smith Clayton, *A Compilation of the Laws of the State of Georgia, 1800-1810* (Augusta, 1812), pp. 396 & 501.

28. Compiled from Flourie Carter Smith, *History of Oglethorpe County, Georgia* (Washington, Georgia, 1970).

29. E. Merton Coulter, "Meson Academy, Lexington, Georgia," *Georgia Historical Quarterly*, XVII (June 1958), 125-162.

30. Compiled from Smith, *History of Oglethorpe County, Georgia* (Washington, Georgia, 1970).

31. Virginia H. Moore, "Historic Sparta and Hancock County," *Georgia Magazine* (1955), p. 16.

32. Lucius Q. C. Lamar, *A Compilation of the Laws of the State of Georgia, 1810-1819* (Augusta, 1821). Hereafter abbreviated as *C.L.G. 1810-1819*, p. 1028.

33. Leodel Coleman, ed., *Statesborough 1866-1966, a Century of Progress* (Statesborough, Georgia, 1969), p. 6.

34. Josiah Everitt, the surveyor for Statesborough, wrote on his plat of the town that the lots were one acre and one-half acre, and that they measured 132 feet square and 132 by sixty-six feet. Neither of these areas equals either a half acre or a whole acre.

35. Lamar, *C.L.G., 1810-1819*, pp. 204-205.

36. Marbury and Crawford, *D.L.G., 1755-1800*, p. 156.

37. *Ibid.*, p. 157.

38. *Ibid.*, p. 165.

39. Compiled from Clyde Hollingsworth, *A History of the Early Years of Screven County* (privately printed, no date).

40. There is always an exception to a rule. In this case it is Gainesville, where two squares were built: one for commercial buildings and one for government buildings.

CHAPTER V

COURTHOUSE TOWNS IN THE LOTTERY LAND

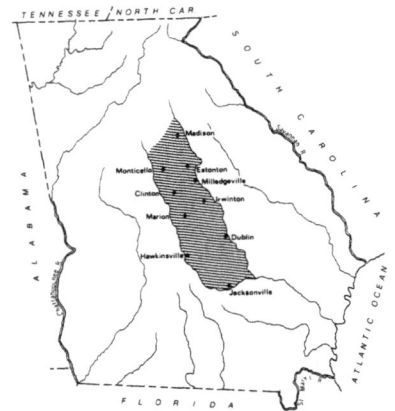

Fig. 43. CREEK CESSION OF 1802-1805.

Courthouse Towns in the 1802-1805 Cession

The Piedmont
  "Washington" plan towns
    Eatonton
    Monticello
    Madison
    Clinton
  Other
    Milledgeville

Red Hills Region
  "Washington" plan towns
    Irwinton
  "Sparta" plan towns
    Dublin
  "Augusta" plan towns
    Hawkinsville

"Savannah" plan towns
    Marion

Pine Barren-Wire Grass Region
    "Augusta" plan towns
        Jacksonville

The Creek cession of 1802-1805 (*Fig. 43*) gave Georgia a valuable strip of land between the Oconee and Ocmulgee rivers and a less valuable one in the south, west of Camden and Glynn counties. The original owners of the lands of this cession were, of course, the lottery winners.[1] These winners did not necessarily become the first settlers as they could and frequently did sell their lots for a good profit, particularly if they were in the Piedmont. If a winner did take up his land, he might sell out in a few years. Within several decades much of the best land had been bought up by large planters. The poor land was not so easily sold and was occupied by the lottery winner or, more frequently, by squatters. These were the subsistence farmers or the Georgia "crackers" as they came to be called. The well-to-do planter settling in the Piedmont and on the better Red Hills land came from the eastern counties of Georgia, from Virginia or the Carolinas. The less affluent also came from the eastern counties and from the Carolina back country. Two ethnic groups—Scots from North Carolina and Irish from eastern Georgia—settled in and around Jacksonville and Dublin, respectively.

The survey and lottery laws of this cession allowed the state to now enforce a certain amount of order in the disposition of land. Before white settlement was allowed, the land was first surveyed into land lots of 202½ acres and, in the less fertile Wayne County, of 400 acres. Out of this newly-acquired territory the state reserved 3,240 acres on the Oconee River as a site for the new state capital, Milledgeville. The first two counties of the cession (Wayne County, in the southern part of the cession, will not be considered as it was almost uninhabited) were Wilkinson and Baldwin. Because of problems connected with the acquisition of Creek land, they were not organized until 1805. The legislature noted "it is necessary and expedient that the counties of Baldin and Wilkinson be organized as speedily as possible," that justices be appointed and that a central place be selected in each for the holding of court.[2] Between 1805 and 1809 ten counties were carved out of the cession. They were Baldwin and Wilkinson (1805); Jones, Laurens, Morgan, Putnam, Randolph (later renamed Jasper) and Twiggs (1807); Pulaski (1808); and Telfair (1809).

The lottery system did not appreciably change the former headright procedure for the actual founding of towns. The main difference lay in the amount of land the town founders were told to purchase. In this cession the land allowed for a county town was a minimum of 100 acres and a maximum of 202½ acres, or one land lot. When the commissioners for the county sites of Putnam and Randolph overstepped these rules and "did proceed and purchase more land for county purposes than was contemplated by said resolution,"[3] the General Assembly took note of it. However, in the case of both of these counties the act declared the proceeds of sales of part of the land had produced some $8,000. This sum placated the lawmakers and since it furnished adequate money to build the courthouse and jail they offered no more resistance to the purchase of extra land.

The aim of the county seat was the same as formerly: to provide a convenient location to dispense local law and justice. The location was important. As had been its custom, the legislature insisted with few exceptions that the seat be in the center of the county. An act of 1809[4] required the justices of Wilkinson County to fix on a county seat within two miles of the geographical center of the county. That same year Twiggs County was set off from Wilkinson. The justices of the Inferior Court of both counties had to lay out new towns, the former courthouse town of Wilkinson no longer being in the center of either county. Exceptions to the usual rule were the four river towns in this cession. Two of them, Jacksonville and Hartford, were required to be located on the cession boundary, the Ocmulgee River. This was apparently an attempt to prevent the Indians from crossing back into their recently-ceded lands. The new capital, Milledgeville, was located at the Fall Line of the Oconee River. Dublin was located at a ford on an east-west trade route crossing the Oconee. In 1810 the legislature appointed five commissioners for Laurens County (Dublin was soon to be the county seat) to purchase or procure by donation any quantity of land not exceeding 202½ acres, at or within two miles of a place known as Sand Bar on the Oconee River as a site for the public buildings of the county.[5] In another act the legislature appointed justices for Telfair County and instructed them "to determine upon any spot or lot of land as the seat of the county" provided that it is in the 8th district and upon the Ocmulgee River."[6] (This was Jacksonville.)

After the justices of the Inferior Court or commissioners had purchased or been donated the 100 to 202½ acres at the location directed by the legislature, they were advised to reserve lots for the county buildings. Four acres was the usual area which the legislature stipulated should be kept for public use. How large, how many, or in what arrangement the lots surrounding the county buildings were laid out were decisions left up to the local planners.[7] The state was interested in the settlement process and law and order and not in the pattern of the town plan. The act providing for the seat of Morgan County (Madison) was typical. It instructed the justices of the Inferior Court to fix on a site for the courthouse and jail, to receive title to the land and "to lay off the same or any part thereof into lots of such size as they deem proper."[8] After having legislated on the location of the county seat and on the amount of public land to be set aside for courthouse and jail, the General Assembly's next duty was to ascertain that funds be acquired for the construction of these buildings. Since the sale of town lots was the source for construction funds, the body prescribed the method of sale. For Dublin it counseled the commissioners to auction the town lots in four equal installments and to give sixty days' notice in a gazette as to the days of the auction. How the buyers were to pay for the lots was also often stipulated. In Madison twelve months' credit was allowed. In the less desirable areas such as Irwinton the legislature was more lenient, allowing the commissioners to "lay off what number of lots they may think proper, and sell the same in the following manner, viz.: one fourth part of the purchase money payable in twelve months from the day of sale; one fourth part payable in two years; one fourth part payable in three years, and the remaining fourth part in four years thereafter."[9]

Once the legislature had successfully coerced the local officials into building the courthouse and jail, the next item of importance to both the state and to the townspeople was the erection of an academy. Any funds from lot sales not used to build the courthouse and jail were usually set aside for education. The legislature saw to it that the academy was incorporated and that trustees were appointed.[10]

As in a headright town, once the county seat was laid out the justices, the elected county officials, dealt with the county business. The commissioners, usually five, generally continued to be appointed by the legislature, but when their town was officially chartered they became elected officials. However, this change did not abate the state's continuing vigilance. Act after act was written endeavoring to regulate the morals, the noise, the springs, the streets, the taxes and general conditions of the county seats.

In spite of the planners' freedom to design a town in any way that might take their fancy, the plans used in the headright period continued to be adopted. The similarity can be explained by the fact that the majority of settlers came from counties directly to the east. Along with their families, slaves and household goods, they brought a desire to recreate the town they had left. The "Washington," "Augusta," "Sparta," and "Savannah" plans are all represented in this cession. Eatonton, Madison, Monticello, the most prosperous of the Middle Piedmont towns, were to continue the popular central Georgia courthouse town layout: the "Washington" plan.

The Piedmont

Eatonton, Monticello and Madison were located in the fertile Piedmont and with the exception of Milledgeville, the capital, were the most successful towns of the cession. Eatonton was the first to be laid out. From the beginning the settlers, tobacco planters from Virginia and from the eastern Georgia counties, seem to have been quite sure of the success of their county seat. They not only purchased more land than the 202½ acres allowed by the legislature but laid out a town of 200 lots, by far the largest in the cession. In this typical "Washington" plan the blocks and streets do not vary in size. It appears from discussion with the townspeople that there has probably always been a plaza (a block long and about twenty-five feet wide) in front of the courthouse square. Starting as a market, it is today used as a parking lot. The unusual aspects of the Eatonton plan lie in the large original layout, which harks back to the colonial and headright towns, and in the wide plaza on Marion Street.

Monticello was laid out at approximately the same time by settlers of the same background using the same "Washington" style plan. The town differed mainly in having a smaller square, 100 by 100 feet, and fewer lots.

Laid out a year later, Madison (*Fig. 44*) was to become one of the handsomest and richest of the Georgia Piedmont towns. Data available on the manuscript plan relate that the justices purchased 105 acres of land for the town and laid out forty-five lots, a more reasonable and less ambitious undertaking than Eatonton's 200 lots. The Madison plan followed the centralized grid pattern of Eatonton and Monticello, with the four main streets entering at the corners of the square. The main streets were approximately twice as wide as the other streets or lanes. Each block was divided into four lots separated by lanes or alleys crossing at right angles. The courthouse, formerly in the center of the public square, has been moved to lot five.

Clinton, also located in productive land and founded the same year as Madison, has today almost disappeared. Its unsuccessful

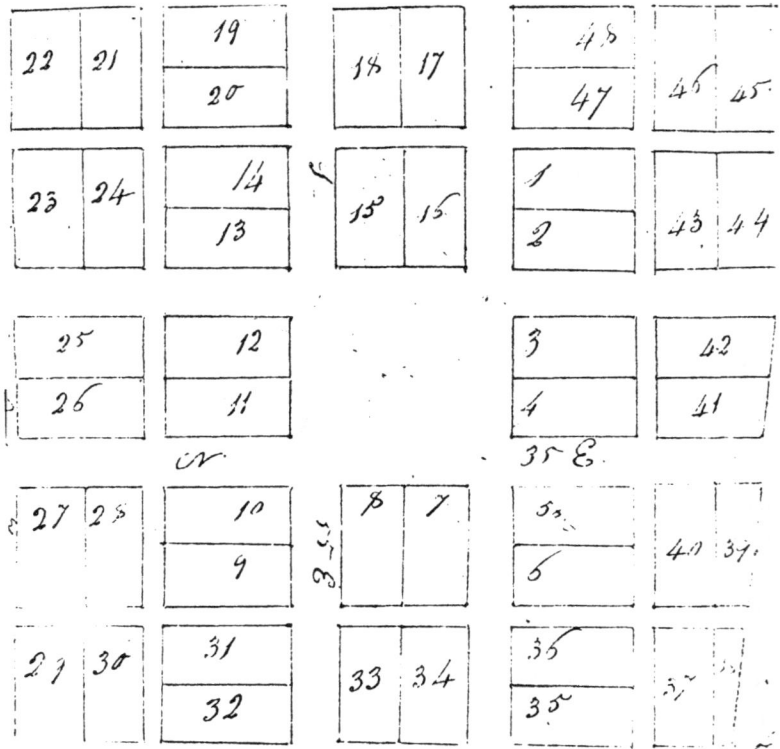

Fig. 44. MADISON, MORGAN COUNTY. Founded 1809. Surveyor: Justices of the Inferior Court. 1802-1805 Cession.

history was probably due to its proximity to Macon, the state town founded in the 1820s. In Georgia's rural society, a courthouse town depended not only on the local planters and periodic courthouse activity for its existence, but also on the activity generated by being a stop on the stage route. A larger and more attractive town nearby could easily capture this scanty but important commerce and severely affect the smaller town. According to historian Carolyn White Williams, the county site at Clinton was chosen in 1809 and a 202½-acre lot was purchased from Thomas Johnson for $2000.[11] Clinton does not seem to have been laid out before 1811 in spite of having been sited two years earlier. The commissioners laid off a typical "Washington" plan county seat with a central square surrounded by a grid of streets. Today only two of the main streets define the limits of the square.

Red Hills Region

Owing to river locations, to former trade-route towns becoming county seats, and to the topography, this region has a complete selection of courthouse town types. Although no original plan exists for Irwinton, visual survey reveals that the "Washington" plan was followed. The important effect of fertility in the surrounding country on the prosperity of a town is clearly demonstrated in Irwinton. Located in an infertile part of the Red Hills region, this minimum "Washington" plan town was not laid out until 1811 by settlers who were predominately poor subsistence farmers from eastern Georgia.

The flat-to-rolling topography of the 1802 cession did not encourage the "Sparta" plan. A rather steep hill rising from the Oconee, however, enabled the planners of Dublin[12] (*Fig. 45*) to use the "Sparta" plan and to make their town one of the handsomest in the cession. A main street climbs up from the river to end facing the courthouse. It continues from the opposite side of the square as a wide two-block boulevard formerly graced with a central tree-lined park. This main street branches into two triangular blocks. The library was built on the first lot and the city hall, formerly a hotel, now occupies the second. This layout shows the sensitivity of Georgia planners in locating important buildings in relation to the town plan.

The circumstances surrounding the siting of Hawkinsville explain the "Augusta" plan which it follows. The original Pulaski County seat was Hartford, located on the east bank of the Ocmulgee. In 1837, long after the Creeks had been moved from their land west of the river and after a thriving town, Hawkinsville, had grown up on this side, the courthouse was moved to the more prosperous town. The plan of Hawkinsville is typical of an "Au-

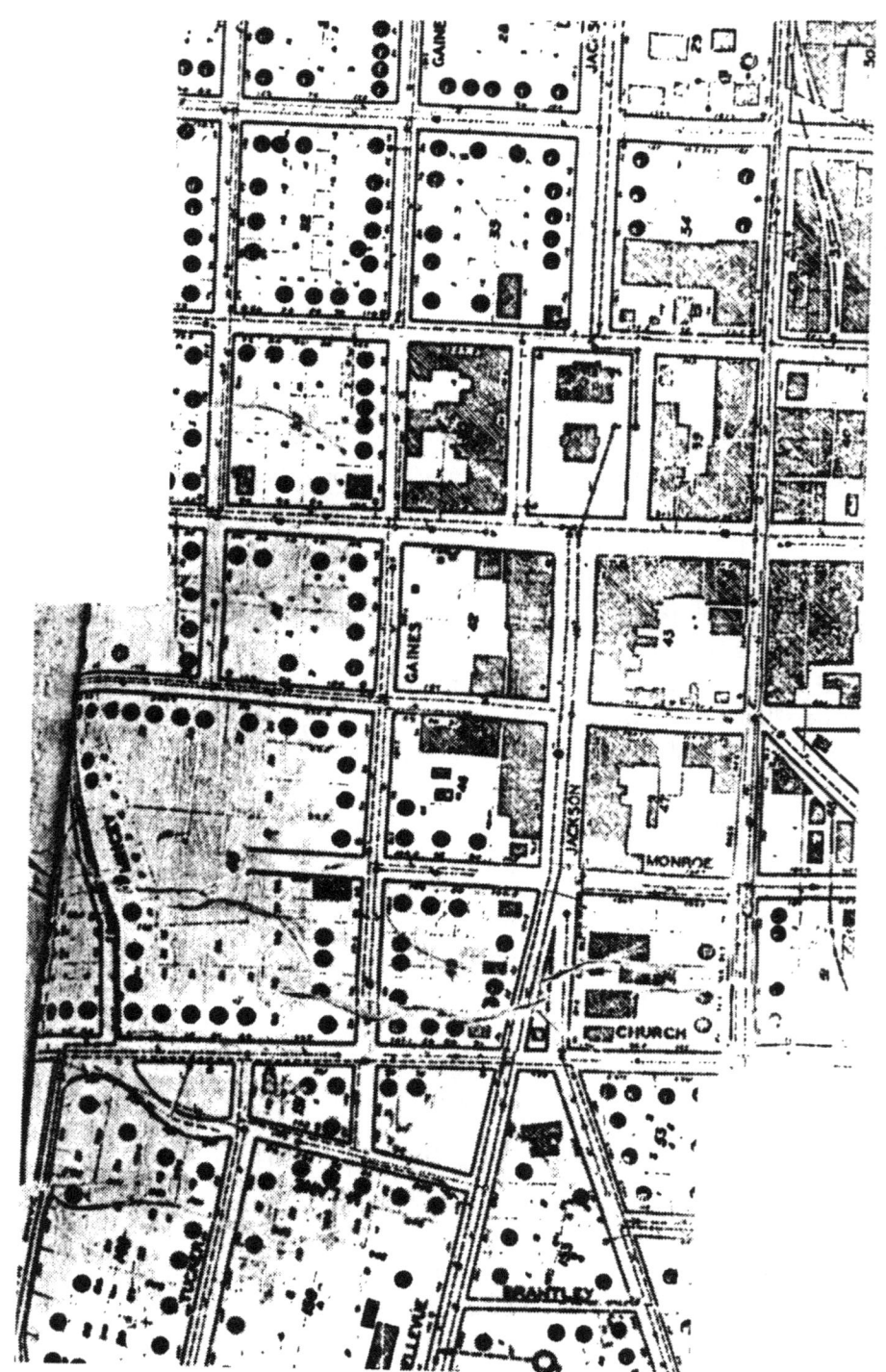

Fig. 45. DUBLIN, LAURENS COUNTY, GEORGIA. Founded 1811. Surveyor: Commissioners. 1802–1805 cession.

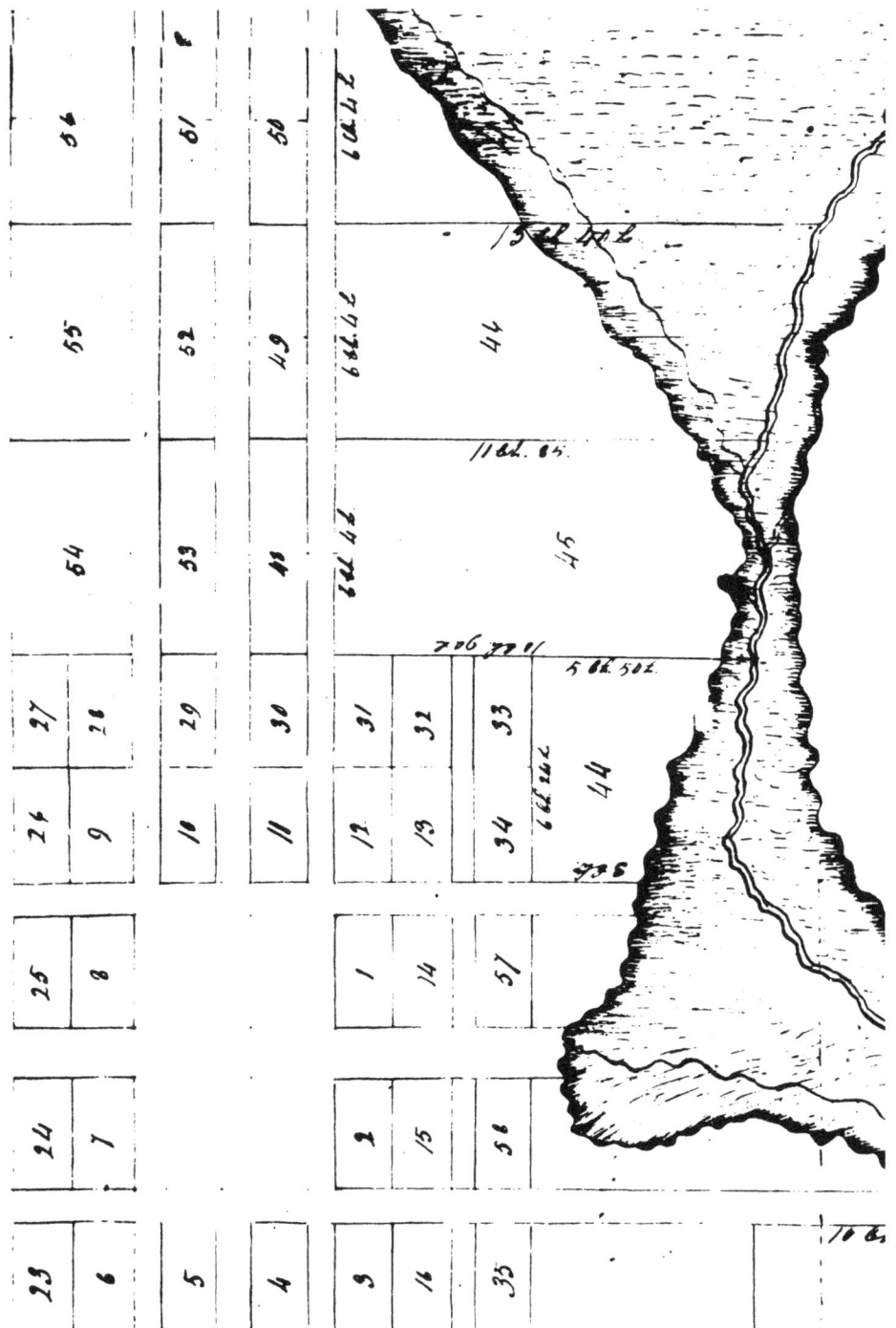

Fig. 46. **MARION, TWIGGS COUNTY.** Founded 1810. Surveyor: Commissioners. 1802–1805 Cession.

gusta" type town. It illustrates the difference between a town originally planned as a county seat and an existing town made a county seat later in its history. In the "Washington," "Sparta" and "Savannah" type towns the courthouse square is central and the town surrounds it. Almost all towns in Georgia which are not county seats follow a linear plan. In Hawkinsville and other "Augusta"-type towns this linear pattern is kept and the courthouse is placed to one side of or a block away from the main street.

Marion (*Fig. 46*), a now-vanished town, had the "Savannah" type layout which is typically located in flat terrain. The freestanding square is centered in the grid, the main streets enter the square at the center of its four sides and the secondary streets at the corners of the four sides. The plan for Marion was unusually sophisticated and well-drawn for this period in Georgia. Mysteriously, the town's main north-south streets dead-end in a creek which, according to the map, seems to be surrounded by a swamp. Such poor siting for a county seat is seldom found in the state. The varying street widths and the three streets leading into sides of the public square are features found in the Georgia colonial towns. The settlers in Twiggs came from the eastern counties and Virginia, and it is possible that they employed a surveyor from one of the coastal towns where they had lived. The forty-one small lots in the plan were mostly one-half acre, although those further from the square were larger. The square itself was exceptionally large—almost five acres.

Pine Barren-Wire Grass Region

Jacksonville was one of the cession's four river towns and the only one located in the Pine Barrens. At the instigation of the General Assembly it was located where a trade route crossed the Ocmulgee River at a ford. It seems likely that along this route, a linear settlement to serve the traffic at the ford had grown up. The commissioners for the courthouse town made this the main street and laid out lots on each side of it. As is typical for an

TOWN PLANNING IN GEORGIA   105

"Augusta" plan, the public park and courthouse occupy only part of a block facing the main street.

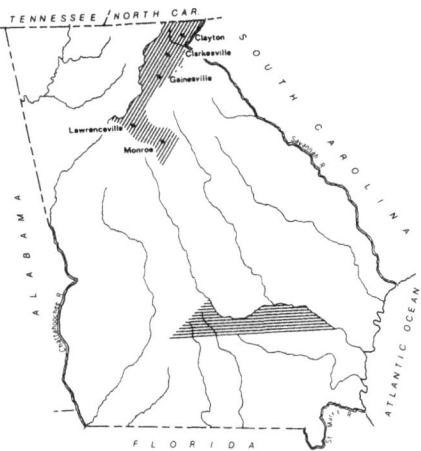

Fig. 47. CREEK AND CHEROKEE
CESSIONS OF 1817-1818 and 1819.

Courthouse Towns in the 1817-1818 and 1819 Cessions

Upper Piedmont
  "Washington" plan towns
    Lawrenceville
    Gainesville
  "Augusta" plan towns
    Monroe

Northeast Georgia
  "Sparta" plan towns
    Clarkesville
    Clayton

The 1814 Fort Jackson treaty gave the state an enormous rectangular area stretching from the old southeastern counties westward to the Chattahoochee River. This all-but-impenetrable Pine Barren-Wire Grass region was neither surveyed nor laid out into counties until after the 1817-1818 cession (*Fig. 47*) gave Georgia land in the north and a strip in the south bordering the 1815 cession. In 1818, the 1814 cession was finally surveyed along with the 1818 cession. The southern strip which abutted the 1814 cession was surveyed as part of the earlier acquisition. A legislative act provided that the state should "dispose of and distribute the late cession of land obtained from the Creek and Cherokee nations of Indians by the United States, in several treaties: Fort Jackson, 1815, Cherokee Agency, 1817 and Creek Agency on the Flint river, 1818."[13] Three counties were laid out in the 1814 cession and in the southern part of the 1818 cession. Early, the most western county, and the one which would yield fine cotton land when later Indian cessions made access to it less hazardous, was surveyed into land lots of 250 acres. The other two counties, Appling and Irwin, were surveyed into land lots of 490 acres. In the northern mountainous counties of the 1817-1818 and 1819 cession,[14] Rabun and part of Habersham were divided into 490-acre land lots, while the more fertile Walton, Hall and most of Habersham counties were surveyed into 250-acre land lots. After the survey the 1820 lottery, which took in all the surveyed land, was held.

The legislative attempts to organize the southern counties had little success. An act concerning these counties, Early, Appling and Irwin, advised that the duty of three or more commissioners which the legislature had appointed for each county was to advertise and superintend the election of five justices of the Inferior Court. These justices were then to be appointed by the governor to site a courthouse town, to buy no more than one lot of land and to build a courthouse and jail on some part of it.[15] Not for almost a decade was the state to be successful in bringing about permanent sites for county justice, and then only in Early and Irwin counties. Under the transportation conditions available until the railroad was built, the settlement and organization of Appling and of most of Irwin were practically non-existent.[16]

TOWN PLANNING IN GEORGIA

In organizing four northern counties the legislature passed an act which by now had become routine. Commissioners appointed by the legislature were to hold elections for the justices of the Inferior Court. The act concerning Walton, Gwinnett, Hall and Habersham counties counsels that

> the elected justices are hereby appointed commissioners of the courthouse and jail and have full power to fix on a site of public buildings, purchase as much land as they may deem necessary on which to erect said buildings—provided no more than 250 acres are acquired, and to contract with persons for purposes of building a comfortable courthouse and secure jail.[17]

Since even in this relatively more fertile land settlement was scanty and thinly scattered, the legislature suggested that the commissioners might first choose a temporary place for the courthouse and jail.

In 1819 an additional treaty concerning land in the northeast was won from the Indians. The legislature advocated that the state "dispose of the territory lately acquired of the Creek Indians by a treaty held by the honorable John C. Calhoun at the city of Washington." The act further directs that this acquisition be added to Hall and Habersham counties and that "all the balance of said territory shall form one county, Rabun."[18] This region was then added to the other lands in the 1820 lottery. The acts organizing Rabun were similar to the others. The legislature appointed commissioners to hold an election for justices of the Inferior Court. These justices were then appointed commissioners of the courthouse and jail and were to fix on a site for them near the center of the county. They were to purchase no more than one land lot (one wonders if the legislature realized that one land lot in this county consisted of 490 acres) and to lay off any portion into town lots reserving a sufficient amount for the public square.[19]

Walton and Gwinnett counties are in the Upper Piedmont where the land is rolling and not particularly fertile. In Hall, Habersham and Rabun the topography ranged from hilly to mountainous with fertile valleys few and far between. Not many Georgians took up their winnings in the 1820 lottery. The majority sold their land lots to settlers from the back country of the Carolinas, a people more used to the solitude of isolated mountain country than they were. It was not an area in which large holdings or cotton growing would be profitable. The yeoman farmers moving into the region had few or no slaves and small grains and livestock became the backbone of their economy. None of these county seats, away from the main tide of immigration and north of the best agricultural land, could compare to the prosperous central Piedmont towns such as Eatonton, Madison and Monticello. The courthouse seats of this cession were small, in out-of-the-way places, and they did not have plantation owners to embellish the towns with fine houses. However, they were still laid out with care and followed three typical plans—"Augusta," "Washington," and "Sparta." As would be expected, the North Georgia towns of Clarkesville and Clayton followed the "Sparta" plan. Gainesville and Lawrenceville in the Upper Piedmont followed the "Washington" plan, and Monroe, a settlement before it became a county seat, the "Augusta" plan.

Although these county towns, with the exception of Clarkesville and Clayton, had been promptly sited, the legislature had not been able to coerce the appointed commissioners to hold an election for county officials. An 1823 act appointed officials who it was hoped would hold office only until an election could be held. These appointed commissioners had full power to extend incorporated laws over all the lots and land adjoining the town "agreeable to the plan of said town laid off for county purposes."[20] In the act concerning elected commissioners the legislature instructed that they must be residents and freeholders within the corporate limits of the town and that they "shall receive no compensation for their services."[21]

Upper Piedmont

Plans for the two "Washington" towns differ considerably. Lawrenceville has a typical "Washington" plan with the streets entering the square at the corners. It was one of the few county seats where the courthouse square was not located on a rise but was considerably lower than the streets to the north. As a result, Lawrenceville lacks the charm of other courthouse towns where the siting of the square on the highest eminence adds greatly to its importance. James C. Flanagan, Gwinnett county historian, recounts the locating and laying out of Lawrenceville. The justices could not agree on the site for the county buildings. To solve the dilemma a single justice was chosen to decide on one of three land lots. Number 146 was finally chosen because of springs in the vicinity and it was purchased for $200 from the lottery winner. William Towers was employed to survey it for the courthouse and jail and then to survey and mark out adjacent lots and streets. He was paid $23.00 for this work.[22]

The most carefully conceived plan of any type in this cession was that of Gainesville (*Fig. 48*). Timothy Terrell IV, a surveyor of some note who had surveyed for both the state and the federal government, laid out the town. The main streets were forty-nine and one-half feet wide and the other streets thirty-three feet wide. The public square was approximately 200 by 200 feet. The blocks were divided into four lots.[23] In this 1820 plan there were seventy-five town lots, an optimistic undertaking for this part of Georgia.[24] The variation of the "Washington" plan which was used here and in various other similar towns consists of two ranges of narrow blocks crossing at right angles and forming the public square at the crossing. This arrangement permitted the square to be reduced to a reasonable size. The other blocks in Gainesville were 400 by 400 feet. If they had been used to surround the square it would have been twice the size of the one which resulted from blocks of 200 feet on each side.

If an owner with a land lot of 250 acres located in an isolated wilderness gave or sold part of it to the county for a town, his remaining acres would substantially increase in value.[25] Gainesville is a typical example of this sort of profit-making gift or sale. In 1820 Duke Williams deeded fifty acres to the Inferior Court of Hall County for county buildings. He was paid $1,000 for this

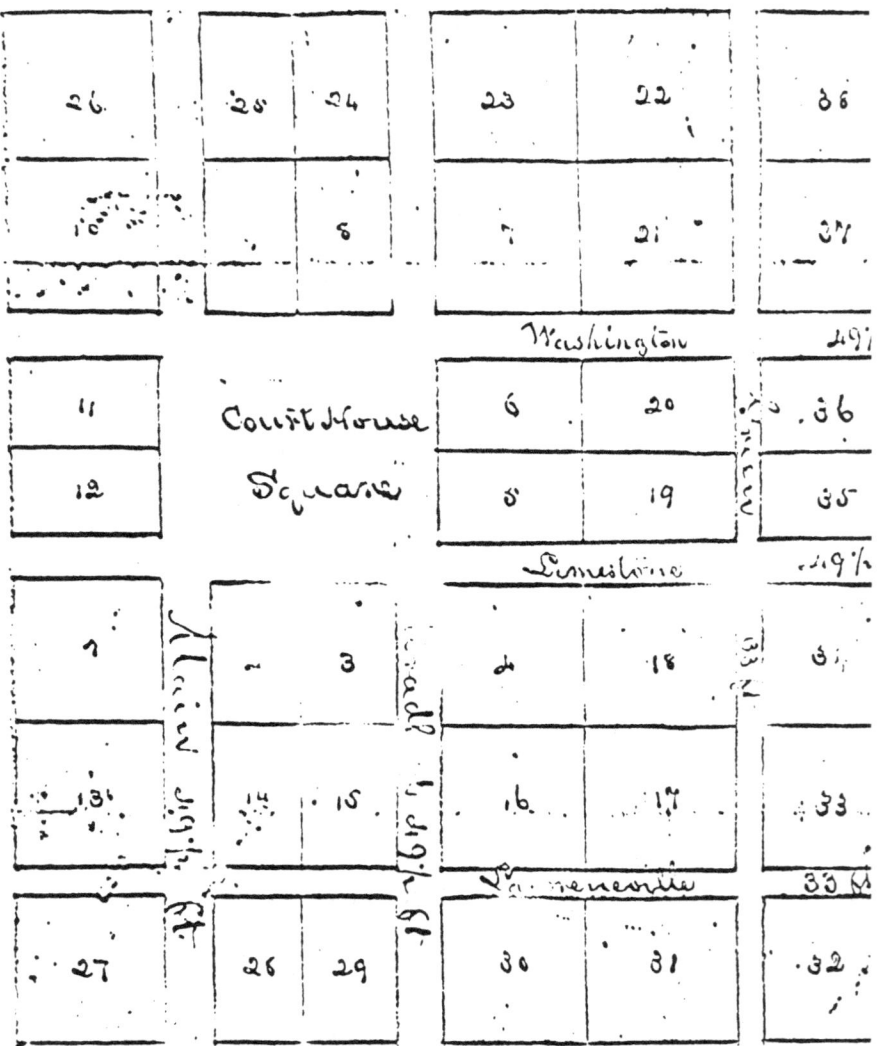

Fig. 48. GAINESVILLE, HALL COUNTY. Founded 1818. Surveyor: Timothy Terrell, IV. 1818 Cession.

land and was also given two lots in the town. In 1823 Col. Stephen Reed donated fifty acres joining the town land, reserving certain lots for himself.[26] Both men probably expected to increase the worth of their remaining land, one by causing a town to be built

TOWN PLANNING IN GEORGIA 111

on part of it, the other by encouraging the direction future growth would take.

Easley's Cowpen, the first Walton County seat, was about two miles from the present one, Monroe. An important north-south route known as Rogue Road was the original reason for the latter settlement. When the courthouse was moved to this more prosperous village Rogue Road was made the main street and a grid of blocks was laid out on either side of it. Alleys, seldom used in Georgia after statehood, were laid out in Monroe where they divide the blocks facing the long sides of the public square. The courthouse was built in a block and faces Broad Street, formerly Rogue Road.[27] This "Augusta" type plan was a typical solution for fitting a courthouse and public square into an existing linear-oriented town.

Northeast Georgia

The two towns in the northeast section of this cession follow the "Sparta" plan. Clarkesville (*Fig. 49*) was the more carefully planned of the two and shows the surprising care taken in siting a town, even in an isolated and poor region. As usual, the conformation of the land was a determining principle in siting the town. However, instead of using the points of the compass, the usual orientation for a surveyor, the main street follows a broad ridge and the plan takes advantage of the flat plateau for the town lots laid out on either side of Washington Street. The wide main road on the ridge leads up an incline to the center of one side of the public square which is located at the highest point of the town. The road leaves the square from the center of the opposite side and follows a steep descent to the Soque River. A variation of the "Sparta" plan used here and in other North Georgia towns consists of one main street entering and leaving the center of opposite sides of the square. On the other two sides of the square the roads enter at the corners.[28]

Clayton was originally more isolated than a town in the Pine Barrens. Until the railroad was built in the early twentieth century

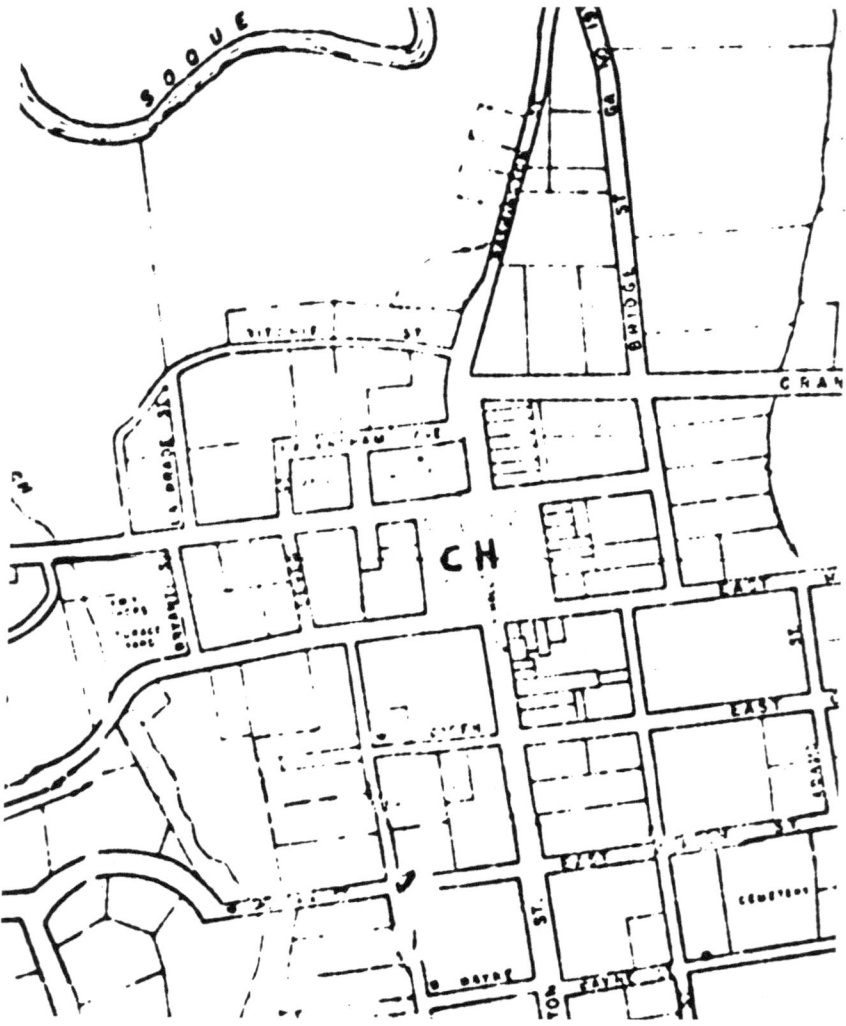

Fig. 49. CLARKESVILLE, HABERSHAM COUNTY. Founded 1823. Surveyor: Commissioners. 1818 Cession.

and it became something of a summer resort, this settlement had only the most tenuous connection with the outside world. The plan is typical of a North Georgia county seat with the main street running up a hill and entering the courthouse square at the center

TOWN PLANNING IN GEORGIA

of one side, then continuing on from the opposite side. It is possible that Main Street may have originally also entered the square at the centers of the other sides. Today the square is no longer in existence and only vestigial remains are found in a tiny park at the crossing of the main streets.

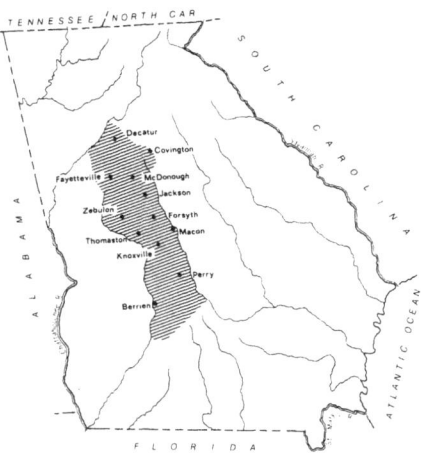

Fig. 50. CREEK CESSION OF 1821.

Courthouse Towns in the 1821 Cession

Upper Piedmont
   "Washington" plan towns
      Fayetteville
      McDonough
      Covington
      Zebulon
   "Sparta" plan town
      Decatur

The Piedmont
   "Washington" plan towns
      Jackson

Forsyth
Thomaston
"Sparta" plan town
　Knoxville
Other
　Macon

Red Hills
"Washington" plan town
　Berrien (Drayton)
Other
　Perry

It had been almost two decades since an Indian cession had included any part of the rich Piedmont. The 1814 and 1818 cessions had given the state hilly country in North Georgia with only narrow valleys to cultivate and Pine Barrens in the south which at that time were considered just about what the name implies.

> Georgia had waited the tide of events and observed the march of time for seventeen years; she had seen two states made out of the territory which she had given up in 1802, other states relieved of their Indians were growing great, while Georgia, to whom the United States owed particular obligations, was languishing because she could not get control of her own possessions.[29]

Finally in the 1821 treaty of Indian Springs the federal government bought from the Creeks a large and valuable region which extended from the Ocmulgee River in the east to the Flint River in the west, from the Chattahoochee in the north to the northern boundary of the 1814 cession in the south (*Fig. 50*). The cession encompassed the rich Upper and Middle Piedmont, the equally valuable cotton country in the Red Hills, and only a small portion of the always-unwanted Pine Barren-Wire Grass region.

The lottery had been conceived in an attempt to stop fraudulent land transactions. In this cession further attempts at control were made. The survey time was shortened to sixty days with particularly exacting requirements for surveyors and the lottery was held almost immediately after the survey. The survey itself began directly after the signing of the treaty. The land was divided into five counties and these into districts nine miles square, "the district lines running parallel to lines dividing counties and crossed by other lines at right angles."[30] The districts were then subdivided into tracts as in the 1802-1805 cession of 202½ acres. Fractional lots and certain land areas were reserved by the state. Lots 1-100 in each district were to be sold for the poor school fund[31] and land on both sides of the Ocmulgee at the Fall Line was reserved for a trading town which the state planned to build.[32] A tract at Indian Springs and the McIntosh Reserve was also kept by the state, to be later laid off into lots and sold for the state.

When the state organized the cession into five counties it was recognized that these would be divided as the population increased. The legislature appointed commissioners for the original counties, Henry, Fayette, Dooly, Houston and Monroe, to hold elections for five justices of the Inferior Court. The justices were then appointed commissioners in charge of fixing on a temporary site for the county buildings, usually someone's house. As in former cessions, the site was to be in the center of the county or of the largest population concentration. Georgians and out-of-state migrants, eager to move from their worn-out land, lost no time in crossing the Ocmulgee into the fertile virgin territory. Within two years the five original counties had been divided into twelve. The new ones were DeKalb, Newton, Upson, Crawford, Pike, Bibb and Butts.

Most of the legislation concerning the county towns of this cession was not written until 1823 after the twelve counties had been organized. The commissioners of each were directed to purchase a centrally-located land lot of 202½ acres and to lay out a county town. Unlike former cessions, the amount of land allowed for the county seat was always one land lot; also unlike earlier cessions, this order was always followed by the commissioners.[33] In a typical act the commissioners were authorized

> to purchase one square or lot of land ... and to lay out a county town on said lot, and dispose of lots under such rules and regulations as they may think most conducive to the interest of said county.[34]

More freedom than formerly was given the commissioners and they were not instructed concerning lot sales or the acreage to be set aside for county buildings. With the exception of Berrien, which was in the sparsely inhabited southern region, there were as usual no instructions as to how the town should be laid out. The legislature apparently took for granted that the commissioners would keep land for the courthouse square and, after funds from lot sales made it possible, construct the county buildings.

After the acts appointing commissioners to site county towns had been carried out, acts to incorporate these towns were enacted. These incorporation acts, though worded with slight differences for different towns, apparently had the same meaning. A typical act states that "the incorporation shall extend to and include all the tract of land originally purchased by the commissioners ... for a site of the public buildings."[35] Concerning McDonough the legislature directed that the commissioners have corporate jurisdiction over all public lots that "are now or may hereafter be laid out in said town."[36] In Forsyth the commissioners were given the power to extend the incorporation laws over all lots laid off in the plan of the town for county purposes.[37] Thus, even if the town layout did not encompass the whole 202½ acres, and none did, the commissioners were responsible for, and the legislature incorporated, the whole land lot. This is further confirmed by acts regulating the residence of elected officials to within the "square or lot of land" as the legislature refers to the 202½ acres, chosen for the county seat. By incorporating the whole land lot the town was given control over its growth. In headright or colonial towns the land outside the town proper would have been referred to as the common.

Though the first acts to incorporate towns in this cession commonly mention the land lot as the incorporated territory, until the town was chartered the state frequently changed the size of this incorporated area. Perry is typical. In 1823 it was made the permanent site of Houston county and the land lot area, 202½ acres, was established for the public buildings.[38] In 1824 an act to incorporate the town included the land one-half mile in all directions "from the center of said corporation, which shall be the center of the public square."[39] (This would be approximately 502 acres.) In 1825 the legislature determined that the incorporation of the town should extend one-fourth mile in all directions from the public site.[40] (This could encompass approximately 125 acres.) In 1828 the corporate limits of Perry consisted "of all lands lying within six hundred yards of the center of the courthouse square"[41] (approximately 233 acres). When the town gained a charter its boundaries became stabilized. The reason for the state's indecision concerning the extent of incorporation is not known. One explanation may be that surveying in a circle with the courthouse as the center, though a simplified method frequently employed after a town was laid out, of necessity changed the acreage.[42]

Adiel Sherwood in his 1827 Gazeteer wrote that almost all towns on the west side of the Ocmulgee seem to have sprung into existence as if by magic, and that four or five years earlier the territory had been solitary wilderness. He was pleased to find that in all villages lots had been provided for churches and academies, that elegant courthouses and jails had already been constructed, and that the houses were handsome.[43] It was routine in this cession for the legislature in the incorporation of a town to authorize the justices to select and donate lots for the Presbyterian, Baptist and Methodist churches.[44] The counties without exception applied for state grants to build academies. The country was becoming less of a rough and tumble frontier. Cultural baggage was not too troublesome to transport into this cession from the adjoining well-settled region to the east. Georgia was gaining on the wilderness.

Upper Piedmont

The Upper Piedmont was a region inhabited by planters owing medium-size farms and few slaves. Most had migrated from the eastern Georgia counties and the Carolinas and many had won their land in the 1821 lottery. Decatur (*Fig. 51*) in DeKalb County is the one town in this region which was laid out in the "Sparta" plan. When James Diamond, a settler living in the county, surveyed the site for Decatur he followed the traditional "Sparta" siting by placing the courthouse square on a rise with two main streets leading into the center at opposite sides. The justices, typically, offered lots to three churches if the congregations would, within a specified time, erect buildings.[45]

The other four towns of the Upper Piedmont follow the most simple form of the "Washington" plan. There is no deviation in the size of lots, blocks or width of streets. If a variation did occur, it was in the wider streets surrounding the courthouse square. In keeping with Georgia's tradition the towns were well sited, with the public square placed at the highest elevation. Covington became a successful town with an embryonic cotton mill industry. Consistent with the attitude of the settlers and the legislature, the commissioners bought twenty acres of land for an academy and the legislature extended the incorporated area to include this addition.[46] In 1828 the handsome Fayetteville courthouse, now the oldest in the state, was built. That such a building could be constructed so soon after Georgia got possession of the region shows how quickly it became settled. (Fayetteville is perhaps best knwon as the town where Margaret Mitchell had the fictional Scarlett O'Hara attend school.) Both McDonough and Zebulon conform to the ubiquitous "Washington" plan. Pike County demonstrates the rising value of land in this region. The land lot for the first county site, four miles south of Zebulon, was purchased for $700. It was subsequently found not be be adequately central and another land lot was purchased from James Whatley for $1000. Zebulon was laid out on this tract.[47]

TOWN PLANNING IN GEORGIA 119

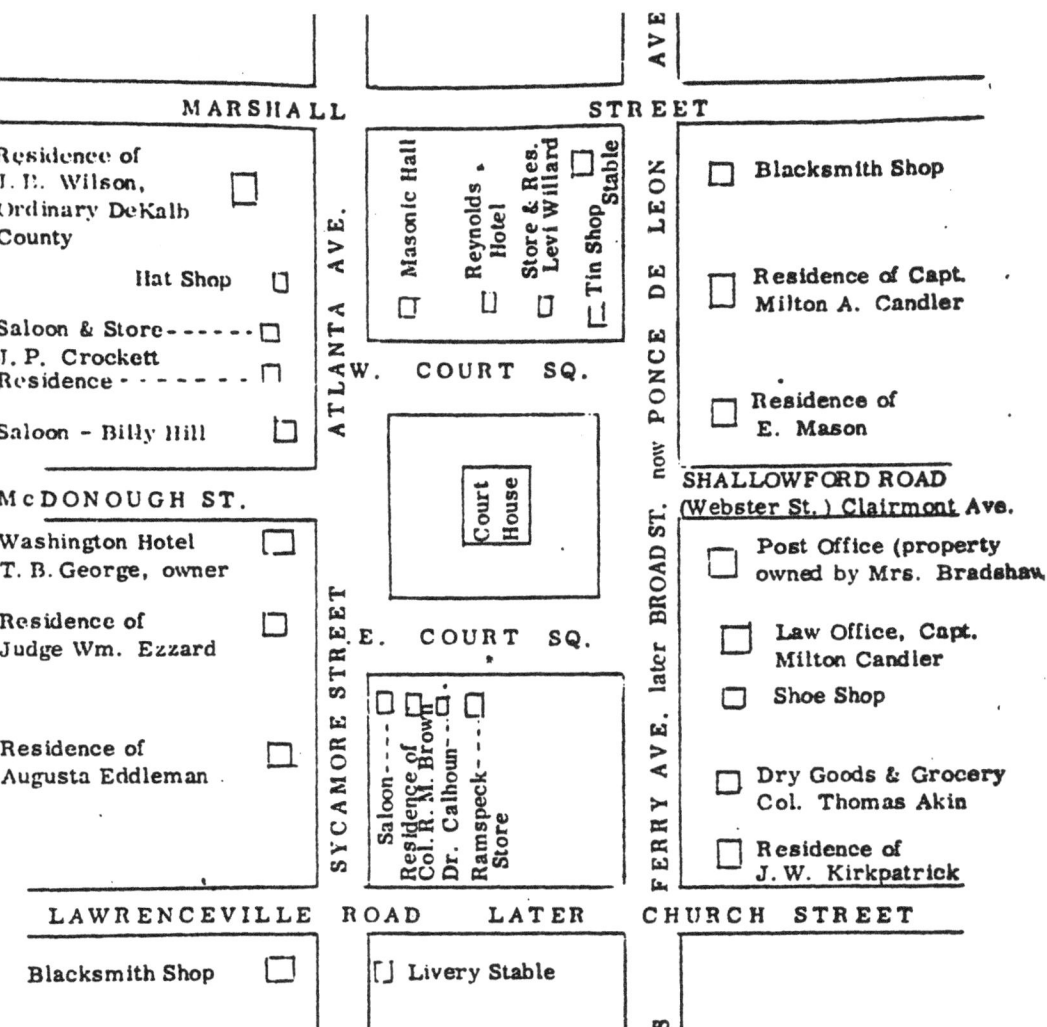

Fig. 51. DECATUR, DEKALB COUNTY. Founded 1823. Surveyor: James Diamond. 1821 Cession.

The Piedmont

The Piedmont towns came into being with the same alacrity as those in the Upper Piedmont. Near the eastern border of the ces-

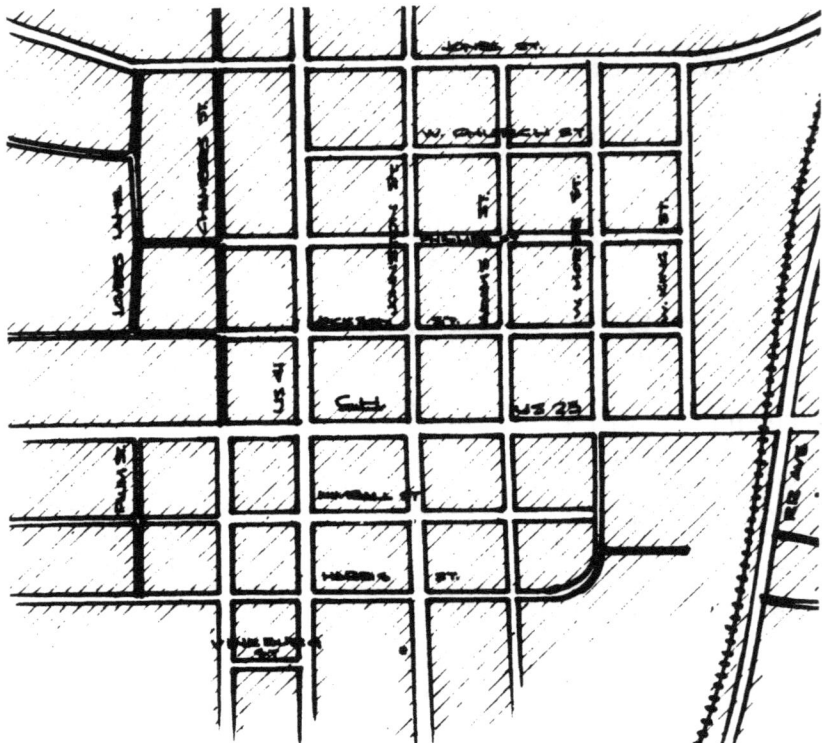

Fig. 52. FORSYTH, MONROE COUNTY. Founded 1823. Surveyor: Lemuel Gresham. 1821 Cession.

sion were Jackson, Forsyth, and Macon, the last being a state-planned town. Further to the west were Knoxville, which was on the main route from Milledgeville to Columbus, and Thomaston, in the Pine Mountains. With the exception of Knoxville, all of these county seats used the "Washington" plan. The towns most popular with the large planters, who in this region of valuable cotton land were often absentee owners, were Forsyth and Macon. Very soon after their founding they were graced with academies, churches and large houses. Forsyth (*Fig. 52*) was originally laid off into lots of two and one-half acres "affording ample room for garden plots and spacious lawns."[48] Today, in the blocks west of the courthouse square, there is still evidence of a few of these large lots and

TOWN PLANNING IN GEORGIA 121

of the houses and gardens which were built on them. Part of two lots making up one land lot were bought by the commissioners for Forsyth for $715.75. The surveyor, Lemuel Gresham, was paid $90 to lay out the town and $50 extra for other chores for the county.[49] Thomaston, in the Pine Mountains, had access to water power and shortly after its founding the beginnings of industrialism began to appear. Jackson was laid out in the usual "Washington" nucleated plan. Unfortunately, it has been badly mutilated by a highway on one side of the courthouse square which turned the town into a linear plan.

Knoxville is one of the few early county seats in Georgia (if not the only one) which today consists of a courthouse deserted by its town. When the railroad came through this area, it passed Knoxville some two or three miles to the south where the town of Roberta developed. Usually in such situations the county seat would be moved to the more lively and convenient location, but that was not done here. Today the attractive 1840 courthouse stands on its hill in solitary splendor. The plan of Knoxville was the "Sparta" type, which is unusual for the Piedmont. The courthouse, located on a high rise, is approached from east and west by roads which run to the middle of two sides of the square. The east-west direction was the route the stage followed from Milledgeville through Macon and on to Columbus. It was the one most travelers took. Few of the 1821 cession towns, with the exception of Macon, are ever mentioned in the letters and journals of early travelers. Knoxville, surprisingly, is noted by both the well-traveled James Stuart and James Silk Buckingham. It was a stop on the stage and they found it a "new village" with "rude fare."

Red Hills

The most interesting town plan, on paper, of the 1821 cession was done by Joel Walker for Perry (*Fig. 53*) in Houston County,[50] one of the largest cotton-producing counties in the state. The plan is unusual in having four symetrically-arranged public squares, the

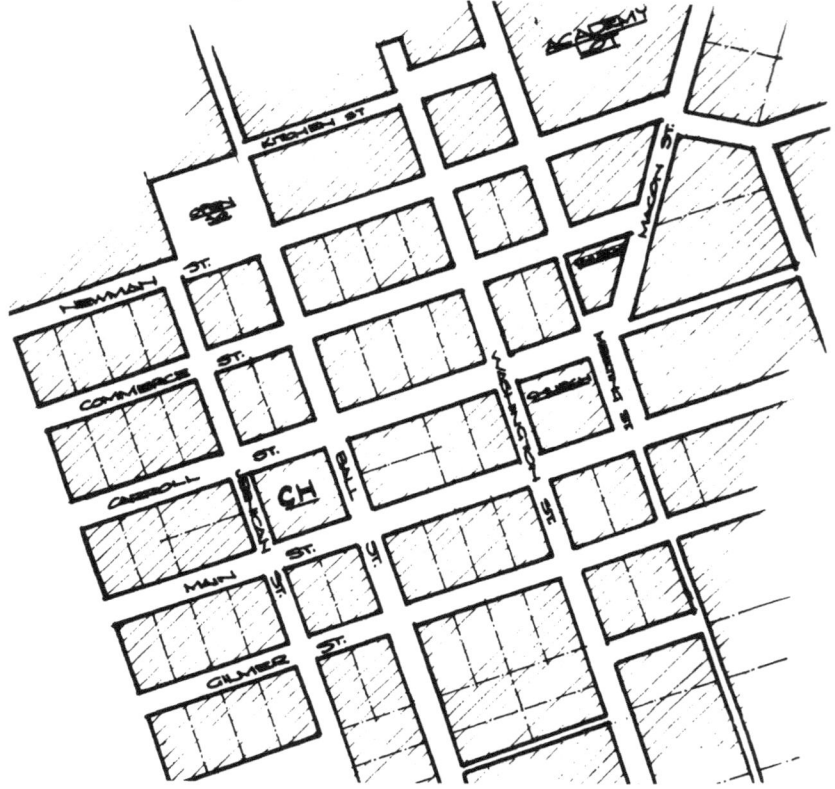

Fig. 53. **PERRY, HOUSTON COUNTY.** Founded 1824. Surveyor: Joel Walker. 1821 Cession.

courthouse square being the southeastern one. A comparable arrangement of public squares is found in courthouse towns in the Carolinas. Raleigh, North Carolina and Camden, South Carolina are typical of this type. Since the original settlers came from South Carolina,[51] it is possible that they brought the idea of this plan with them. The plan not only has four squares but also blocks of varying sizes which are reminiscent of earlier and more elaborate Georgia plans. Perry has developed around the courthouse square, and viewing it today it is difficult to visualize the more interesting original layout of four squares of equal size.

With the exception of Macon, Berrien, in the southern part of the cession, was the only town to be located on a river (the Flint).

TOWN PLANNING IN GEORGIA

It had a rather slow birth, as was to be expected in this less-populated region. The legislators, seemingly worried about bringing it into existence after appointing commissioners several times with no results, finally added extra instructions. They exhorted the commissioners to lay off for the town "not less than 10 nor more than 20 acres of land,"[52] a very small area indeed. Shortly after Berrien was laid out, the name was changed to Drayton and in 1854 the county seat was moved eight miles east to Vienna. No plan of Berrien was available but Vienna follows the usual "Washington" plan and it is probably reasonable to conclude that Berrien followed the same design.

Fig. 54. CREEK CESSION OF 1826.

Courthouse Towns in the 1826 Cession

The Piedmont
  "Washington" plan towns
    Newnan
    LaGrange
    Talbotton

Hamilton
"Sparta" plan towns
Greenville
Other
Columbus (Chapter 6)

Upper Piedmont
"Washington" plan towns
Franklin
"Sparta" plan towns
Carrollton
Other
Campbellton (dead)

Southwest Georgia
"Washington" plan towns
Lumpkin
Americus
"Savannah" plan towns
Cuthbert
Other
Starkville (dead)
Horry (dead)

The next-to-last Indian cession (*Fig. 54*) took in the land between the Flint and Chattahooche rivers and stretched from the Cherokee nation in the north to the 1814 cession in the south. The treaty was first signed at Indian Springs in 1825 and again in Washington in 1826. It was not until 1828 that Georgia legally got possession of the remaining land under Creek ownership, an area west of the Chattahoochee which was to include Carroll County. Without waiting for this fine point to be settled the state began the survey of the entire region in 1826. The Creeks did not take the loss of their lands without protest. Uprisings and raids made the region west of the Chattahoochee and the southwest relatively unsafe for some years.

The legislative act ordering the survey was similar to the 1821 act. The surveyors were to be bonded and the survey was to be completed within ninety days. The territory was first to be divided into districts, approximately nine miles square, then into land lots of 202½ acres.[53] The land lottery, which had become a well-established and regulated institution, was held in 1827. As formerly, the state reserved certain lands. All fractional lots were reserved, one square mile at Marshall's Ferry, including the ferry on the Flint River, one square mile at McIntosh's, including the ferry on the Chattahoochee River, and five square miles at Coweta Falls where the state planned to build a trading and industrial town.

In general this cession follows the topography of the 1821 cession. The region extending north of the Fall Line was the rich Piedmont. It was the territory most quickly settled and was an area of large cotton plantations. The tract west of the Chattahoochee was rolling and heavily wooded. This was a region of yeoman farmers as was the small area of the Upper Piedmont. The portion south of the Fall Line included the Red Hills. It became a region of large cotton plantations and absentee owners. In the southeastern corner of the cession was a large tract of Pine Barren wilderness.

The majority of settlers came from the eastern counties, a large number from the Carolinas and a smaller number from Virginia. In this cession, before the rich southwest was appreciated, the best lands were thought to be in Coweta, Troup, and Talbot counties. As in the last cession, the settlers brought with them their cultural baggage which included the way a town should be planned. With a few startling exceptions, such as Carrollton and Cuthbert, the towns follow the familiar "Washington" plan.

In an act "to organize the territory lately acquired from the Creek Indians" the legislature fixed the boundaries of the first counties: Lee, Muscogee, Troup, Coweta, and Carroll.[54] It instructed the settlers to elect justices of the Inferior Court who were to fix on a site for county buildings. The act also directed the elected officers to purchase a land lot for the county town and reserve a fraction as the public site. The judges were to assess the value of this fraction, then lay out a county town and dispose of the lots in a manner they thought most conducive to the public interest. It was further the duty of the Inferior Court to reserve two lots of one acre each for academies, and four lots of one acre each for religious purposes.[55] A duty newly spelled out for the justices was the selection of other sites besides the county seat for voting purposes. Some of these sites would eventually become towns, though not planned developments. Vernon in Troup County had such a beginning.[56] The above acts show the most advanced type of planning which the legislature had done. The indecisions of former years were resolved and these decisive acts show clearly the result of a quarter of a century of organizing the settlement of large areas of virgin land.

The Piedmont

The Piedmont towns—Newnan, LaGrange, Hamilton and Talbotton—followed the "Washington" plan. In Newnan, nine blocks were laid out in the original survey. At the sale of the lots $7,000 was realized, an unusually large sum.[57] Large acreage bought by a planter in the county land lot would frequently border on the original town plan. As a result streets could often not be extended from the town but stopped at the boundary of the planters' land. Their large houses were usually built facing a town street. This tradition is evident in the older eastern counties and carries over in many instances into the newer settlements. It has made for pleasant vistas in Newnan and also in such other towns as Hamilton.

Talbotton (*Fig. 55*) was a much larger venture than either Newnan or Hamilton. Its importance came partly from being on the stage route from Macon to Columbus. It is even mentioned by two early travelers: James Silk Buckingham noted that it was a pretty little place, whereas Tyrone Power found the town "wild and wooly." The plan has small lots facing the square with larger ones in the blocks further from it.

TOWN PLANNING IN GEORGIA 127

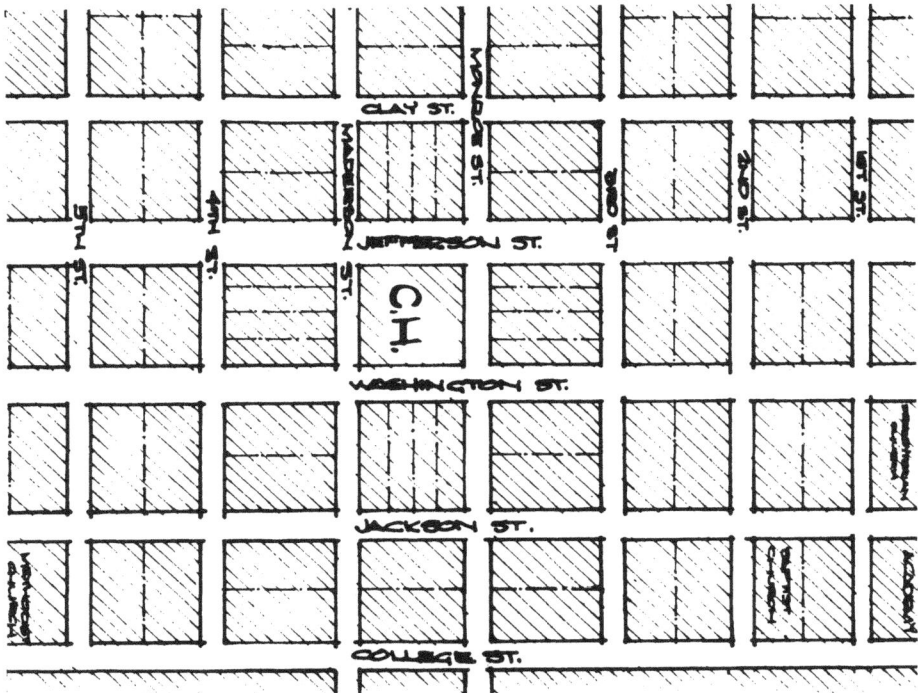

Fig. 55. TALBOTTON, TALBOT COUNTY. Founded 1827. Surveyor: Commissioners. 1826 Cession.

LaGrange (*Fig. 56*) was laid out by the county surveyor, whose training was probably more extensive than was usual for a planner. This could be the reason for its greater elaboration. Similar to Gainesville in the Upper Piedmont, two narrow ranges of blocks, perpendicular to each other, cross at the courthouse square. As has been pointed out, this makes for a square of reasonable size. The lots around the LaGrange square which were intended for commercial purposes had small frontages, while the other town lots were one acre with four lots making up a block. The commissioners followed the legislature's instructions and kept out from the lot sale two lots for academies and four for churches.[58] In a region of productive land such as this, the price of land lots rose

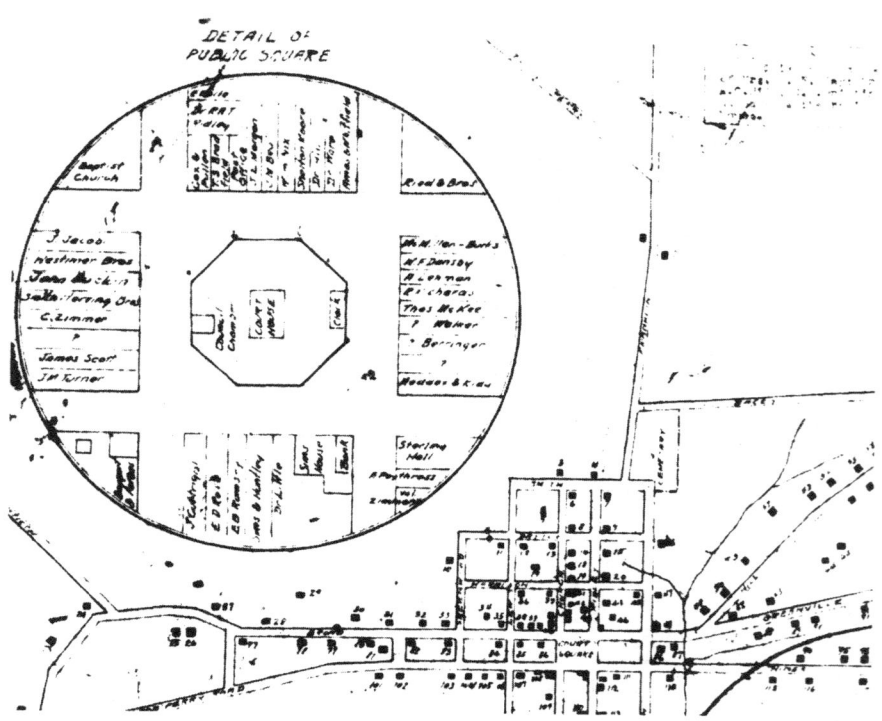

Fig. 56. LaGRANGE, TROUP COUNTY. Founded 1828. Surveyor: Samuel Reid. 1826 Cession.

rapidly after the lottery. Land lot 109, for example, had been drawn by Baily Reed, who some months later sold it for $300. It changed hands two weeks later for an additional $200, and only one week after that the owner sold it to the Inferior Court justices for $1,350.[59]

The lots indicated on the Greenville plan (*Fig. 57*) are those which had been sold at the time the survey was filed in the deed book. The plan of the single main street entering the center of the square is the familiar North Georgia or "Sparta" plan, and one used when the topography was steep enough to allow the courthouse square to be sited on a considerable rise. It is the only one of its kind in this cession. Carrollton and Cuthbert are somewhat

TOWN PLANNING IN GEORGIA

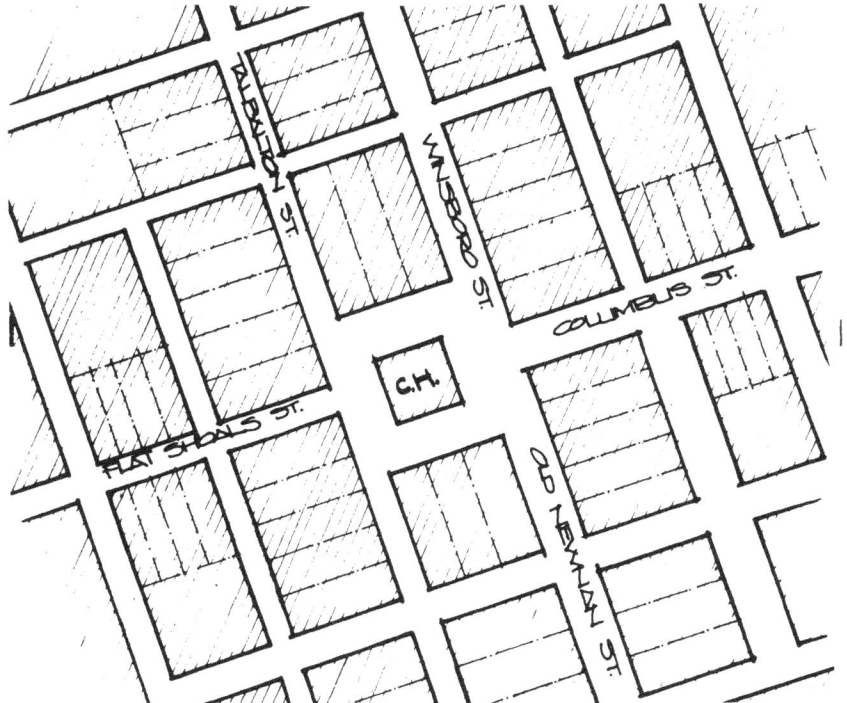

Fig. 57. GREENVILLE, MERIWETHER COUNTY. Founded 1828. Surveyor: Commissioners. 1826 Cession.

similar, but have main streets entering the center of all four sides of the public square.

Upper Piedmont

In the northern part of the Piedmont the siting of the now-dead town of Campbellton showed the type of speculation found in some earlier towns. In 1829 the owner of a large piece of undeveloped land laid out a town which he hoped would become the seat of Campbell County. From visual survey of this ghost town the plan seems to have been patterned after the "Washington" type. The owner then offered free building lots to anyone who

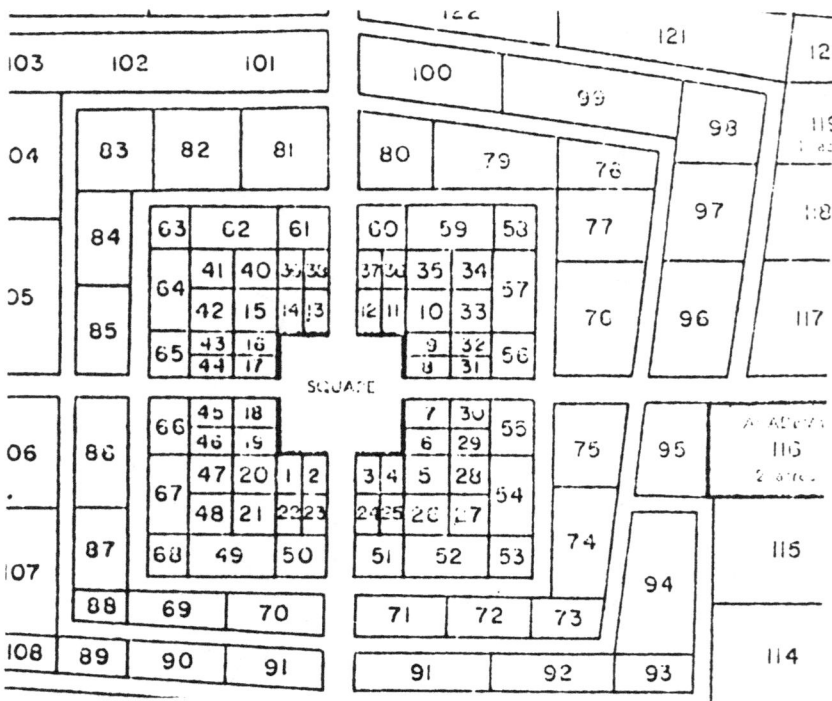

Fig. 58. CARROLLTON, CARROLL COUNTY. Founded 1826. Surveyor: Ulysses Lewis. 1826 Cession.

wished to settle in his town and free land for the public buildings.[60] His scheme was successful and through it he no doubt was able to increase the value of his adjoining land. This kind of speculation was unusual for the period; more typically, the county site was selected by the state-appointed commissioners and purchased from the owner.

Because of Indian raids and isolation, another town in the Upper Piedmont was not laid out until 1830. This was Carrollton (*Fig. 58*), whose unusual plan is illustrated in James C. Bonner, *Georgia's Last Frontier*.[61] It bears a faint resemblance to a type popular in the 1820s in the old Northwest, of which Indianapolis and Sparta, Ohio are examples.[62] This may give a clue as to Carrollton's provenance. In a region where land was selling for ten cents an acre, a town plan containing 148 lots was highly unrealistic; it is reminiscent of some of the headright towns or of Eatonton. With the exception of the state-planned town of Columbus, it is the most ambitious plan of the cession. According to Bonner, there were sixteen prime lots on the square with fifty-foot frontages that ran back 100 feet. Behind these was a group of lots of one acre and behind these two-acre lots and then four-acre lots. As might have been predicted, many of the lots were unsold ten years after the founding. In spite of an unauspicious beginning, Carrollton has kept her unusual plan intact and it is easily recognizable today.

Franklin, the other town west of the Chattahoochee, is a small "Washington" type county seat offering none of the fanciful exoticism of Carrollton. It is, however, beautifully sited on a hill. The flat top of the elevation forms the square which is surrounded by lots forming the main part of the town.

Southwest Georgia

In certain localities of the southwest portion of the cession the land was unhealthful but excellent for growing cotton. As a result, in an area at least twice the size of the Piedmont only three early towns managed to survive: Lumpkin founded in 1828, Cuthbert founded in 1831 and Americus founded in 1832. Lumpkin and Americus were run-of-the-mill "Washington" plan towns. Lumpkin is notable both for its handsome siting on a hill which allows a wide view from the courthouse square of the rolling countryside, and for some interesting restorations which are today being made to a tavern and other nineteenth century buildings. Americus (*Fig. 59*) is more notorious than notable as being the only courthouse town in Georgia, in the first 100 years of Georgia town planning, which sold her public square. In the late nineteenth century the Windsor Hotel was built on half of the square and the local post office on a portion of the remainder. The effect of losing the central open space gives an unpleasant crowded feeling to

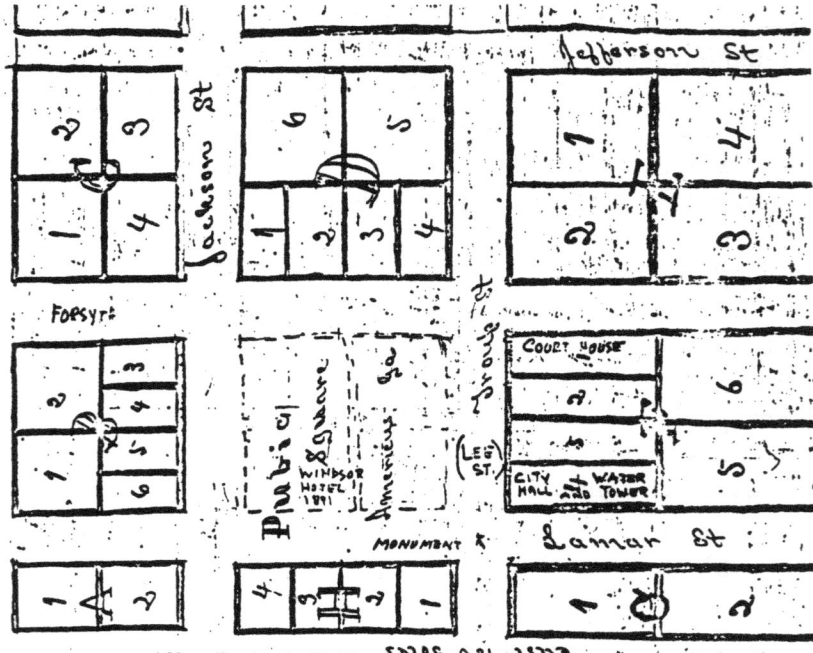

Fig. 59. AMERICUS, SUMTER COUNTY. Founded 1832. Surveyor: Commissioners. 1826 Cession.

the downtown area. The importance of the public park graced with a courthouse in the center can be truly appreciated in Americus where it has been lost.

Cuthbert *(Fig. 60)*, laid out in 1831, is a case where an interesting plan developed into an equally interesting city. The plan is similar to Blakely *(Fig. 64)*, where the four main streets enter the square at the middle of each side. In Cuthbert, however, the "Savannah" plan is followed and smaller streets also enter the square at the corners. There are two ranges of narrow blocks placed at right angles whose crossing forms the public square. The other blocks in the plat are square with dimensions corresponding in size to the longer side of the oblong blocks.[63] As in the more carefully designed plans, a module is established which allows for a tidy fitting together of the various sized blocks. The extent of the

TOWN PLANNING IN GEORGIA 133

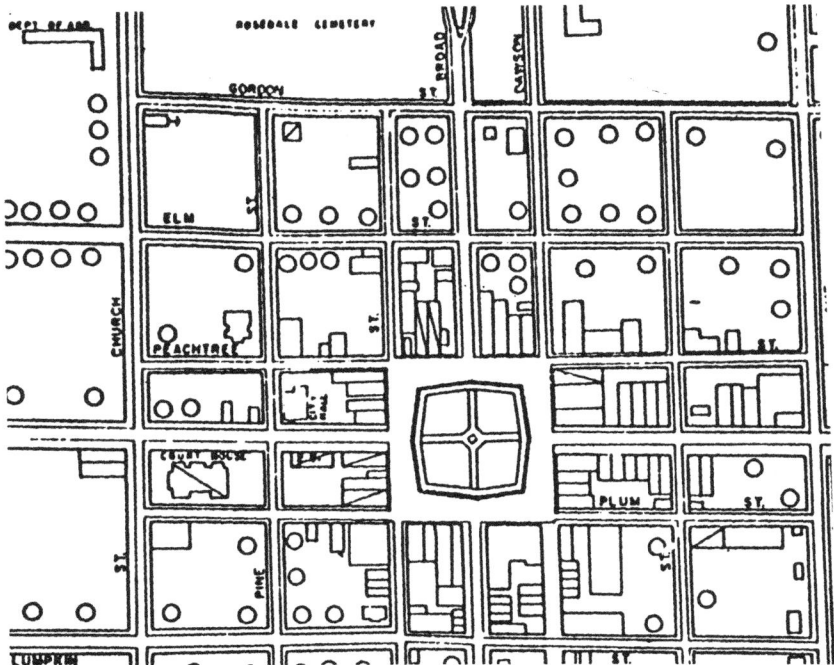

Fig. 60. CUTHBERT, RANDOLPH COUNTY. Founded 1831. Surveyor: Commissioners. 1826 Cession.

original boundaries can easily be recognized from the map. Cuthbert furnishes a good illustration of streets of the original grid which dead-end at the boundary of the plan. It is, as has been pointed out, opposite these dead-end streets that many of the typical Greek Revival houses were sited. They give a handsome focal point to the street which they front and form one of the typical characteristics of Georgia courthouse towns. In Cuthbert the courthouse, once in the center of the square, has been moved two blocks north.

The 1826 cession was given to Georgia only five years after the 1821 cession, and as settlers had not been waiting for almost two decades to move to new land it was not as quickly settled as the previous one. Towns away from the popular Piedmont took a considerable time to be founded, some original county seats not being founded until four or five years after the lottery. However, with the exception of Horry, the first county seat of Marion; Starkville, in Lee County several miles east of Leesburg; and Campbellton, all of the county towns continued to exist if not to thrive.[64]

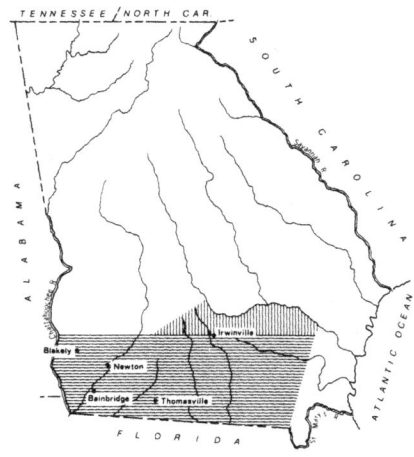

Fig. 61. THE 1814 CESSION AND THE SOUTHERN PART OF THE 1818 CESSION.

Courthouse Towns in the 1814 Cession and the Southern Part of the 1818 Cession

Southwest Georgia

    "Washington" plan towns
        Bainbridge
        Newton
        Thomasville
    "Sparta" plan towns
        Blakely

TOWN PLANNING IN GEORGIA

Pine Barren-Wire Grass Region
  "Washington" or "Augusta" plan towns
    Irwinville

Out of the War of 1812, which in Georgia was fought between the United States and the Creek Indians, came the 1814 Fort Jackson treaty.[65] This treaty gave Georgia an enormous tract of land across the southern part of the state (*Fig. 61*). At the time this was acquired it was isolated from the rest of the state by Indians inhabiting the area to the north and Spaniards controlling the region to the south and few settlers were attracted to it.[66] The eastern part of the cession was flat, consisting mostly of the Pine Barren-Wire Grass region. It was considered useless until many decades later when lumber companies discovered its potential as a rich source of timber. The western section consisted partly of the so-called hummocks and the fertile limesink region. After the 1821 and 1826 cessions made this area accessible it was found to contain valuable cotton land.

The first five county towns in the 1814 cession were founded between 1823 and 1831. Before this time, in spite of numerous acts passed by a frustrated legislature attempting to organize these large empty counties, there had been little interest on the part of the sparse and mostly illiterate population to site courthouse towns. It was not until 1823 that the original Early County was adequately populated to be divided into a less cumbersome size. Decatur County was formed and the legislature recommended that the commissioners fix on a permanent courthouse site for it and a temporary site for Early, as it was supposed that this latter county would soon be divided again.[67] It was two years, however, before two more counties, Baker and Thomas, were formed from Early. Irwin County was even less successful. In 1823 commissioners were appointed to fix on a county site, but it was not until 1827 that Irwinville, the second courthouse site, was incorporated. Appling County was still without an incorporated county town by the end of the 1830s.

Although the state had fewer recommendations than was customary for a cession, the legislature did pass the usual organizational acts and a few unusual ones. An act in 1831 counseled moving the Baker County courthouse from Byron, ten or twelve miles northwest of Albany, to Newton, on the Flint, because "the courthouse is not central by many miles to the great inconvenience of the inhabitants." It specified further that two acres be purchased for public buildings and the old Byron courthouse be sold or moved.[68] An act which made permanent the public buildings in Bainbridge also directed the commissioners to designate one or more additional sites in the county for holding elections. This had been done in the 1826 cession, but here the act directed punishment for "those that may attempt to defeat the provisions of this act."[69] In an act familiar from other cessions, the commissioners for Thomasville, Irwinville and Bainbridge were instructed to give one acre of land to each religious society and to erect an academy on land purchased for county purposes.[70]

The background of the settlers in this diverse region differed considerably. In the eastern part, poor farmers from the Carolina back country and from the poorer sections of Georgia formed the population. In Baker County (Newton was the courthouse town) the land, although highly productive in certain areas, was unhealthy and malarial. It contained what was considered in 1830 to be a large population (1,253 persons, mostly black). These people lived on plantations run by overseers. Large landowners from the Piedmont and eastern Georgia moved to the Thomasville area. The owners of plantations surrounding Bainbridge and Blakely were rich planters who frequently built their houses on the Flint and Chattahoochee rivers. Here they reproduced the earlier life style which had existed on Virginia's James River and Georgia's Sea Islands. Their contact with urban life was not through Georgia but by way of the Apalachicola River to the Gulf and New Orleans.

Southwest Georgia

Bainbridge (*Fig. 62*) was the most important of the three river towns. Sited on a high bluff on the east bank of the Flint River, it

TOWN PLANNING IN GEORGIA   137

was at the head of reliably navigable water. It was located near
Fort Hughes and at a ford which was on the traditional trade
route through this part of the country. The town was not far from
where the Flint and Chattahoochee join to make the Appalachicola. With these advantages Bainbridge became the collection center for agricultural produce, mainly cotton, from counties to the

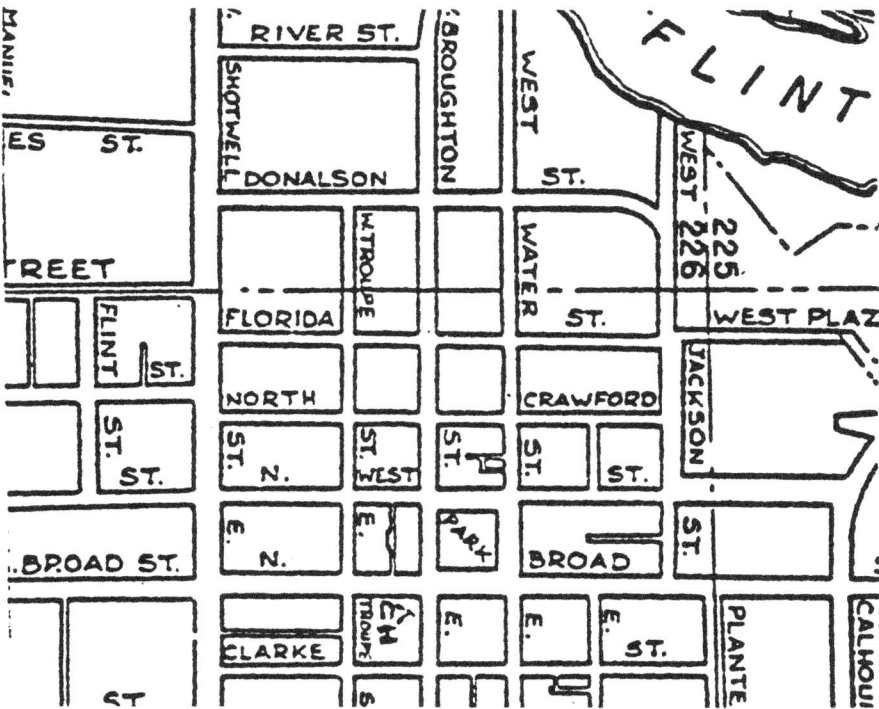

Fig. 62. **BAINBRIDGE, DECATUR COUNTY.** Founded 1824. Surveyor: Commissioners. 1814 Cession.

north. At Bainbridge produce was transshipped down the river
to ports in the Gulf, to Europe or to the east coast. The plan of
Bainbridge is a simple "Washington" grid. While some of the
blocks away from the center seem double the size of those at the
center, others are divided in a way which suggests that originally
all blocks were separated by alleys.

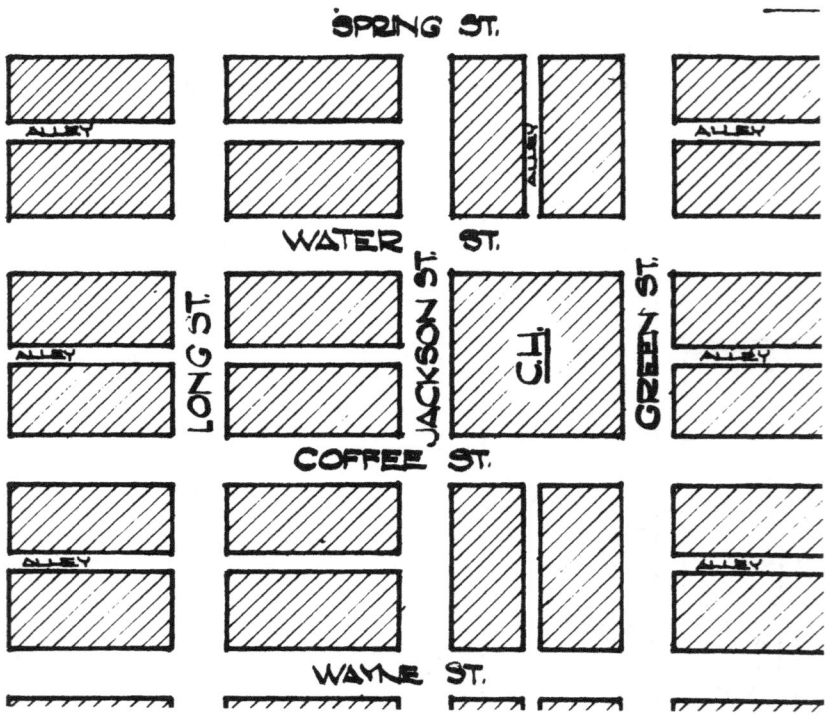

Fig. 63. NEWTON, BAKER COUNTY. Founded 1831. Surveyor: Commissioners. 1814 Cession.

When the Baker County seat was moved to the site of Newton in 1831, the commissioners were told by the legislature to lay off a new town into one-half acre lots.[72] The resulting plan is a typical orthogonal "Washington" type with a large central square. The one-acre blocks, containing the two one-half acre lots stipulated by the legislature, are divided in half by alleys. As today Newton has lost most of its original layout, it is fortunate that the original plan for it (*Fig. 63*) still exists. This plat suggests that Newton probably was identical in layout to the neighboring town of Bainbridge. Not only does Newton resemble Bainbridge; both towns show a striking similarity to Sandersville in the headright region (*Fig. 34*). It is tempting to assume that the settlers came from

TOWN PLANNING IN GEORGIA   139

Sandersville and simply copied their hometown plan. Newton was not a successful town, probably because it was located in an unhealthy region and at a point where the Flint River was too shallow for commercial use and often flooded over its banks.

In the original town plan of Thomasville blocks were divided into eight lots, a surprisingly small lot size for a southern town. The plan follows a pattern used in LaGrange, Gainesville and other towns. It is the "Washington" plan with the variation which uses two ranges of oblong blocks at right angles to each other to form the public square at their intersection. As has been pointed out, this made for a square one-half the size it would have been if the larger-size blocks had been used throughout the plan.

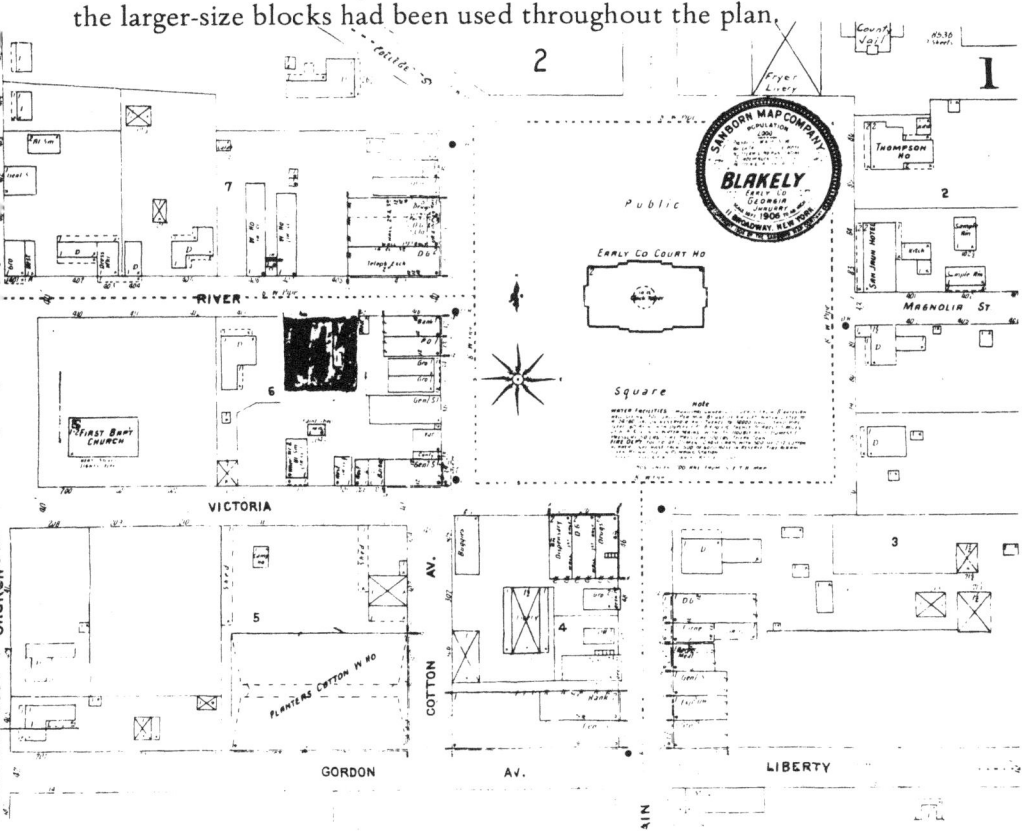

Fig. 64. BLAKELY, EARLY COUNTY. Founded 1826. Surveyor: Commissioners. 1814 Cession.

Fig. 65. IRWINVILLE, IRWIN COUNTY. Founded 1831. Surveyor: Commissioners. 1818 Cession.

Tradition has it that in 1821 Benjamin Collier donated four acres for a courthouse site in Early County and that Blakely was laid out around this gift. If the dimensions of the Sanborn map (*Fig. 64*) are correct, the courthouse square is exactly four acres. Blakely has one of the most graceful of all squares in Georgia. Four streets enter the square at the middle of each side. The courthouse is centered in the four-acre square and was designed with four entrances which face down the four main streets. With the courthouse located at the crest of a rise, the entrances to the town provided a pleasing vista. Cuthbert (*Fig. 60*). thirty miles north of Blakely, is surprisingly similar to the older town. It seems likely

TOWN PLANNING IN GEORGIA 141

that Blakely was the model because these two plans are unique in the western section of the state.

In 1831 Irwinville (*Fig. 65*) was made the county seat for the enormous Irwin County. Originally the courthouse had been in the northern part of the county two miles from the Ocmulgee River and twelve miles southwest of Jacksonville.[73] Both the first county seat and Irwinville were in the southern part of the 1818 cession, and both were on the main trading path to the southwest. The plan of Irwinville probably was drawn at a time when it was hoped a railroad would be built through the town.[74] It was customary to lay out commercial lots around an expected depot and this seems to have been the case of this plat. If the original layout were a "Washington" type, then the plan shows only one-half of the town, that to the left of the courthouse. If the main street followed the trading route which existed long before the town was built, Irwinville could be considered to have been laid out in the "Augusta" type linear plan. The town eventually languished, largely because of the poverty of the surrounding countryside.

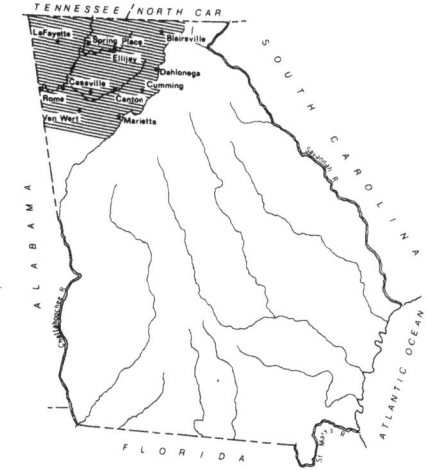

Fig. 66. CHEROKEE CESSION OF 1835.

Courthouse Towns in the 1835 Cherokee Cession

Eastern Section
  "Sparta" plan towns
    Dahlonega
    Canton
    Ellijay
    Blairsville
  "Washington" plan towns
    Cumming

Western Section
  "Sparta" plan towns
    Lafayette
  "Savannah" plan towns
    Marietta
  Other
    Rome
  Unknown
    Spring Place
    Paulding Courthouse,
    Cassville (dead)

The Cherokee cession (*Fig. 66*) consisted mainly of mountainous lands bordered by Alabama on the west, the 1826 cession on the south, the Chattahoochee and Chestatee rivers on the east and Tennessee on the north. The western section was made up of table lands and wide, deep valleys. It was in this area that the main route from Georgia through Tennessee to the old Northwest was built. Later a railroad was constructed here to bring produce to Georgia from the rich Ohio valley. As a result of the topography, land trade routes, and navigable waterways, it was less isolated than the eastern section. Broken land with narrow valleys and abrupt, inaccessible mountains and hills characterized the area to the northeast. In the southern part of this northeastern section, the land gradually flattened out in the locality of Cumming to form the Upper Piedmont.

The region was originally part of large Cherokee land holdings. Since the Revolution the Cherokees had gradually ceded most of their lands in Virginia, Kentucky, the Carolinas, and Tennessee, and were reduced, by the 1820s, to the region in North Georgia. Most Cherokees had by this time given up their hunting culture for an agricultural life. The federal government had helped in this transformation by supplying them with cattle and farm implements. The Indians had invented an alphabet for their language, had become Christians and many had attended missionary schools. The richer members of the tribe even followed western ways to the extent of owning slaves. A census taken of the Cherokees in Georgia in 1825 showed that they numbered 13,563; they had 1277 slaves; and 220 whites lived among them. Into this emerging third-world culture, the discovery of gold in 1828 came as a lethal bomb.

The mountains and valleys of North Georgia were used by the Cherokees for small farms, villages and hunting. The discovery of gold near Dahlonega brought a disruptive foreign element into the Indian territory. The greed and lawlessness of the white miners created, in the gold districts, a ruined and abused land. After the Indians were sent west and Georgia had taken control of the region, the white settlers who came there were not miners but yeoman farmers mainly from Tennessee and the back country of the Carolinas. They too had small farms and few, if any, slaves. In the middle of the century, industry began to appear in the western section, particularly in Rome where water and land transportation and water power were available. The whole northern region, beginning in the late 1830s, became a popular summer retreat for planters from the hot and unhealthy climate to the south.

The state's maneuvering to gain control of the Cherokee territory amounted to about a decade of political finagling with the federal government. The 1826 cession had finally rid the state of the Creeks and had extended it to the western boundary. Up to this time Georgia had virtually ignored the mountainous Cherokee region to concentrate on acquiring the Creek land where cotton grew best. With the final expulsion of the Creeks and the discovery of gold in Cherokee territory, Georgia's attention was turned to incorporating her remaining unceded land. In accordance with her agreement with the United States government early in the century, Georgia believed that the Cherokees' land belonged to her. The finding of gold and the emergence of the independent Cherokee Nation brought the situation to a head and gave Georgia reasons to push for state control and removal of the Indians. The new government in Washington headed by Andrew Jackson was, contrary to former administrations, in complete sympathy with Georgia. When asked to by the Georgia governor, the President promptly removed federal troops attempting to keep order in the gold region and allowed Georgia to perform this function. In retaliation against the newly-founded Cherokee Nation which Georgians considered illegal, the General Assembly put all white people living in the Nation under Georgia law and decreed that by 1830 all Indians would be subject to Georgia law.

In its determination to gain control over Cherokee territory the legislature's almost-five decades of experience in organizing new state land stood it in good stead. An act was passed in 1831 which directed that all unceded territory be surveyed and distributed by land lottery to the people, meaning the white people. With the survey and the succeeding lottery accomplished, the state managed to produce a sort of squatters'-right situation. This became an important factor in dealing with the United States government concerning occupation of Cherokee lands. In spite of lawsuits and delayed actions by the Cherokees and public sympathy in the rest of the country for the Indians, the outcome was never really in doubt. In 1838 the federal army was sent into the short-lived Cherokee Nation to round up the inhabitants. In a forced march they were sent to their new reservations in Oklahoma.

The distribution of land in the two 1832 gold and general lotteries was not carried out in the tradition of the earlier lotteries. The state had granted a number of gold lots before the first lottery, and to this confusion was added the problem of Cherokees still living in the territory on their farms and in their villages. The greed which the discovery of gold engendered in the state government, compounded by a problem the state had not dealt with before—that of ridding the land of settled inhabitants (the Creeks had given up their villages long before the state acquired their land), caused what might be called a moral collapse in the legislature. It was fortunate these were the last public lands the state would have to assign or there might have been a return to the disorder and speculation of headright years.

The Cherokee land was surveyed into four sections, each divided into districts nine miles square. The districts were made up of 490-acre mountain lots, 160-acre land lots and forty-acre gold lots. The latter were mostly in the vicinity of Dahlonega, Cumming and Canton. The original county was Cherokee. It was almost immediately divided into ten counties: Union, Lumpkin, Forsyth, Cobb, Paulding, Cherokee, Floyd, Cass, Gilmer and Murray.[75] In no other cession had the original county or counties been divided so quickly. The state was extremely eager to get North Georgia organized and many acts point to this hurried incorporation.[76] The act to form the counties was passed in December 1832. By March of 1833 an act provided that residents who could vote were to meet at designated places in their respective counties "under the superintendence of three suitable and capable persons" and elect five justices of the Inferior Court.[77] Never before had the legislature phrased in this way an act concerning the organization of a county. There is the sense throughout the acts dealing with the Cherokee land that the legislature was not going by the rule book but was acting hastily and cutting corners in order to complete the county structure. This haste was necessary to establish legal sanctions needed in the state's dealing with the federal government; in order to lay out militia districts in case of trouble with the Indians; and to bring order to the gold tracts belonging to the state and to lottery winners.

The General Assembly instructed that the justices in their respective counties "shall designate the site for necessary county buildings as they may think most conducive to the public good and they shall have power of erecting all necessary county buildings."[78] In the urgency to organize county seats the legislature neglected to make the usual requirements concerning how town lots were to be sold and how money from the lots was to be used, or to insist on a central location for courthouse towns and on the reservation of lots for churches and academies. On the other hand, the incorporation of the county seat was attended to with care. Duties of commissioners were spelled out, when and where elections were to be held was noted, and courthouse towns which changed their location or name were legalized. The 1835 act concconcerning the removal of public buildings in Floyd County from Livingston to Rome directs that "the site of the public buildings of the county of Floyd shall be removed from the town of Livingston and permanently located on lot number 245." With its usual paternalism, the legislature directed the justices to refund the money with interest to lot purchasers in Livingston.[79]

In spite of having no direction from the legislature, most county seats were centrally located in their county. Some were sited on purchased land lots, others on donated land. In Dahlonega the public buildings were made permanent by the legislature on lot 950. In Rome, Ellijay, Marietta, and Canton land was given for the county seat. Some towns were laid out in the wilderness, as were Rome and Blairsville, while others were in or near former habitations. Spring Place was located at the site of a Moravian mission, Ellijay near what had been one of the largest concentrations of Cherokees, and in LaFayette the county courthouse had originally been an Indian courthouse. Between 1832, the year of the survey and first lottery, and 1835, eleven county seats had been incorporated. The state had succeeded in organizing the last of her unceded land. The federal government had capitulated and the Indians were fated to be removed.

Eastern Section

Four towns in the eastern section of the Cherokee cession followed the "Sparta" plan and one the "Washington" plan. Because

TOWN PLANNING IN GEORGIA

Fig. 67. DAHLONEGA, LUMPKIN COUNTY. 1835 Cession.

of the topography the siting in most cases does not follow that of the Piedmont towns. Cumming, southwest of Gainesville, follows a simplified version of the earlier town's plan with streets entering the corners of a large public square. Cumming was sited in a flat area with an unusual downhill approach from the west. Dahlonega (*Fig. 67*), Canton and Ellijay follow the "Sparta" plan, and the siting of Dahlonega and Ellijay are similar. Both of the latter are approached by and laid out on a flat plain with the hills to the north of the square. Canton had a "Sparta" plan sited like towns in the Piedmont districts, and it seems likely that Blairsville, the most northern town in the cession, originally had a "Sparta" plan.

The justices purchased land lots for the county seats of Dahlonega, Blairsville and Cumming. For Ellijay and Canton land was given. Clement Guillion procured ten acres of land from a lottery winner and, after reserving one lot on the square for himself, donated the rest for the site of Ellijay. The Inferior Court accepted his offer, ran boundaries and designated the center of the plat for the courthouse park. Guillion surveyed the rest of the tract, allowing one acre for the public square, nine acres for streets and twenty lots.[80] In Canton two landowners offered to contribute land for the county seat if the justices would locate it on their lots. The justices seem to have procrastinated, for county records contain these telling minutes:

> We the grand jurors, have . . . a just cause of regret, to wit: The situation of our courthouse, if indeed, we might be said to have any. We therefore recommend to our Inferior Court and hope they will without further delay proceed to select a site for the town . . . with due regard to the beauty, eligibility and central situation for the public buildings of our county.[81]

The gift of the two landowners was finally accepted and the town duly laid out.

Western Section

Of the six towns in the western section of the Cherokee cession, one has lost its county seat status, one no longer exists and one is in doubt. Spring Place, the original courthouse town for Murray County, was located at the site of an Indian mission established by the Moravians. Today the courthouse has been moved and the town is marked by only a crossroads. Vague boundaries of the square in Cassville, once the seat of Cass County, are all that is left of this once-important west Georgia town. Cassville residents had voted not to allow the railroad to enter their town. This proved the beginning of the end. The railroad was built through a nearby town which then captured the commerce and population of the area. Georgia historian George G. Smith gave Dallas the honor of being the first Paulding County seat, while today's Paulding County Clerk considers Van Wert the first county seat. Considerable research is needed to settle the problem of the wandering Paulding courthouse.

The history of Rome is different. Rome was a speculative venture meant for trade and commerce whose location at the junction of two navigable rivers was ideally suited for these purposes. Four men, two lawyers and two landholders, on their way to court in Livingston (the original Floyd County seat) were camping at the future site of Rome. Convinced that the county seat would be better located at this strategic place, they formed a company, purchased the land and surveyed it. One of their members who was in the legislature drew up a bill of removal. The founders then pledged themselves to the Floyd County justices to give sufficient land for public buildings, provide ferries, build bridges and lay out a town if the justices would consent to move the courthouse to this new location. The gift was accepted and Col. Daniel R. Mitchell, one of the founders, laid out the town of Rome.[82]

The plan which Col. Mitchell devised was a grid laid out between the Oostanaula and Etowa rivers (*Figs. 68, 69*). Two main streets, Broad and Fourth, were a generous 132-feet wide, the others were sixty-six feet and lanes were thirty-three feet. Keeping the southern tradition of large residential lots, the planner located them on a bluff in the southern section of the plan. Commercial lots were smaller and were located at the confluence of the two rivers. Broad Street had a tree-lined park running down the center. The public square was completely omitted and the courthouse was located on a lot on Fifth Avenue one-half block north of Broad Street. In this plan Col. Mitchell followed the trend already evident in Columbus toward a linear layout and away from the centralized plan. Across the river a handsome cemetery, laid out in the romantic English landscape style, is reminiscent of Macon's earlier Rose Hill. The plan of Rome was specifically designed for the site and for the town's commercial, industrial and governmental functions. Because of these factors it is one of the more successful town plans in the lottery region. It became an important industrial and transshipment center form-

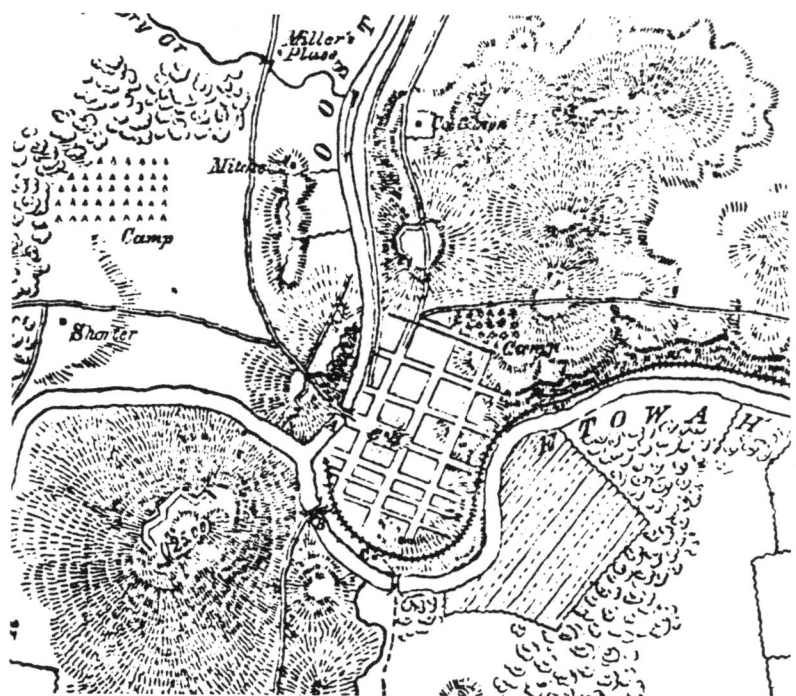

Fig. 68. ROME, FLOYD COUNTY. Founded 1834. Surveyor: Col. Daniel Mitchell. 1835 Cession.

ing a connecting link between Georgia and Tennessee and acting as a clearing house for produce from the Coosa valley and northeast Alabama.

Marietta (*Fig. 70*), located at the northern limits of the Upper Piedmont in a healthy area with ample water power, was settled mainly by people from old North Georgia, Franklin County and the Pendleton district of South Carolina. Land was given by John Hayward Glover for the courthouse square and around this James Anderson, one of the surveyors for the Cherokee cession, laid out the town.[83] He used a traditional "Savannah" plan that differed from others of this genre in having the corner streets leading into the square more important than the center streets. The square was formed by sides of equal size which resulted in an

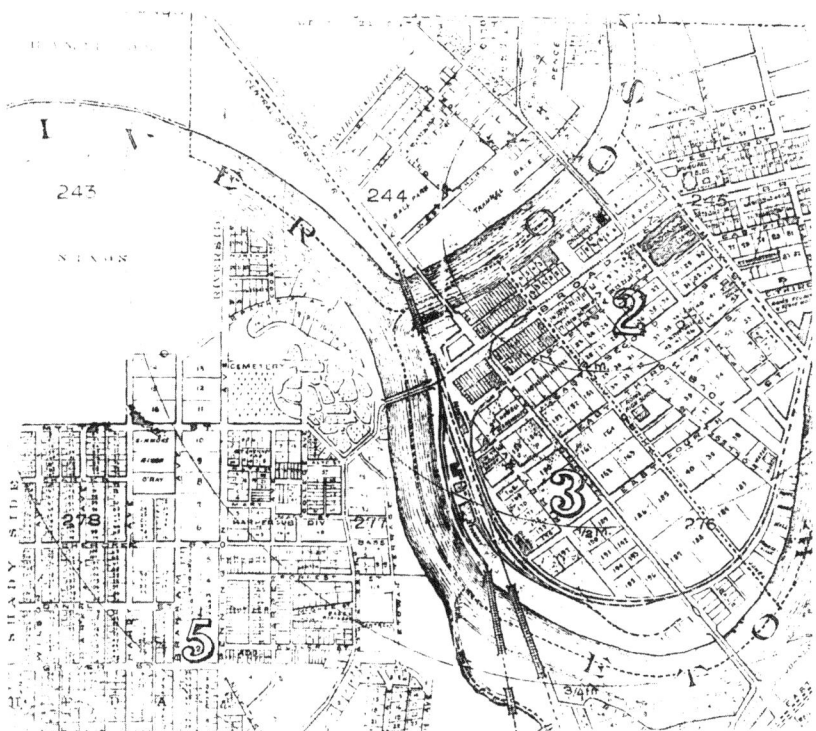

Fig. 69. ROME'S GROWTH BEYOND ITS ORIGINAL BOUNDARIES FOLLOWED SIMILAR GRID PATTERN.

extremely large courthouse park. Because of its location Marietta flourished as a summer resort and as a budding industrial center.

LaFayette was formed when Walker County split off from Murray. Most settlers came from Tennessee. The surprisingly narrow secondary streets may reflect, as was so often the case in town plans, the origin of the inhabitants. Otherwise the plan has the typical North Georgia "Sparta" type with the main streets entering the square at the center of two sides and two streets entering at the corners of the other two sides. The square has today lost

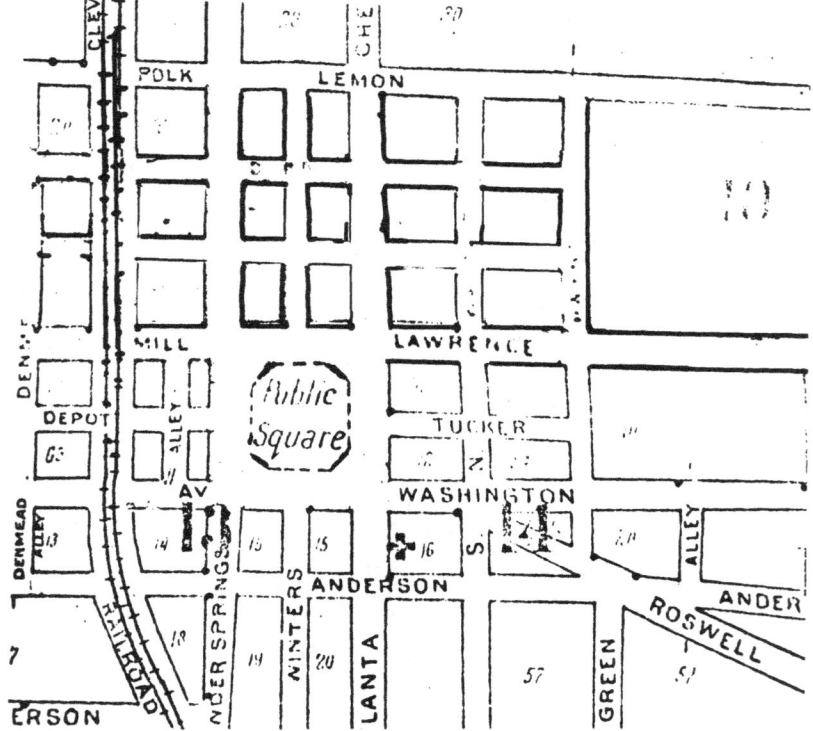

Fig. 70. MARIETTA, COBB COUNTY. Founded 1833. Surveyor: James Anderson. 1835 Cession.

most of its importance and is recognized only as a widening of the main street. The courthouse has been well relocated a block away facing one of the streets entering the square.

The plans used in these courthouse towns in the lottery lands were first used in the headright region. The "Washington" plan was the most popular and was used almost exclusively in the Piedmont. The "Augusta" plan was used less, one reason being that there were fewer settlements to convert to county seats. The "Sparta" plan was used in northeast Georgia with a scattering in the Red Hills and in the southwest. The "Savannah" plan was used in a few widely separated sites. The state-planned cities were the most important towns of the lottery lands and will be taken up in Chapter VI. With the exception of them and of Rome, the courthouse towns do not show any evolution from the headright towns. Certain situations seemed to call for a certain type plan and this did not change. The "Washington" plan was used in flat topography, the "Sparta" plan where a steep ascent to the courthouse could be laid out, the "Augusta" plan when an already-existing town was made into a county seat and the "Savannah" plan used in flat topography. Whatever the type of town, it was almost always laid out with care and attention to the amenities of life or, as the grand jury of Gilmer County advised, that its justices site their county town "with due regard to . . . beauty, eligibility and a central situation."

Notes

1. Chapter I, p. 9.
2. Augustin Smith Clayton, *A Compilation of the Laws of the State of Georgia, 1800-1810* (Augusta, 1812). Hereafter abbreviated as *C.L.G., 1800-1810.*, p. 279.
3. *Ibid.*, p. 481.
4. *Ibid.*, p. 482.
5. *Ibid.*, p. 642.
6. *Ibid.*, p. 603.
7. The exception to this is the five towns planned by the state: Augusta, Louisville, Milledgeville, Macon, and Columbus.
8. Clayton, *C.L.G., 1800-1810*, p. 483.
9. *Ibid.*, p. 624.
10. Dorothy Orr, *A History of Education in Georgia* (Chapel Hill, 1950), pp. 20-35.
11. Carolyn White Williams, *History of Jones County, Georgia, From 1807 to 1907* (Macon, Georgia, 1957), p. 19.
12. Bertha Sheppard Hart, *History of Laurens County, Georgia, 1807-1941* (Dublin, Georgia, 1941), p. 11.
13. Lucius Q. C. Lamar, *A Compilation of the Laws of the State of Georgia, 1810-1819* (Augusta, 1821). Hereafter abbreviated as *C.L.G., 1810-1819*, pp. 416-417.

14. The 1817-1818 and 1819 cessions will hereafter be noted, for simplicity, as the 1818 cession.

15. Lamar, *C.L.G., 1810-1819*, p. 236.

16. Because of the late settlement pattern of the southern counties, they will be dealt with after the 1826 cession.

17. Lamar, *C.L.G., 1810-1819*, p. 227.

18. *Ibid.*, p. 429.

19. *Ibid.*, p. 241.

20. William C. Dawson, *A Compilation of the Laws of the State of Georgia, 1819-1829* (Milledgeville, 1831). Hereafter abbreviated as *C.L.G., 1819-1829.*, p. 432.

21. *Ibid.*, p. 145.

22. Information compiled from James C. Flanigan, *History of Gwinnett County, Ga. 1819-1960* (Hapeville, Georgia, 1959).

23. Typescript in the uncatalogued files of the Gainesville Public Library, Gainesville, Georgia.

24. Existence of a town plan did not necessarily mean the town would be built right away. In some cases it took years for a plan to be completed. Gainesville was such a case.

25. The seller was frequently one of the appointed commissioners: thus, speculation did exist, but only to a limited degree. This was probably because through the state survey greater control was now exercised over the new lands.

26. Typescript in the uncatalogued files of the Gainesville Public Library, Gainesville, Georgia.

27. Anita B. Sams, *Wayfarers in Walton. History of Walton County, Georgia, 1819-1967* (Monroe, Georgia, 1967).

28. Joan Niles Sears, "Town Planning in White and Habersham Counties, Georgia," *Georgia Historical Quarterly*, LIV (1970), 27.

29. E. Merton Coulter, *Georgia—A Short History* (Chapel Hill, 1960), p. 225.

30. Dawson, *C.L.G., 1819-1826*, pp. 246-247.

31. *Ibid.*, p. 275.

32. Chapter VI.

33. The land lot was purchased for varying prices, usually from a lottery winner. Differing from former cessions, there seems to have been no one in this fertile territory willing to donate his land, and all lots to be used as courthouse seats were bought.

34. Dawson, *C.L.G., 1819-1829*, p. 122.

35. *Ibid.*, p. 451.

36. *Ibid.*, p. 251.

37. *Ibid.*, p. 453.

38. *Ibid.*, p. 447.
39. *Ibid.*, p. 458.
40. *Ibid.*, p. 461.
41. *Ibid.*, p. 477.
42. Howard Alan Schreiter, "Circular Corporate Limits in the U.S., Their Origin, Distribution, and Implications" (Unpublished M.A. Thesis, University of Georgia, Athens, Georgia, 1959), p. 379.
43. Adiel Sherwood, *A Gazeteer of the State of Georgia* (Charleston, 1827), p. 550.
44. Dawson, *C.L.G., 1819-1829*, p. 470.
45. DeKalb Chamber of Commerce, *Early DeKalb History* (Decatur, 1970). No pagination.
46. Dawson, *C.L.G., 1819-1820*, p. 441.
47. Zebulon Historical Society, *Pike County, Georgia* (Zebulon, 1970). No pagination.
48. Lucian Lamar Knight, *Georgia's Landmarks, Memories, and Legends* (Atlanta, 1913), II, 878.
49. W.P.A., "Historical Sketch of Forsyth" (Atlanta, no date), p. 6 (typescript).
50. Fussell M. Chalker, *Pioneer Days Along the Ocmulgee* (Carrollton, Georgia, no date), p. 157.
51. George G. Smith, *Story of Georgia and the Georgia People* (Macon, Georgia, 1900), p. 372.
52. Dawson, *C.L.G., 1819-1829*, p. 451.
53. Oliver H. Prince, *A Digest of the Laws of the State of Georgia Enacted Previous to 1820* (Milledgeville, 1832). Hereafter abbreviated as *D.L.G. to 1820*, p. 555.
54. Dawson, *C.L.G., 1819-1829*, p. 132.
55. *Ibid.*, p. 136.
56. *Ibid.*, p. 481.
57. Mary G. Jones and Lily Reynolds (Eds.), *A History of Coweta County from 1825-1880* (Newnan, Georgia, 1928), p. 14.
58. Clifford L. Smith, *History of Troup County*.
59. *Ibid.*, p. 48.
60. Mark C. Lindsay, "Ghost Town Close to Atlanta," *Atlanta Journal and Constitution Magazine*, XXIII (January 11, 1973), 28.
61. James C. Bonner, *Georgia's Last Frontier* (Athens, 1971), map follows p. 52.
62. John W. Reps, *The Making of Urban America: A History of City Planning in the United States* (Princeton, 1965), p. 274.
63. Compare with Marion, Fig. 46.

64. Of the two dead towns in the south-west region, Horry and Starkville, nothing remains. Both were surrounded by poor land and were too near Columbus to survive after their courthouses were moved.

65. Chapter V, "Courthouse Towns in the 1817-1818 and 1819 Cession," pp. 105-106.

66. E. Merton Coulter, *Georgia—A Short History* (Chapel Hill, 1960), p. 224.

67. Dawson, *C.L.G., 1819-1829*, p. 126.

68. *Ibid.*, p. 478.

69. *Ibid.*, p. 159.

70. *Ibid.*, p. 468.

71. George G. Smith, *Story of Georgia and the Georgia People, 1732-1860* (Baltimore, 1963), p. 400.

72. Dawson, *C.L.G., 1819-1829*, p. 478.

73. Adiel Sherwood, *A Gazeteer of the State of Georgia* (Charleston, 1827), p. 27.

74. The railroads eventually were built to the north and south of Irwinville.

75. Georgia, *Acts and Resolutions of the General Assembly* (1833), p. 56.

76. It should be remembered that until 1835 no treaty had been signed between the Cherokees and the United States, and that the Indians were not only living in North Georgia but had proclaimed their Nation an independent entity.

77. Georgia, *Acts and Resolutions of the General Assembly* (1833), p. 58.

78. Georgia, *Acts and Resolutions of the General Assembly* (1834), p. 250.

79. Georgia, *Acts and Resolutions of the General Assembly* (1835), p. 259.

80. George Gordon Ward, *Annals of Upper Georgia* (Carrollton, Georgia, 1965), p. 65.

81. Lloyd G. Marlin, *History of Cherokee County* (Atlanta, 1932), p. 44.

82. Compiled from George McGruder Battey, Jr., *A History of Rome and Floyd County* (Atlanta, 1922).

83. Compiled from Bowling C. Yates, *Historic Highlights in Cobb County* (Marietta, Georgia, 1973).

Chapter VI
Five Towns Planned by the State

A society whose main focus was limited to slavery and cotton was not the sort to encourage large urban development, which historically has flourished on diversity. If urban centers were to exist in Georgia, it was the state which would have to bring them into existence. Even in a society as specialized as Georgia's, commercial centers for selling and buying were a necessity. Macon and Columbus were the state's answer to the need for "trading" towns. The other ventures into larger urban planning revolved around the state capitals: Augusta, Louisville and Milledgeville. (The state hoped that the capitals would also prove to be successful commercial centers.) The five state towns were laid out on rivers at the Fall Line, at the head of navigation. Much of their success or failure depended upon the degree to which the rivers could be used for transportation of produce to and from the coast. The Chattahoochee and Savannah rivers were the largest and most reliable for shipping and for passenger travel. The Ocmulgee and Oconee were less reliable and the Ogeechee the least desirable of all (*Fig. 71*).

Of the five state-planned towns, Augusta and Columbus were the most successful. They were located on the largest rivers and were the outlet and transshipment centers for produce from some of the state's most fertile lands. Because of the water power generated by the falls of the Savannah and Chattahoochee rivers, both Augusta and Columbus became industrial centers. In Macon, business was cotton or cotton-related, and industry was at a minimum. Handsome houses and a lively social life gave the town a refined atmosphere equalled only by Savannah. Besides being the seat of the legislature, Milledgeville had little to offer. Poorly sited, and on a river unsatisfactory for transportation, the main business of the town centered around government. Louisville, the earlier capital, had the same problems, but to a greater degree: poor siting, swamps and an unsatisfactory river for commerce.

The mechanics for founding the five state towns did not differ appreciably from those used in founding courthouse seats. Acreage was prescribed for both, but for the state towns more generous sums were allotted; the amount varying from 1000 acres in Louisville to 21,000 in Macon. This larger amount gave the state control of the town's growth and of funds from the sale of lots in the town reserve. The terminology which the legislature used for these reserves retained the British designations of common, gardens and farm lots. The instructions concerning the plan itself, and the method of selling the town, garden and farm lots, were more detailed than for the courthouse towns. The legislature appointed commissioners (in the case of Macon they were elected) to bring the legislative acts into operation. In some cases the commissioners laid out the town themselves; in others, specifically Macon and Columbus, surveyors were hired.

The plans of the towns show surprising variety. Louisville, it is conjectured, followed the one-square "Washington"-type courthouse plan. In Milledgeville the General Assembly was more ambitious and imaginative in its planning. Three, later four, sixteen-acre squares interrupt a grid of four-acre blocks. Savannah may well have been the prototype for this multi-square plan. As Macon was expected to be a "trading" town and not a capital, the legislature laid it out with one main square for the county courthouse and wide streets, some with central parks. All of these state towns were planned not only for their primary function, but also as county seats. The reduced importance of the square in the overall plan begins to show in Macon and becomes more evident in Columbus. Here the courthouse square is located in a block within the grid, as are the other squares reserved for public use. A gradual development is seen here away from the nucleated design featuring a central square surrounded by streets and blocks, toward a linear pattern which emphasized a wide main street often planned to include a central tree-planted park.

TOWN PLANNING IN GEORGIA 159

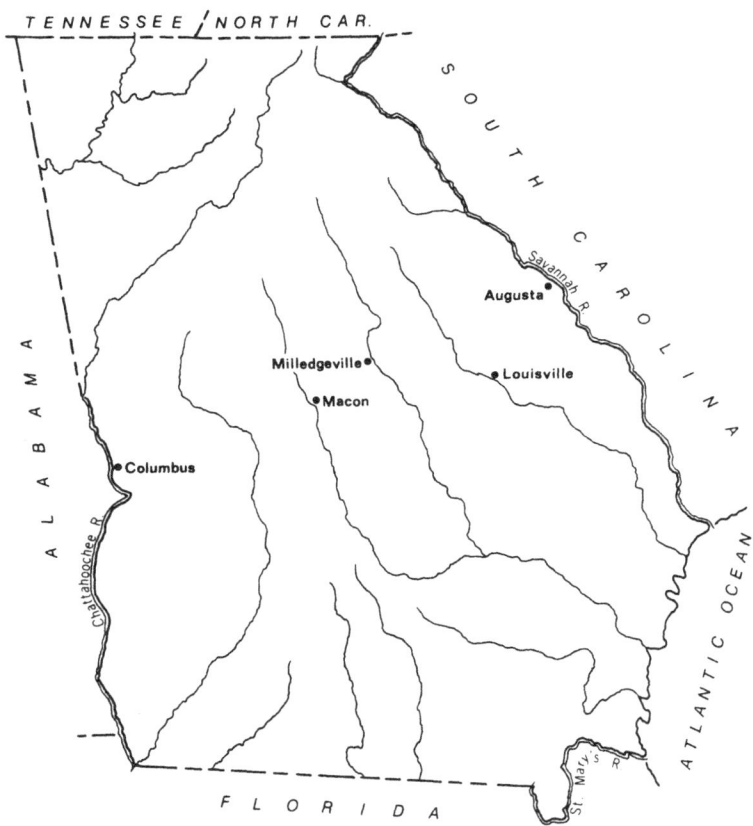

Fig. 71. FIVE TOWNS PLANNED BY THE STATE.

In these plans the size of the blocks did not vary from the original four-acre blocks planned in the new section of Augusta. There was, however, a change in lot size. The state-planned sections of Augusta and Louisville and Milledgeville had an unvarying one-acre lot layout. By the time Milledgeville was planned, most courthouse towns had reduced the size of their lots to one-half acre, but the conservative state legislature insisted on the older one-acre division.[1] By 1823 in Macon, and later in Columbus, the General Assembly had changed to the more up-to-date one-half acre lots. The legislature specified alleys for Louisville, Macon and Columbus. In Columbus they were not laid out and in Louisville they were removed in 1803. The indecisive situation concerning the alleys lay in their problematical use by slaves. When this use became too disruptive or aroused suspicions and apprehensions among whites, the alleys were removed by legislative directive.[2]

Three Georgia State Capitals

Augusta
Louisville
Milledgeville

The copy of the Ordinance authorizing the selection of a site for Louisville and the sale of lots within it which is reproduced on page 161 shows how the first "created" capital of Georgia was legislated into existence. It was a far cry from legislative act to actual creation. That a decade was necessary to implement this act gives some indication of the disorganized condition of the state at that early time. To most Georgians Savannah still symbolized British colonialism. The population and activity, even as early as 1783, were in the Piedmont, and the upstate Republican faction there was strong enough to wrest the government seat from its past colonial home and move it to an area of more populist sentiments. So while Louisville was in the making, Augusta served as the temporary capital of the new state.

Shortly after Oglethorpe arrived in Georgia, he built a fort at the falls of the Savannah River. Ever since, first as a fort and later as a trading post, Augusta had been continually inhabited. The General Assembly first met there in August 1780, having fled from Savannah. It optimistically passed an act to lay out more lots and sell them for the state, and "to lay out, measure and post in the best and most regular way the streets and highways."[4] Since the British soon retook the town, no action was taken until 1783 when the Americans regained possession. The Thursday, Novem-

An ORDINANCE for empowering Commissioners to fix on a Place convenient for a Seat of Government, and to erect publick Buildings thereon.

BE it Ordained, by the Representatives of the Freemen of the State of Georgia, in General Assembly met, and by the authority of the same, That Nathan Brownson, William Few, and Hugh Lawson, Esquires, shall be commissioned and appointed, and they, or a majority of them, are hereby authorized and empowered, to proceed and fix on a place, which they may think most proper and convenient, for erecting of Publick Buildings, and establishing the Seat of Government and the University, provided the same shall be within twenty miles of Galphin's Old Town; and the said Commissioners are hereby authorized to appropriate any publick lands, or to purchase, or otherwise procure, in behalf of the state, a tract of land, for that purpose, which shall not exceed one thousand acres, and to lay out a part thereof in lots, streets, and alleys; which shall be known by the name of Louisville; and, after reserving a sufficient quantity of land for the State-House, University, and other publick buildings, to sell the remainder of the lots, or so many as they shall judge most conducive to the publick interest, and also to sell the Government-House and Lot in the town of Savannah, and the money arising from the sale of the said house and lot shall, by them, be applied to the sole purpose of paying for the aforesaid land and erecting the said publick buildings: And the said Nathan Brownson, William Few, and Hugh Lawson, or a majority of them, are hereby vested with full power to bargain, sell, and convey, the said Government-House and Lot, together with the lots in the said town of Louisville so as aforesaid to be laid out, with the appurtenances, and take bonds in their own names; and to their successors in office, and, on receiving full payment, to convey to the purchaser or purchasers thereof, and make a sufficient title in fee simple to the same, which shall be held and considered as good and valid in law or equity.

And be it further Ordained, That the said Commissioners shall, before they enter on the business aforesaid, give bond and security to his Honour the Governor, for the due performance thereof, in the penalty of six thousand pounds; and shall, before him, take the following oath: "I A. B. appointed a Commissioner to fix on a place most convenient for a seat of government, and for erecting publick buildings thereon, do solemnly swear, that I will faithfully discharge the duties required of me by law, to the best of my skill and judgment, for the interest of this state, and the convenience of the inhabitants thereof; so help me God:" And the said Commissioners shall receive compensation for their expences while on actual service, provided the same does not exceed two dollars each per day.

And be it Ordained, by the authority aforesaid, That the place for the meeting of the Legislature, the residence of the Governor, the Secretary, Treasurer, Surveyor General, and Auditor, shall be at Augusta, until the State-House and other publick buildings shall be erected, and the next meeting of the Legislature thereafter shall be at Louisville.

By Order of the House,
W^m. GIBBONS, Speaker.

Augusta, 26th January, 1786.

ber 30, 1783 issue of the *Georgia Gazette* related the General Assembly's charge to the Richmond County Grand Jury.

> *It is a gratification to be able to inform you that the Legislature, at its last session in Augusta, passed a law upon the most liberal basis for extending and speedily building up the town . . . in addition to this the assembly has ordered an academy to be erected for the instruction of youth.*[5]

In 1786 another act was passed showing the legislature's intimate concern with its temporary capital by continuing its control of the sale and laying out of lots.[6] Although Augusta was originally a colonial town it is acts such as these that place it in the state-planned town category.

When the General Assembly returned to Augusta in 1783, it was to a town ruined by war. The act cited previously for the rehabilitation and enlargement of the community reiterated and expanded the 1780 act. A later act provided for a board of commissioners to act as trustees for all purposes mentioned in the act. Augusta was from this time until 1798, when it was incorporated, governed by legislative acts which were carried out by the appointed commissioners. This board eventually evolved into a governing body usually referred to as the Trustees of the Academy.[7] Even after incorporation and a firm resolve to let the town manage its own affairs,[8] the legislature continued to control the growth and changes in Augusta. An important act as late as 1814 appointed the state surveyor to remeasure, lay off and define all of the public streets and highways in the city.[9]

The earlier British settlement held the key to the planning of future developments. Broad Street, laid out apparently as a parade ground, was the essential feature of the town. Originally 350 feet wide, it had to be reduced twice by legislative acts to a final and more manageable 170 feet. However, as travelers' accounts note, it continued to be the focal point for the town. Figure 72 is a plan of Augusta after the "new part" had been laid out to the north and south of the "old town." The width and importance of Broad

Street are easily recognizable. The lots in the new part were one acre, the size which the legislature had recommended for other 1780s towns. Some lots predating the state town along Broad Street were one-fourth and one-half acre. Outlined in Figure 73 are the additions of 1783 and 1798.

At the beginning of Independence the legislature granted Augusta 1,000 acres, confiscated from royalists, which covered most of the downtown, and 600 acres of public reserve or common laid out by the British around the fort. With this much land belonging to the city it could control growth and allow due concern for urban amenities. A wide tree-planted park was laid out between Bay Street and the river, Green Street was made wide enough to have a tree-lined park in the center, and Broad, narrowed to 170 feet, was also tree-lined with a central park. The courthouse (no statehouse was built in this temporary capital) on Green Street faces Monument Street which runs at right angles to Broad. A handsome approach such as this to an important building would become typical of Georgia towns. Lots for public buildings were reserved between Telfair and Walker streets, with church and academy lots reserved here and elsewhere in town.

With the exception of Savannah, more travelers wrote about Augusta than any other Georgia town. From William Bartram in 1773 to William Makepeace Thackeray in 1856 the comments are surprisingly complimentary. All travelers mention Broad Street as the most outstanding feature of the plan. Its width is given as anywhere from 130 to 170 feet and the length from one to two miles. Travelers call it variously a rambling great street, a handsome well-built street with a row of trees for nearly a mile on each side, or an avenue that seemed at least a mile long, full of small stores and some low taverns. One visitor found Augusta to consist mainly of one very wide street a couple of miles in length composed of a mixed description of buildings, many very humble and others handsome. It was noted that Pride of India trees grew on each side of the main streets: Broad, Greene and Telfair. Augusta was generally considered the most enterprising and thriving

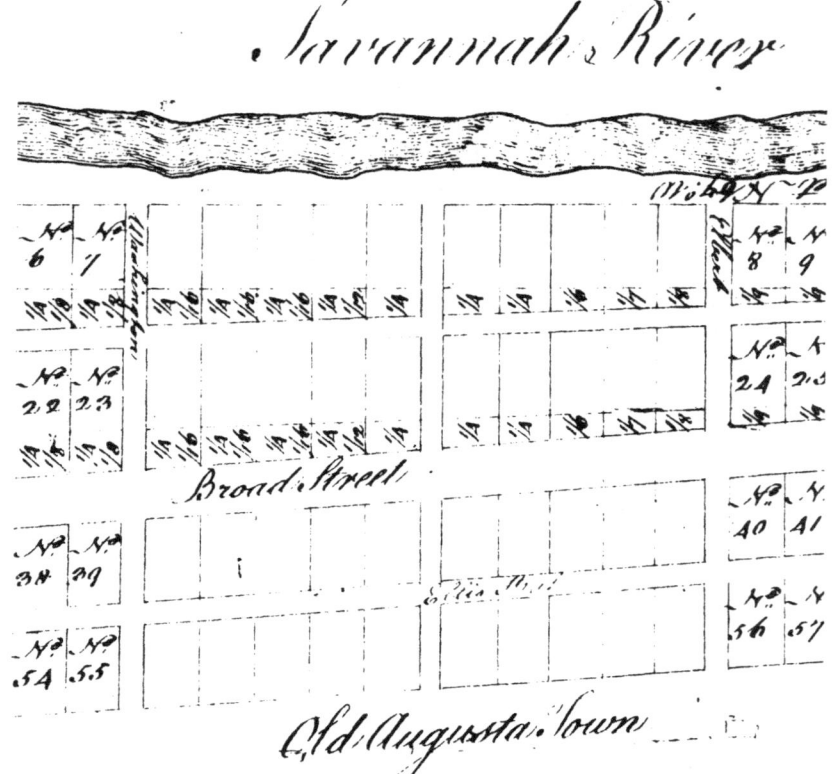

Fig. 72. AUGUSTA, RICHMOND COUNTY. Founded 1736 as a British Fort. Surveyors: British. 1733 Grant.

community in Georgia, and one visitor declared that no city of the same size was more wealthy than Augusta. Travelers seemed relieved to find good hotels and food,[10] and most agreed with Bartram that "the site of Augusta is perhaps the most delightful and eligible of any in Georgia for a city."[11]

From its inception by the British, Augusta flourished. The location at the foot of the Savannah River falls and at the head of navigation made it a transshipment center for produce from the north and west. The falls also gave water power for mills and other industry. It was, until the founding of Columbus, the most successful town in Georgia.

TOWN PLANNING IN GEORGIA   165

...... 1783
- - - 1798
⊛   Court House

Fig. 73. THIS PLAN OF AUGUSTA, GEORGIA'S CAPITAL FROM 1780 TO 1786, shows the additions of 1783 and 1798. Surveyor: State Commissioners.

Louisville

In January of 1786 the legislature authorized commissioners to procure 1,000 acres of land on which to establish a seat of government for the state. A decade later the capital was laid out on forty acres of the reserve into lots, streets and a statehouse square. Originally, Louisville seems to have been patterend after the "Washington" type plan. A large central square sited on a rise

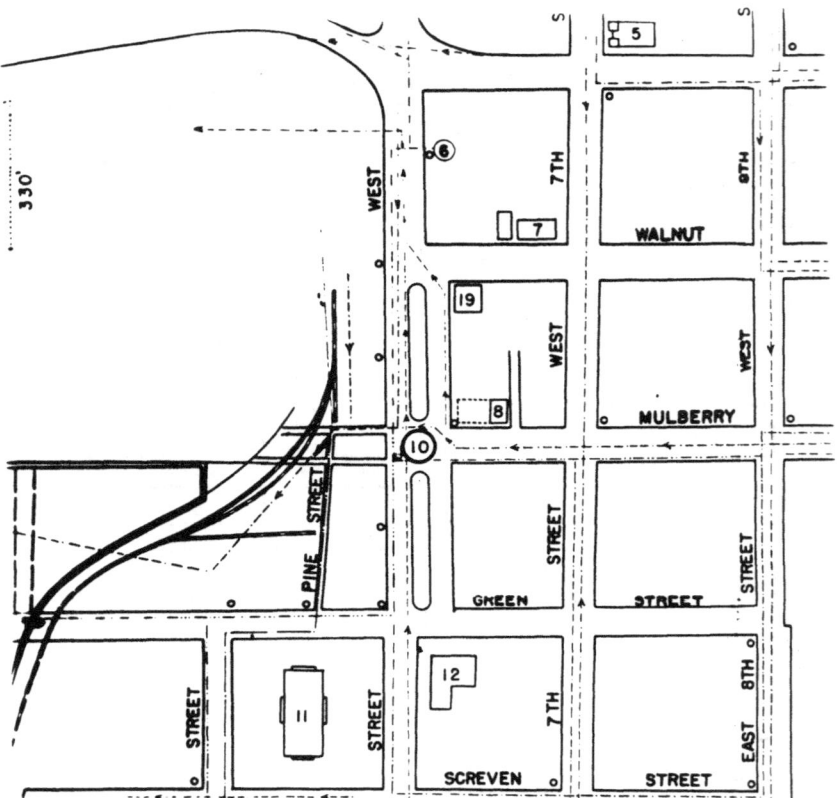

Fig. 74. LOUISVILLE, JEFFERSON COUNTY. Founded 1796. Surveyors: Nathan Bronson, William Few, Hugh Lawson. 1790 Cession.

was surrounded by streets and town blocks. In accordance with legislative direction, the lots were one-acre in area, with four to a block. The legislative instructions also directed that alleys separate the lots, but an 1803 act noted that they "have not answered the beneficial purposes for which they were intended" and directed that they be sold.[12] In Figure 74 the vestigial remains of one of the alleys can be seen one block to the east of Broad on Mulberry Street.

The first Georgia statehouse, built in Louisville, cost $10,000. The site is considered to have been in the large square where the Jefferson County courthouse stands today. It is said that when this late-nineteenth century courthouse was being constructed foundations and bricks of the old statehouse were uncovered.[13] John Melish, a visitor to Louisville in 1806, described the capitol as being built of brick and having two stories with three rooms on each floor. It was fifty feet square, a relatively large building for the times.[14]

Extensive research has failed to turn up an early plan of this apparently unloved capital. If the original plan were as described, and from travelers' accounts and legislative acts it seems more than likely that it was, it has changed drastically. In Figure 74, number 11 refers to the county courthouse (also the site of the old statehouse) and the square. Originally this was the center of town. When the railroad was built, it cut off blocks to the north of the square. Broad Street then became the central business section, leaving the square off to the side and away from the main commercial district. Following a pattern which was developing in larger Georgia towns in the late 1820s and 1830s toward linear planning, Broad Street was widened and a park built down the middle.

As outlined in the 1786 act, the location for Louisville was to be within twenty miles of Galphin Old Town. The location chosen by the commissioners was near the Ogeechee River and turned out to be unhealthy and malarial. After the 1802-1805 cession, the state determined that Louisville, besides being unhealthy, was too far from the center of population. In 1805, having served as the capital for less than ten years, Louisville was abandoned and the seat of government moved to Milledgeville.

Milledgeville

In the 1802 act which outlined the lottery system, the legislature also enacted laws to lay out a new state capital. It directed

That immediately after the boundry line shall be run agreeable to this act, five commissioners to be appointed by the Legislature, shall at the

> *most eligible and suitable place, at or near the head of navigation on the east side of the Oconee River, lay out a tract of land containing 3240 acres of sixteen tracts of 202½ acres each ... which is hereby reserved and set apart for a town to be called and known by the name of Milledgeville, and shall on such part as they may deem most proper, lay off lots containing one acre each. ...* [15]

Although the tract of land and the land lots were surveyed, the town was not located until 1804. A letter at that time from one of the commissioners to Governor Milledge stated:

> *... we have agreed on a plan and laid it to the ground. We have made reserves of 3 squares of 16 acres each which I think are eligible and well chosen,—any one for a State House; one for the Governor's residence, and the other for a penitentiary. ... Two main streets of 120 feet wide are intended to run to the State House. The Blocks are laid off in square of 4 acres which are to be checked into acre lots. The other streets are 100 feet wide. The place is well watered with good springs as any place I ever saw and every other appearance are in favor of its being a healthy situation.* [16]

The plan of the capital presents a confused mixture of details from colonial and early state planning. Colonial town features are echoed in the four squares (the surveyor mentioned three; however, Figure 75, the 1808 plan, shows four) with main streets running to the centers of the squares. The British influence stops here. The squares were not, as in a colonial town, left vacant and landscaped as parks, but were reserved for special purposes and public buildings. The lots, one acre in size, with four to a block, were similar to towns planned in the 1780s. Alleys seem to have been omitted in Milledgeville, perhaps because of the problems they were causing in other towns such as Greensborough and Louisville. No consideration was given to laying out smaller lots for commercial purposes. In fact, no specific business district seems to have been planned anywhere in the town.

Milledgeville has the unique distinction in Georgia of having four sixteen-acre outsized squares. The rationale behind this over-enthusiastic allotment for public buildings may have been

TOWN PLANNING IN GEORGIA 169

Fig. 75. MILLEDGEVILLE, BALDWIN COUNTY. Founded 1804. Surveyors: Commissioners. 1805 Cession. Succeeded Louisville as the seat of Georgia's government, 1806.

an abortive attempt to plan an impressive capital—the bigger the square, the more impressive the square. Each of the public squares was planned for one major purpose: statehouse, penitentiary, governor's square and cemetery. The land remaining in the square after the main building had been built in it was to be given away acre-by-acre for churches, county buildings and academies. In the 1829 *Gazeteer for the State of Georgia*, a map shows the Statehouse Square containing the statehouse in the center with street approaches from the four sides. Arranged haphazardly around the sides of the square are three churches, an academy and a powder magazine. There is also an arsenal placed within the square, which would seem somewhat too near the statehouse for comfort. Besides containing the penitentiary, Penitentiary Square included the county jail, the courthouse and an academy. The Governor's Square is to this day a wilderness and the fourth square contains a particularly handsome cemetery.

In laying out a large grid with large squares and wide streets running to the center of them, the planners may have hoped to produce a town somewhat similar in appearance to Savannah. However, the all-important fact that Savannah (and other colonial towns as well) was laid out on flat topography was not taken into consideration by the Milledgeville planners. In Savannah the level land which gives long vistas between the squares is an important component part of the plan. In Milledgeville the undulating land effectively prevented long vistas which would have offered a striking element to the town plan.

Although staked out, the town had not attracted many inhabitants. An act passed by the legislature at the end of 1804 pointed out that since the State had approved the site and plan, "it is expedient that a part of the lots of the said town should be sold to raise a fund for the erecting of a State House and other public buildings." More commissioners were appointed and told to advertise the lots in the state gazettes for sixty days. They were "to sell and dispose of any number of lots not exceeding twenty lots of one acre each." The town contained 336 one-acre lots, and the reason why the State was so chary of selling them remains problematical. Another provision made in this act was that no more than two lots could be sold in a block and no one person could buy more than two lots. The reason for this restriction may have been that the legislators were still smarting from their land speculation scandals. The act further stipulated that within two years the purchaser must improve his lot to the value of $100.[17] Ten months later the legislators became more bold and authorized the sale of lots not exceeding 100 in number. The money from these lots was to be deposited with the state treasurer and was to help pay for the new statehouse. Twelve more lots were allowed to be sold in 1812. In addition to selling lots the commissioners were to give any church which requested it one acre of land on the state house square, as "the promotion of religion and morality at the seat of government is an object of primary importance."[18]

Most travelers to Milledgeville remarked on the wide distances between houses and on the large gardens. A Frenchman visiting in the 1820s, described Milledgeville:

> We arrived on the banks of the little Oconee near to which Milledgeville is built. This town which for its dispersion of its houses, and the multitude and extent of its beautiful gardens, rather resembles a fine village than a city containing a population of 2,500 souls.[19]

In the 1830s an English traveler found the capital an open, airy place with fine broad streets. James Silk Buckingham visited Milledgeville in 1839 and he had little good to say of it. He found the inn miserable, and the appearance and manner of the guests the worst he had witnessed in the United States. He described the road to Milledgeville as being through a dense gloomy forest and the worst he had travelled on.[20]

With the exception of Augusta, the state's ventures in town founding had not been strikingly successful. Although the commissioners felt they had sited the new capital well, in fact it proved to be about as unhealthy as Louisville. The location near the Oconee River swamps and the poor drainage on one side of the town caused the usual illnesses. The Oconee proved too shallow for reliable commercial traffic and the legislature attempted to make it more navigable by passing numerous acts to provide for clearing it. Unfortunately no lasting results were achieved. Milledgeville also suffered, as did all of Georgia, from lack of passable roads. After more than the usual failures to attract a railroad, the capital was finally successful and in 1851 was connected to the Central of Georgia by a spur road. The advent of the train was a convenience for the local planters, but did not noticeably cause the hoped-for growth and boom. The train had come too late and the center of commerce and industry had moved west to Macon and Columbus.

Two Trading Towns Planned by the State

Macon
Columbus

Macon

LaFayette's secretary noted in his diary during the General's trip through the States in 1824 and 1825:

> Macon which is a small and handsome village, tolerably populous, did not exist eighteen months since; it has arisen from the midst of the forest as if by enhantment. It is a civilized speck lost in the yet immense domain of the original children of the soil. Within a league of this place we were again in the bosom of virgin forests.[21]

British Capt. Basil Hall, who visited Macon in 1827, wrote:

> Macon appeared to be in the South exactly such a town as Utica or Syracuse in the North, or any other of those recently erected towns in the western parts of the State of New York. The woods were still growing in some of the streets and the stumps were not yet grubbed up in others. The houses looked as if they had been put up the day before, so that you smelt the sawmill everywhere. As yet the streets had no names, but they were laid out with perfect regularity, as I could discover by stakes here and there at the corners, and by rows of the Pride of India trees planted along both sides in a sort of mockery, as it seemed, of the grim old forest which was frowning all round on these pigmy works of man.[22]

The 1821 cession had given the state a large segment of land from the Oconee to the Flint rivers. Near Fort Hawkins, a Federal Indian Trading Post on the Ocmulgee River, the state reserved 21,000 acres for a "trading" town. The trading town, Macon, was located near the middle of this cession at the Fall Line and the head of navigation of the Ocmulgee.

The Macon survey was made by James Webb early in 1823. In March of that year the first auction of lots took place. Briefly, the legislative acts concerning the lot sales provided: forty lots were to be auctioned the first year, but no lots on the river were to be sold; twenty lots, to be auctioned in 1824, must adjoin those already sold, and no lots were to be auctioned within 100 yards of the river. The following year, twenty lots were auctioned, along with a few river lots, and the town streets were extended into the north and west commons. In 1827 the State advertised the sale of all remaining town and reserve lots. At this time the State appointed commissioners to survey two ranges of lots to the west and north of the commons in the State reserve; the first range to contain ten acre lots, the second to contain twenty acre lots, the rest to be laid off in 100 acre lots (*Fig. 76*). This act then carefully outlined a plan for the portion of the community on the east side of the river, the site of old Fort Hawkins,[23] which is now called East Macon.

Macon was laid out on a bluff above the river with hills rising on the west and the north. There were 480 one-half acre lots and thirty-seven river or fractional lots (*Fig. 77*). A four-acre square was carefully lined up opposite (*i.e.*, west of) where the bridge across the Ocmulgee was to be built. The center of the square was planned for the county courthouse. One block, number 35, was designated as a graveyard and another, number 1, for the use of the academy. Unlike the courthouse square, which interrupted the Macon grid plan (two of the 180-foot streets are the co-ordinates for the courthouse square), the other two squares were blocks within the grid. There were seven streets parallel to the river, alternating between 180- and 120-feet wide. Perpendicular to the river there were eleven streets with the same alternating widths. Because of the low-lying land in the south part of the town, not all of these were built. A diagonal street cutting through the town, Cotton Avenue, had started as an Indian trail, grown to a trader's path, and then become the Federal Road which ran through the middle of Georgia. So strong was the pattern developed by this road that it managed to persist even in the face of the usually obliterating grid. As in Milledgeville, each block consisted of four acres. In Milledgeville the lots were one acre, but in Macon the

Fig. 76. MACON, BIBB COUNTY. Founded 1823. Surveyors: Commissioners and James Webb. 1821 Cession.

block was broken up into eight one-half acre lots which were divided by two alleys, one of twenty feet and the other of ten feet. The 180-foot streets seem, from the beginning, to have been planned with idea of a park in the center. John C. Butler, a Macon historian, wrote that one of the first acts of the new board of commissioners was "the planting of shade trees along the sides and in the center of the streets."[24]

Vineville, a suburb, was built shortly after Macon was founded. Hills in a hot country are always desirable locations for homes and, as would be true in Columbus, it was in the higher land that the town's leading citizens built their Greek Revival mansions (*Fig. 78*). The plan of Vineville did not follow the uncompromising grid of the town proper, and the somewhat irregular layout of the streets and lots showed a certain recognition of the hilly topography.[25] Even the cemetery moved to this fashionable northern section. Simri Rose, editor of the local newspaper and a leading

TOWN PLANNING IN GEORGIA 175

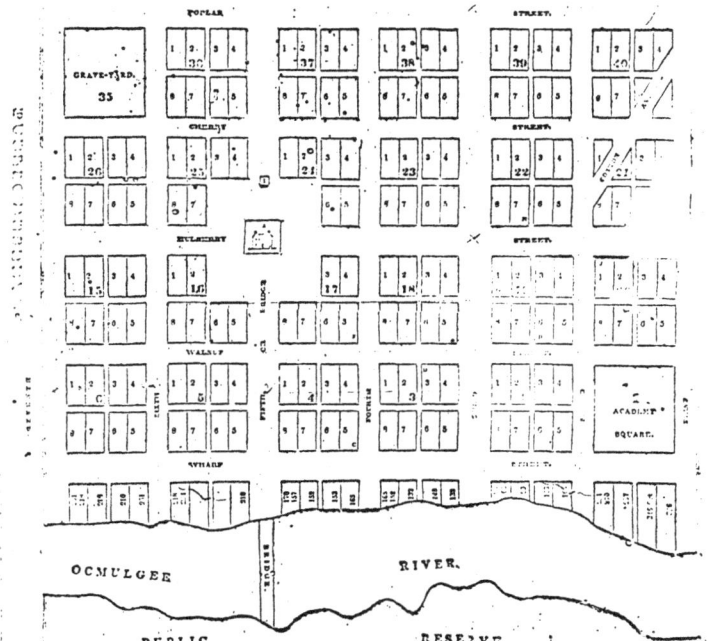

Fig. 77. DETAILED VIEW OF PLAN OF MACON, looking south from "Public Reserve" on north side of Ocmulgee River.

citizen of the town, gave to the city in 1840 a large tract of land along the bluff of the river. Here he laid out a cemetery in the latest fashion. To quote from the designer himself, "many who have visited the cemeteries of the north, and even far famed Mount Auburn, in Cambridge, Massachusetts, think them far inferior in natural beauty and location to Rose Hill."[26]

Another important development in the original plan, though occurring somewhat later, was the advent of the railroad. When the tracks were laid out on the west side of the river, they were located south of Fifth Street. From the town's founding most traffic had entered the city center along Cotton Avenue then turned onto Cherry or Mulberry and continued to the wharves or to Fifth Street and across the bridge. The street entering the square from the south was little-used (the southern section of

Fig. 78. AN EARLY VIEW DOWN MACON'S MULBERRY STREET FROM WHAT LATER WAS NAMED COLEMAN HILL. Long the site of princely post-bellum mansions, this promontory is now largely devoted to business structures on the fringe of the downtown area.

Macon was low and swampy, and early in its history much of it had been reserved for a city park) and the railroad tracks did not appreciably upset traffic patterns. The state had planned Macon as a trading town. That it happened also to be a county seat was of secondary importance in its development. Also, that the tracks were allowed to cut off one-half of the market square without undue disruption to the town seems to suggest that this was not the center of the town's activity. In keeping with beginning trends toward linear planning, Macon, from its inception, had built its most important buildings along Cherry and Mulberry streets. By 1850 the market square was no longer essential to serve the important function which it was originally intended to have, and the railroad tracks, although invading the square, did not destroy the town's plan as it had developed.

By 1860, Macon had a population of about 7,000 people, one-third probably slaves. There were three railroads, six hotels, 175 stores, two banks, four agencies, an academy for the blind, and a women's college.[27] All the furnishings for a prosperous medium-sized town had been acquired. Though there were some industries, Macon's fame and fortune rested on being a cotton-selling center: a trading town as the state had hoped. Town historians mention with pride that cotton was never sold on the streets in Macon but in the more select way through factors and in warehouses. The certain elegance which Macon retains is due to its planter background and to the insistence of these citizens upon handsome public buildings and surroundings.

Columbus

After the 1826 treaty with the Creeks was signed, giving the state land between the Flint and Chattahoochee rivers, the legislature passed an act to "lay out a trading town, and to dispose of all the lands reserved for the use of the state near the Coweta Falls on the Chattahoochee River and to name the same." The state appointed five commissioners to lay out the town and instructed them "to have special regard to the future commercial prosperity of said town and the health of its inhabitants." The state must have been concerned about the town-founding business, for at this time even her latest hope, Macon, was languishing, and the act for founding Columbus was more specific than had been the case with her other towns. The commissioners were told to lay out a square or oblong fronting the river of 1,200 acres to contain the town and commons. The town was to have not less than 500 building lots of one-half acre each with an appropriate number of streets and alleys and a suitable number of reserved squares for public buildings. The county of Muscogee, in which the town was located, was to be given ten acres in the town to sell for funds to build a courthouse and jail. For the State, two ranges of lots adjoining the commons were to be laid out in ten-and twenty-acre lots and beyond these the reserve was to be divided into 100-acre lots (*Fig. 79*). The act further stated that the auction of the lots was to be advertised sixty days in advance in Georgia newspapers and also in those of Charleston and Tuscaloosa. Unless there was a lack of interest, the lots were to be auctioned each day until all were sold.[28] Out of 632 building lots, 488 sold in a two-week period netted the State $131,000. In Macon after five years of careful selling the State had made only $120,000.[29]

A few months before the sale the peripatetic Captain Hall and his wife had arrived at Columbus. Mrs. Hall, in a letter concerning this embryonic town, wrote

> *as yet the town is a thick forest, with the exception of some temporary wooden buildings erected to shelter the numerous bidders from all parts of the union who are waiting for the sale of lots which is to commence in July"*[30]

Five years later Tyrone Power, another English traveler, wrote that Columbus was a thriving frontier town, with stores well-stocked and warehouses filled with cotton. He rhapsodized, as did most Columbus visitors, about "the wildly beautiful scenery along the falls of the river." He also mentioned that he observed several dwellings of mansion-like proportions.[31] Harriet Martineau, another well-known commentator of the American scene, visited Columbus the same year, 1833. According to her more matter-of-fact report, there were three main streets, Front, Broad and Oglethorpe, with many smaller ones branching out into the forest. She said there were five hotels and a population of 1000.[32]

TOWN PLANNING IN GEORGIA 179

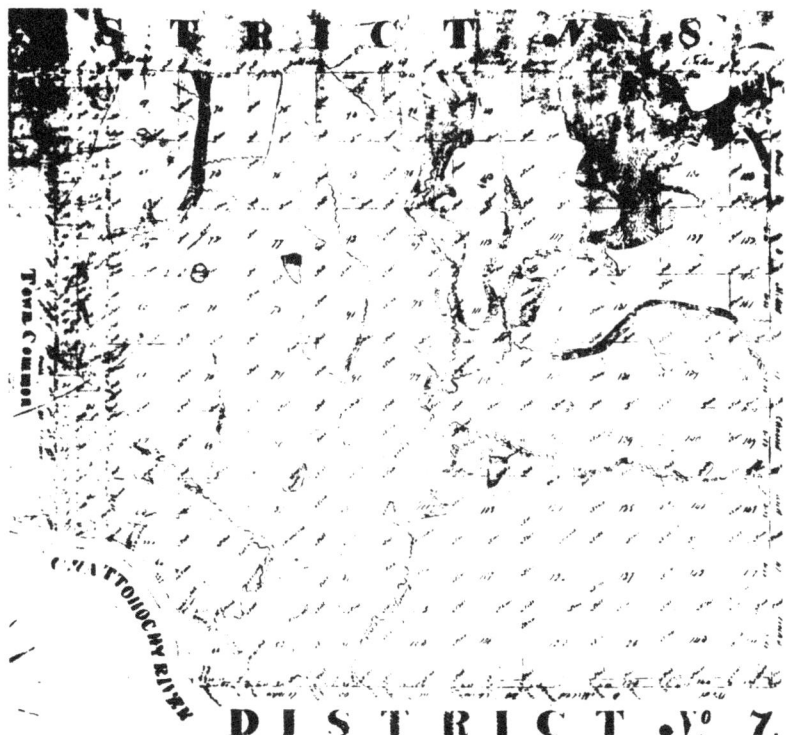

Fig. 79. COLUMBUS, MUSCOGEE COUNTY. Founded 1828. Surveyors: Commissioners and E. L. Thomas. 1826 Cession.

The commissioners appointed a surveyor, Edward Lloyd Thomas, to lay out the town. The field book which Thomas kept while surveying the site has survived.[33] Happily for the historian, Thomas was not averse to using his field book as a diary. He described in detail the hardships of the three-months survey and other daily occurrences. The intense interest in this new town is confirmed by various entries noting that all or some of the commissioners were always on the site, that the federal engineers visited the location, and that the county officials came to inspect the ten acres which the state had given them. Early in the survey, Thomas ran lines for the purpose of enabling the commissioners to fix on the most suitable place for the location of the 1,200 acres of town and commons. He made an entry concerning the lots which he was told to survey for the academies, churches and courthouse, and described carefully the beauties of the site chosen for the cemetery.

The plan which resulted was neither as sophisticated as that of Macon nor did it develop with age the amenities of the earlier town. The blocks were the usual four acres laid out in one-half acre lots. In Figure 79, five squares are shown, two for academies, two labelled A, B, C and D for churches, and one for the courthouse. The ten acres which the legislature deeded to the county, and which are labelled "courthouse square" on this map, were meant to be sold for funds for building the courthouse. Although alleys were prescribed in the legislative act, there is no plan which shows them and they were apparently eliminated. The streets parallel to the river were 132 feet wide, with Broad Street 164 feet. The cross streets were all ninety-nine feet wide. The falls of the Chattahoochee were spectacular enough to demand from the planners a public viewing place, and a promenade along the river at the south end of town was laid out. The reserves for public buildings were four-acre blocks placed in a balanced pattern in the grid. As at Macon, the linear elements of the plan (rather than the squares) became the important feature of the town. The park in the center of Broad Street was stretched the full length of the town. Accenting the linear pattern, the lots were arranged to form oblong blocks rather than the usual square ones.

The railroads in Columbus were not handled with the same care as in Macon. Arriving in 1853, they extended the entire length of the east and west boundaries of the town. To the west this eliminated the river promenade, and the wide expanse of tracks on the east boundary isolated the suburbs developing in the hills, allowing them to become practically another city.

With Columbus, Georgia finally hit the jackpot. The enormous advantages gained from the extensive water power at the falls, from the Chattahoochee being a truly navigable river, and from the fortunes to be made growing cotton in the rich virgin lands of west Georgia, led not only to a quick sale of the lots but also to the founding of a real industrial complex which was (with the possible exception of Augusta), the first in the state. Columbus was a true trading town and remains so today.

Notes

1. One-half of the population of a southern city usually consisted of slaves. The reasons for the large one-acre and one-half acre lots, laid out in most slave-owning states, were not only health and fresh air but also the need for extra space to house the lot owner's slaves.

2. Richard C. Wade (who does not seem to have studied Georgia conditions to any great extent) wrote in *Slavery in The Cities of the South 1820–1860* (New York, 1964), p. 61:

> *Urban housing in the South . . . omitted alleys. Local officials felt they would upset the basic scheme embodied in the enclosure system. To cut through city blocks would have broken into each lot, required rear entrances to the residential units, and induced interior traffic somewhat removed from public view. But, most compellingly, whenever alleys were opened they created an alternative center for slave activity. Soon Negro life in the neighborhood gravitated to the middle of the block and away from the supervision of slave owners or white authority. The isolation of the compound [town lot] could no longer be maintained, and the bondsman's orientation moved away from his master in the yard to his contacts in the back streets. . . . Unlike the thinly sliced commercial and residential areas, elsewhere, the city blocks in the South remained solid.*

3. Henry Marbury and William H. Crawford, *Digest of the Laws of the State of Georgia, From 1775 to 1800* (Savannah, 1802). Hereafter abbreviated as *D.L.G. 1775–1800*, p. 96.

4. Charles C. Jones and Salem Dutcher, *Memorial History of Augusta, Georgia* (Syracuse, New York, 1890), p. 133.

5. *Ibid.*, p. 132.

6. Marbury and Crawford, *D.L.G., 1775–1800*, pp. 132–136.

7. Richmond Academy was an integral part of Augusta. The fact that the commissioners gradually took over the title of Trustees of the Academy gives an idea of the importance attached to this institution. From statehood, the legislature had offered largess to counties in the form of land grants and confiscated royalist properties for county academies. The Richmond Academy

Trustees received from the Assembly a tract of 2000 acres and were allowed to lease land in the common for academy funds.

8. Jones and Dutcher, *Memorial History of Augusta, Georgia*, p. 135.

9. Augustin Smith Clayton, *A Compilation of the Laws of the State of Georgia, 1800-1820* (Augusta, 1812). Hereafter abbreviated as *C.L.G., 1800-1810*, p. 610.

10. These remarks have been taken from various travel accounts in Mills Lane (ed.), *The Rambler in Georgia* (Savannah, 1973).

11. Mark Van Doren (ed.), *The Travels of William Bartram* (New York, 1928), p. 219.

12. W.P.A. (comp.), "Louisville, Jefferson Co." Manuscript is in the Special Collection of the University of Georgia Library, no date, no pagination. (Typescript.)

13. Z. V. Thomas, *History of Jefferson County* (Macon, Georgia, 1927), p. 34.

14. Mills Lane (ed.), "John Melish 1806-09," in *The Rambler in Georgia* (Savannah, 1973), pp. 22-23.

15. Clayton, *C.L.G., 1800-1810*, p. 107.

16. Harriet M. Salley (ed.), *Correspondence of John Milledge, Governor of Georgia 1800-1806* (Columbia, 1947), p. 122.

17. Clayton, *C.L.G., 1800-1810*, p. 209.

18. *Ibid.*, pp. 390-391.

19. A. Levasseur, *Lafayette in America in 1824 and 1825* (Philadelphia, 1829), II, 66.

20. Mills Lane (ed.), "James Silk Buckingham 1839" in *The Rambler in Georgia* (Savannah, 1973), pp. 149-150.

21. Levasseur, *Lafayette in America in 1824 and 1825*, II, 70.

22. Basil Hall, *Travels in the United States* (Edinburgh, 1830), p. 277.

23. William C. Dawson, *A Compilation of the Laws of the State of Georgia, 1819-1829* (Milledgeville, 1821). Hereafter abbreviated as *C.L.G., 1819-1829*, pp. 437, 454, 444, 462-463, 466.

24. John C. Butler, *Historical Record of Macon and Central Georgia* (Macon, Georgia, 1958), p. 91.

25. Vineville is an early example of the type of plan which would be found in resort towns, particularly in North Georgia. Tallulah Falls is a good example of what could be called a relaxed grid layout which took into account the hilly terrain.

26. Rev. George White, *Historical Collections of Georgia* (New York, 1855), p. 270.

27. *Ibid.*, p. 270.

28. Dawson, *C.L.G., 1819-1829*, p. 470.

29. Nancy Telfair, *History of Columbus Georgia 1829-1928* (Columbus, Georgia, 1928), p. 33.

30. Etta B. Worsley, *Columbus on the Chattahoochee* (Columbus, Georgia, 1951), p. 75.

31. Tyrone Power, *Impressions of America, 1833, 1834, 1835* (London, 1836), II, 137.

32. Harriet Martineau, *Society in America* (New York, 1837), II, 214.

33. Edward Lloyd Thomas, *Field Book of Columbus Survey*. Manuscript. G.S.G.

Chapter VII
A Valuable Legacy

The most important town in colonial Georgia was Savannah. Its elaborate plan was a highly sophisticated conception dependent on the planners' background of aristocratic philosophical philanthropy. Its influence on colonial and state town planning was seminal. Colonial public towns copied Savannah's plan and towns founded after Independence used features both from the plan and from the ideals behind the plan.

After statehood, two distinct types of town plans were laid out concurrently: those planned by the state as capitals and as trading towns and those laid out as county towns by commissioners appointed by the legislature. The state-planned towns were laid out as large urban centers, which echoed Savannah's multi-square plan as well as her reserve-land divisions. The plans for the county towns came from a different root. However, an inheritance of the Trustees' ideals is evident in legislative acts which show a determination to keep speculation at a minimum and to give everyone equal opportunities to acquire property. Thus, although the state evolved methods for town founding which suited the changed political background, there was still a continuing use of the colonial planning ideals, ideas, and physical features in all Georgia towns founded by the legislature. After Independence the towns of greatest consequence were those planned by the state: three capitals and two trading towns. Milledgeville shows the influence of the colonial towns in her four symmetrically arranged squares laid out to interrupt the grid. In Macon a large tract of 21,000 acres was reserved for the town. Following the Savannah reserve-land pattern, Macon was divided into farm and garden lots and a common. Although a smaller tract was reserved for Columbus, the state continued to divide it after the colonial fashion: farm and garden lots and a common for the town. Both towns followed the colonial multi-square plan, though in Columbus none of the squares interrupt the grid.

The plans of the county courthouse towns followed a distictly different drummer, the focus being on the single central courthouse square which formed a nucleus for the town lots laid out around it. This plan had no connection with the multi-square colonial plan, which did not have the central courthouse focus. It was, in all likelihood, a pattern brought to Georgia by immigrants moving down the Great Wagon Road from Pennsylvania through the backcountry of Virginia and the Carolinas. It was in the other elements, such as the siting and organization, that the inheritance from colonial Georgia became positive forces in the county towns.

It can safely be assumed that in the colonial period under the Trustees Oglethorpe was the colony's town planner. Under the Crown, the governor and his Council explicitly outlined to the surveyor the plans for the colony's public towns. After Independence, state towns were laid out from exact specifications made by the General Assembly. In nearly every case the government of the colony or the state was the town planner. The exception was Milledgeville, where the appointed commissioners were apparently given *carte blanche* concerning the town's plan, since no acts of the General Assembly exist detailing any particular layout. That body appointed commissioners and directed them concerning most of the factors necessary for bringing a courthouse town into existence, but as in Milledgeville did not regulate how the town was to be laid out. The planners of the courthouse seats and of Milledgeville thus seem to have been the commissioners or a surveyor hired by the commissioners to lay off the town.

In these first hundred years of Georgia's history, town planning was done with extraordinary care, not only for providing urban amenities, but by enacting the legal machinery necessary to inhibit land speculation and to give the small landholder an equal chance with the large planters. Determined to put into effect "the greatest good for the greatest number," the General Assembly kept an almost absolute control over the founding of courthouse and state towns and, if it was thought necessary, over the sale or auction of lots and over the town's development until the legislature felt it was ready to be chartered. A quotation from Governor Milledge concerning the land law of 1803 explains this populist sentiment which was so frequently evident in town legislation:

We must smother in the bud all hopes entertained by individuals of accumulating in the western parts of the state a large landed interest. Let us secure the industrious poor from the grasping hand of the rich speculator.

As a final point, let us briefly consider how the early Georgia towns, in general, stand up against the rigors of contemporary life. Savannah, Brunswick, Washington and Athens are a few examples of towns where citizen organizations have worked hard to preserve their town's plan and buildings and have been successful. On the other side of the coin, the central sections of the handsome state towns, Macon, Columbus and Augusta, have been allowed to deteriorate. Streets denuded of their trees are a tragedy in a northern town; in a southern town to cut down trees which shaded the wide boulevards during the hot summers seems even more thoughtless. Yet this has been done in all three towns. Other equally disasterous changes have made a travesty of the State's fine planning.

Certain towns have been so isolated that time seems to have passed them by. These retain, with no apparent effort, their original plan and charm. Danielsville, Elberton, Carrollton and Zebulon come to mind. Again there is another side to the coin. An equally attractive town which happened to be in the path of a highway could easily be ruined. The central nucleus originally formed by the square could be completely destroyed by a main thoroughfare. Jackson, Fayetteville, Lincolnton and Jefferson are a few towns which became the victims of highways.

Georgians today are becoming increasingly aware of their heritage. If this awareness leads to positive action, it may not be too late to save the fine downtown districts of the larger towns which are being destroyed by lack of planning, outdated taxation, suburbs and shopping malls. Much still needs to be done to preserve fine examples of town planning. The hour is late; the need is great if we are to pass along to the next generation an inheritance which adapts the best of the past to the needs of the future.

Notes on the Illustrations

Frontispiece. Crawfordville, Georgia: 1826. Manuscript plan:
Plan of Crawfordville. Explanations, "Lots divided into three parts are one by three chains; lots in two parts are one and one-half by three chains; square lots 3 by three chains; lots 23 and 24 are three by four chains; main street one chain, 12-3/4 L.; back streets, one chain; lot 44, Jail; lot 17 Tavern; lot 30, Methodist Church; lot 46, Spring." Office of the Georgia Surveyor General, Atlanta (hereafter abbreviated as G.S.G.)

Fig. 1. Georgia River Systems. From James C. Bonner, *The Georgia Story*, Oklahoma City-Chattanooga: Harlow Publishing Corp., 1958. Used by permission of the author.

Fig. 2. Indian Cessions. From Milton S. Heath, *Constructive Liberalism–The Role of the State in the Economic Development in Georgia to 1860*, Cambridge, Massachusetts, 1954. Copyright © 1954 by the President and Fellows of Harvard College. Used by permission of Harvard University Press.

Fig. 3. Treaty and Lottery Dates. *Idem.*

Fig. 4. "Washington" Type Plans.

Fig. 5. "Augusta" Type Plans.

Fig. 6. "Sparta" Type Plans.

Fig. 7. "Savannah" Type Plans.

Fig. 8. Monticello, Georgia: 1972. "Monticello Quadrangle Georgia–Jasper Co. 7.5 minute series (Topographical) Monticello, Ga. 1972." United States Department of the Interior Geological Survey (hereafter abbreviated as U.S.G.S.).

Fig. 9. Sparta, Georgia: 1972. "Sparta Quadrangle Georgia–Hancock Co. 7.5 minute series (Topographical) Sparta, Ga. 1972." U.S.G.S.

TOWN PLANNING IN GEORGIA 189

Fig. 10. Dublin, Georgia: 1972. "Dublin Quadrangle Georgia—Laurens Co. 7.5 minute series (Topographical) Dublin, Ga. 1974." U.S.G.S.

Fig. 11. Cuthbert, Georgia: 1972. "Cuthbert Quadrangle Georgia—Randolph Co. 7.5 minute series (Topographical) Cuthbert, Ga. 1972." U.S.G.S.

Fig. 12. Petersburg, Georgia: 1965. "Petersburg Georgia:" Frontispiece of E. Merton Coulter, *Old Petersburg and the Broad River Valley of Georgia*, Athens, Georgia, 1965. "This plan was constructed from the deed records in the Elbert County Courthouse, Elberton, Ga."

Fig. 13. Indian Springs, Georgia: *circa* 1827. Unsigned, undated manuscript plan of Indian Springs. G.S.G.

Fig. 14. Athens, Georgia: *circa* 1825. Unsigned, undated manuscript plan: "Date unknown, after 1810 prior to 1835." Georgia Collections, University of Georgia, Athens, Georgia (hereafter abbreviated G.C.U.G.).

Fig. 15. Oxford, Georgia: 1827. Unsigned manuscript plan of Oxford and college square: "Plan of the Town of Oxford." Special Collections, Emory University Library, Atlanta, Georgia.

Fig. 16. Towns founded in colonial Georgia, 1733-1776.

Fig. 17. Savannah, Georgia: 1757. "Plan of the City Savannah and Fortifications" drawn by John Gerar William DeBrahm, from *History of the Province of Georgia*, Wormsloe, Georgia, 1875.

Fig. 18. Savannah, Georgia: 1818. "Plan of the City and Harbor of Savannah, Chatham County, State of Georgia, Taken in 1818," drawn by I. Stouf. G.S.G.

Fig. 19. New Ebenezer, Georgia: 1736. Undated map: "Plan von Neu Ebenezer" drawn by I. Stouf. G.S.G.

Fig. 20. Darien, Georgia: 1767. Manuscript plan:
"Plan of the new town of Darien containing 30.72 acres of land. The old town which was a square of 720 feet every way was laid out in the year 1736 and marked by pricked lines in this plan. . . . Note, the new town is laid out from the front of the old town from the river and at equal distances from each side of it. Lachlan McIntosh 1767." G.S.G.

Fig. 21. Darien, Georgia: 1806. Manuscript plan: "Darien resurveyed and arranged by order of the Proprietors, Commissioners of the Academy of McIntosh County & Comm. of the Town by Thomas McCall Geometrician." G.S.G.

Fig. 22. Hardwick, Georgia: 1974. Manuscript map:
"Georgia Bryan County. The above plan represents the township of Hardwick, surveyed by an order of the commissioners of the Twentieth day of May 1794 under the authority of an act of the Legislature . . . surveyed and recorded by Tho. Collier, County Surveyor." G.S.G.

Fig. 23. Brunswick, Georgia: 1829. Section of manuscript plan: "Plan of the Town of Brunswick and Commons. A true copy of the resurvey of January 1826 by John Conty, Feb. 1829." G.S.G.

Fig. 24. Wrightsborough, Georgia: 1807. Manuscript plan: "State of Georgia, Wrightsborough in Columbia County . . . by M. Marrifz Daley." G.S.G.

Fig. 25. Courthouse Towns in the Headright region before 1790.

Fig. 26. Washington, Georgia: 1805. (Redrawn) unsigned manuscript map of Washington:
We certify that the above is an approved plan of the town of Washington, Wilkes County. Witness our honor and seal this 14 of May 1805. Recorded 17 of May 1805 at the request of the county.
On the reverse of the framed plat is written:
The 48 lots within the painted lines are what is formerly left for commons, but since laid out by an act of April . . . the first lots laid out are 3 chains. . . . [Wilkes County Courthouse, Washington, Georgia.]

Fig. 27. Waynesborough, Georgia: 1857. Unsigned Manuscript plan:
"Georgia, Burke Co. The plan of Waynesboro copied July 10, 1888 from a copy in the possession of Col. J. J. Jones, said copy being made Sept. 19 1857 from a paper in possession of Edward Garlich by John R. Sturgis, [signed] R. C Neely. Lots 2½ by 4 chains. Liberty and Pease streets 96' wide all others 60' wide."

Fig. 28. Greensborough, Georgia: 1812. Manuscript plan: "Greensborough" drawn by William W. Strain. Deed Book EE, Greene County Courthouse, Greensboro, Georgia.

TOWN PLANNING IN GEORGIA   191

Fig. 29. St. Marys, Georgia: 1788. Unsigned manuscript plan of St. Marys (text illegible). G.S.G. Public squares outlined by the author.

Fig. 30. Courthouse Towns in the Headright Region After 1790—in the Piedmont and Red Hills.

Fig. 31. Elberton, Georgia: 1791. Manuscript plan:
"Lot no. 2 of the original Plan of Elberton Georgia, Elbert County. The above plat represents lot #2 on map of the town of Elberton Ga. made in 1791 by R. Kennedy S.E.C. Surveyed for the Town Council of Elberton Ga. April 4th 1892 Recorded May 11th 1892." Deed Book LL, Elbert County Courthouse, Elberton, Georgia.

Fig. 32. Warrenton, Georgia: 1974. Manuscript redrawing done in 1974 from visual survey by the author.

Fig. 33. Lexington, Georgia: 1897. Manuscript plat: "Meson Academy, Georgia, Oglethorpe County. The above plat represents the location of New Meson Academy in Lexington Georgia. Surveyed Dec. 24, 1896 Thos. B. Moss Surv." Oglethorpe County Courthouse, Lexington, Georgia.

Fig. 34. Sandersville, Georgia: 1974. Manuscript redrawing done in 1974 from a visual survey by the author.

Fig. 35. Sparta, Georgia: *Circa*. 1960. Section of current undated map. Sparta Chamber of Commerce, Sparta, Georgia.

Fig. 36. Lincolnton, Georgia: 1854. Manuscript plan:
"The above plat of Lincolnton is a true representation of a portion of land in a rectangular form, containing 100 acres. The lines enclosing the town of Lincolnton and also showing the prisoner his bounds. Surveyed on the 14 of August 1854 by Thomas Searles, C. Sur." Lincoln County Courthouse, Lincolnton, Georgia.

Fig. 37. Courthouse Towns in the Headright Region after 1790—in the Colonial Lands and Pine Barren-Wiregrass Region.

Fig. 38. Statesborough, Georgia: 1806. Manuscript plan: "Georgia, Bulloch County: Statesborough—Plan of the lots in said Borough . . . by Josiah Everitt C.S. 1806." Deed Book A, Bulloch County Courthouse, Statesborough, Georgia.

Fig. 39. Springfield, Georgia: 1821. Manuscript plan: "This is a representation of the Town of Springfield. Laid out in pursuance of an order of the Interior Court to me directed . . . laid out 8th May 1821. Lara [?] Powers C.E." Deed Book D, Effingham County Courthouse, Springfield, Georgia.

Fig. 40. Riceborough, Georgia: 1796. Manuscript plan:
"Plan of a Town laid out by Matthew McAllister, Jan. 7, 1796 at North Newport. The lotts containing 50 feet front and at North Newport. The lotts containing 50 feet front and 75 feet deep, corresponding with the lotts on the opposite side of the main road, and the square for public buildings, being 230 by 150 feet-exclusive of the lanes and alleys." G.S.G.

Fig. 41. Mount Vernon, Georgia: *Circa* 1813. Undated, unsigned manuscript plan: [The date of the plan is probably around 1813, the date of the founding of the town. 1860 is the date it was first recorded.] Deed Book AA, Montgomery County Courthouse, Mount Vernon, Georgia.

Fig. 42. Williamsburg, Georgia: 1793. Manuscript plan: "Town of Williamsburg situated on the south side of the Altamaha River about forty miles from its mouth . . . (signed) Farr Williams, Will. Limbert, Roswell King. Recorded November 8, 1793." G.S.G.

Fig. 43. Creek Cession of 1802-1805.

Fig. 44. Madison, Georgia: *Circa* 1809. Unsigned, undated manuscript plan of Madison. Deed Book A, Morgan County Courthouse, Madison, Georgia.

Fig. 45. Dublin, Georgia: *Circa* 1935. A section of current undated plan of Dublin. Laurens County Courthouse, Dublin, Georgia.

Fig. 46. Marion, Georgia: 1814. Manuscript plan:
"The above is a correct representation of the Town of Marion in the County of Twiggs laid out agreeably to a plan proposed by the Commissioners of the courthouse and jail of said county. Certified by me this 28th June 1814, Francis Spann, Cty. Sur." G.S.G.

Fig. 47. Creek Cessions of 1817-1818 and 1819.

Fig. 48. Gainesville, Georgia: 1820. Manuscript plan: "Gainesville." Typescript on map: "This is the original map of the city of Gainesville, Ga., as prepared by Timothy Terrell IV, who was a civil engineer and surveyor of some note. . . ." Gainesville Public Library, Gainesville, Georgia.

TOWN PLANNING IN GEORGIA

Fig. 49. Clarkesville, Georgia: *Circa* 1970. Current undated plan. Clarkesville Chamber of Commerce, Clarkesville, Georgia.

Fig. 50. Creek Cession of 1821.

Fig. 51. Decatur, Georgia: 1866. Plan of "Decatur Court Square." *DeKalb New Era*, August 6, 1970. DeKalb County Library, Decatur, Georgia.

Fig. 52. Forsyth, Georgia: 1955. Redrawn section of map: "State Highway Department of Georgia. City Map, Forsyth, Monroe County, 1955."

Fig. 53. Perry, Georgia: 1925. Redrawn from manuscript plan: "This map of the town of Perry has been surveyed partly from the original map and from actual survey's and may be relied upon to be correct. September, 1925." Plat Book T, Houston County Courthouse, Perry, Georgia.

Fig. 54. Creek Cession of 1826.

Fig. 55. Talbotton, Georgia: 1828. Redrawn from manuscript plan: "A copy of the map of Talbotton, Ga. as made by Wm Bacon 1828. A true copy. 3/16/66." Plat Book C, Talbot County Courthouse, Talbotton, Georgia.

Fig. 56. LaGrange, Georgia: 1860. Section of plan: "LaGrange Georgia in 1860. Compiled by W. W. Turner, 1923." G.S.G.

Fig. 57. Greenville, Georgia: 1828. Redrawn section of manuscript plan of Greenville: "Sales of Town Lotts." Deed Book A, Merriwether County Courthouse, Greenville, Georgia.

Fig. 58. Carrollton, Georgia: 1971. "The Original Plan of Carrollton" from James C. Bonner, *Georgia's Last Frontier: Carroll County*. Athens, Georgia, 1971. Used by permission of the University of Georgia Press.

Fig. 59. Americus, Georgia: 1869. Section of Manuscript plan: "Plan of the Town of Americus with the square laid out on the public lot which will fully show the area. J. B. Pilsbury, Dept. Clk. June 29, 1869." Guarantor's Book P, Sumter County Courthouse, Americus, Georgia.

Fig. 60. Cuthbert, Georgia: 1962. Section of map: "Cuthbert, Georgia. J.B. McCrary Eng. Corp. Atlanta, Ga. July 1962."

Fig. 61. Southern Cession of 1814.

Fig. 62. Bainbridge, Georgia: *Circa* 1974. Section of current undated map: "Map of Bainbridge." Bainbridge Chamber of Commerce, Bainbridge, Georgia.

Fig. 63. Newton, Georgia: 1832. Redrawn from unsigned manuscript plan: "A plan of the Town of Newton, Baker County, Geo. Surveyed August 1832. The streets are 66 feet wide, Alleys are 10 feet wide, Lots are 213 feet 8½ inches one way and 101 feet 10½ inches the other way." Plat Book I, Baker County Courthouse, Newton, Georgia.

Fig. 64. Blakely, Georgia: 1906. "Sanborn Map Company. Blakely, Early Co., Georgia, January, 1906. 11 Broadway, New York." G.S.G.

Fig. 65. Irwinville, Georgia: *Circa* 1845. Undated, unsigned manuscript plan of Irwinville, Georgia. Irwin County Courthouse, Ocilla, Georgia. Original now in G.S.G.

Fig. 66. Cherokee Cession of 1835.

Fig. 67. Dahlonega Georgia: 1832. Manuscript plan: "Representation of the Town of Dahlonega in Lumpkin County, Georgia. The Figs. A, B & C on Lots 951 and Fig. D on 925; E on 949 and Fig. F on 985 are eminences. The lots were originally to be twenty chains square but by innacurracy of the surveyor vary. 11th May 1835." Dahlonega Court House Gold Museum. Dahlonega, Georgia.

Fig. 68. Rome, Georgia: 1864. Manuscript plan: "Rome and Vicinity. Compiled from Information by Sergeant N. Finegan under the direction of Capt. W. E. Merrill, Chief Topl. Engr., Jan. 26, 1864." G.S.G.

Fig. 69. Rome, Georgia: 1890. Section of manuscript plan: "Plan of Rome 1890, Dietz Bros." Floyd County Courthouse, Rome, Georgia.

Fig. 70. Marietta, Georgia: 1911. Section of map: "April 1911 Marietta, Ga." Sanborn Map Company. Cobb County Courthouse, Marietta, Georgia.

Fig. 71. Five Towns Planned by the State.

Fig. 72. Augusta, Georgia: 1783. Unsigned manuscript plan of Augusta. Plat Book A. G.S.G.

TOWN PLANNING IN GEORGIA 195

Fig. 73. Augusta, Georgia: 1937. Redrawn section of map: "Map of Augusta, Georgia, Federal Writers Project, 1937." Augusta, Georgia. Sections outlined by the author.

Fig. 74. Louisville, Georgia: 1938. Section of Georgia State Highway Map. G.S.G.

Fig. 75. Milledgeville, Georgia: 1808. Detail of Manuscript plat:
"A Plan of Milledgeville, the Capital and permanent seat of the Government of the State of Georgia. Also a representation of the whole Tract or Body of land reserved as an appertenance or Common to the same. Copied from the original PLAN on the 2nd day of September 1808 by Daniel Sturges Sur. Gen'l." G.S.G.

Fig. 76. Macon, Georgia: 1828. Manuscript map of Macon and reserves:
"The Public reserves on both sides of the Ocmulgee River at Macon. Surveyed in pursuance of an act of the General Assembly of the State of Georgia under the direction of Wm. N. Harmon, Ch B. Strong, O. H. Prince commissioners, by Richard W. Ellis Surveyor." G.S.G.

Fig. 77. Macon, Georgia: 1831. Map of Macon, Georgia drawn by Oliver H. Prince. From *Macon Advertiser and Agricultural and Mercantile Intelligencer*, July 29, 1831, Washington Memorial Library.

Fig. 78. "View of Macon, Georgia," 1855. Department of Archives and History, Atlanta.

Fig. 79. Columbus, Georgia: 1828. Detail of a manuscript map of "that part of the Reserve at the Cowetah Falls in Muscogee Co. laid off in Conformite to an act of the Legislature of the State, passed the 24th day of December, 1827 with 10-20- and 100-acre lots forming an area of 9240 acres. Certified June, 1828 by E. L. Thomas, Surv'r." G.S.G.

Bibliography

General

Abott, William W. *Royal Governors of Georgia 1754-1755*. Chapel Hill: University of North Carolina Press, 1959.

Bonner, James C. *The Georgia Story*. Oklahoma City-Chattanooga: Harlow Publishing Corp., 1958.

Boogher, Elbert W. G. *Secondary Education in Georgia*. Philadelphia: I. F. Huntzinger Co., Inc., 1933.

Callaway, James E. *The Early Settlement of Georgia*. Athens: University of Georgia Press, 1948.

Coulter, E. Merton. *Georgia, A Short History*. Chapel Hill: University of North Carolina Press, 1960.

Cummings, William P. "Mapping of the Southeast: The First Two Centuries." *The Southeastern Geographer*: XI, 3-19.

DeBrahm, J. G. William. *History of the Province of Georgia*. Wormsloe, Georgia: Privately printed by George Wymberley Jones, 1849.

DeVorsey, Louis, Jr. (ed.). *DeBrahm's Report on the General Survey in The Southern Districts of North America*. Columbia, South Caroline: The University of South Carolina Press, 1960.

Ettinger, Amos Aschback. *James Edward Oglethorpe, Imperial Idealist*. Oxford: Clarendon Press, 1936.

Georgia, A Guide to Its Towns and Countryside. American Guide Series. Athens: University of Georgia Press, 1940.

Green, E. R. R. "Queensborough Township: Scotch-Irish Emigration and Expansion of Georgia, 1763-1776." *William & Mary Quarterly*: XII (April 1960), 183-199.

Heath, Milton S. *Constructive Liberalism—The Role of the State in the Economic Development in Georgia to 1860.* Cambridge: Harvard University Press, 1954.

Hibbard, Benjamin H. *A History of Public Land Policies.* New York: P. Smith, 1939.

Hitz, Alex M. "Georgia Bounty and Land Grants." *Georgia Historical Quarterly*: XXXVIII (December 1954), 337-348.

Jones, Charles C. "The Dead Towns of Georgia." *Georgia Historical Collections*, IV, Savannah: Morning News Steam Printing House, 1878.

———. *The History of Georgia.* 2 vols. Boston: Houghton Mifflin Co., 1883.

King, Spencer Bidwell. *Georgia Voices.* Athens: University of Georgia Press, 1966.

Knight, Lucien Lamar. *Georgia's Landmarks, Memorials, and Legends.* Atlanta: The Byrd Printing Co., 1913.

Krakow, Kenneth K. *Georgia Place-Names.* Macon, Georgia: Winship Press, 1975.

Library of Congress Exhibition. *Settlement of Georgia 1733-1948.* Washington: Government Printing Office, 1948.

McLendon, Samuel G. *History of the Public Domain of Georgia.* Atlanta: Foote and Davies Co., 1924.

Nichols, Frederick Doveton. *The Early Architecture of Georgia.* Chapel Hill: University of North Carolina Press, 1957.

Orr, Dorothy. *A History of Education in Georgia.* Chapel Hill: University of North Carolina Press, 1950.

Park, Orville A. "The Georgia Scotch-Irish." *Georgia Historical Quarterly*: XII (June 1928), 115-135.

Phillips, Ulrich B. *A History of Transportation in the Eastern Cotton Belt to 1860.* New York: Columbia University Press, 1968.

———. *Georgia and State Rights*. Massachusetts: The Antioch Press, 1968.

Price, Edward T. "The Central Courthouse Square in the American County Seat." *The Geographical Review*: LVIII (1968), 29-60.

Reps, John W. *The Making of Urban America*. Princeton: Princeton University Press, 1965.

———. *Town Planning in Frontier America*. Princeton: Princeton University Press, 1969.

Salley, Harriet Milledge (ed.). *Correspondence of Gov. John Milledge 1802-1806*. Columbia, South Carolina: State Commercial Printing Co., 1949.

Saye, Albert Berry. *New Viewpoints in Georgia History*. Athens: University of Georgia Press, 1943.

Sherwood, Adiel. *Gazetteer of the State of Georgia*. Charleston: Riley, 1827.

———. *Gazetteer of the State of Georgia*. Philadelphia: J. W. Martin & W. K. Boden, 1829.

———. *Gazetteer of the State of Georgia*. Washington City, Georgia: P. Force, 1937.

———. *Gazetteer of the State of Georgia*. Macon, Georgia: S. Boykin, 1860.

Smith, George G. *The Story of Georgia and the Georgia People, 1732-1860*. Baltimore: Geneological Publishing Co., 1968.

Stevens, William Bacon. *History of Georgia*. 2 vols. New York: D. Appelton & Co., 1897.

Wade, Richard C. *Slavery in the Cities, The South 1820-1860*. New York: Oxford University Press, 1964.

White, George. *Statistics of the State of Georgia*. Savannah: W. T. Williams, 1849.

———. *Historical Collections of Georgia*. New York: Pudney and Russell, 1855. 3rd ed.

The Laws of Georgia

Candler, Allen D. (ed.). *The Colonial Records of the State of Georgia.* Atlanta: The Franklin-Turner Co., 1908.

Clayton, Augustin Smith (comp.). *A Compilation of the Laws of the State of Georgia, 1810-1819.* Augusta: Adams and Dubckinck, 1812.

Dawson, William C. (comp.). *A Compilation of the Laws of the State of Georgia, 1800-1810.* Milledgeville: Grantland & Orme, 1831.

Foster, Arthur. *A Digest of the Laws of the State of Georgia.* Philadelphia: Towar, J. & Hogan, D.M., 1831.

Georgia, Acts and Resolutions of the General Assembly. Milledgeville, 1833, 1834, 1835, 1836.

Lamar, Lucius Q. C. (comp.). *Compilation of the Laws of the State of Georgia, 1810-1819.* Augusta: T. S. Hannon, 1821.

Marbury, Henry and William H. Crawford (comp.). *Digest of the Laws of the State of Georgia, From 1775 to 1800.* Savannah: Seymour, Wollhopter & Stebbins, 1802.

Prince, Oliver H. (comp.). *A Digest of the Laws of the State of Georgia Enacted Previous to 1820.* Milledgeville: Grantland & Orme, 1831.

Watkins, Robert and George Watkins (comp.). *A Digest of the Laws of the State of Georgia From Its Establishment to 1798.* Philadelphia: R. Aitken, 1800.

W.P.A. (comp.). "Louisville, Jefferson Co." Georgia Collections, University of Georgia Library, Athens. Typescript of legislative acts concerning Louisville, no date.

———. "Milledgeville, Baldwin Co." Georgia Collections, University of Georgia Library, Athens. Typescript of legislative acts concerning Milledgeville, no date.

Travelers' Accounts

Bartram, William. *Travels Through North and South Carolina, Georgia.* Dublin: J. Moore, W. Jones, R. McAllister, and J. Rice, 1793.

Featherstonhaugh, G. W. *Excursion Through the Slave States.* New York: Harper & Bros., 1844.

Hall, Basil. *Travels in North America in the Years 1827-1828.* Edinburgh: Cadell and Co., 1829.

Hall, Margaret (Hunter). *The Aristocratic Journey.* Una Pope-Hennessy, ed. New York: G. P. Putnam Sons, 1931.

Henderson, Archibald. *Washington's Southern Tour 1791.* Boston and New York: Houghton Mifflin Co., 1923.

Krepper, George W. (ed.). *Travels in the Southland 1822-1828, The Journal of Lucius Verus Bierce.* Columbus, Ohio: Ohio State University Press, 1966.

Lambert, John. *Travels Through Canada and the United States of North America in the Years 1806, 1807 & 1808*, vol. II. London: C. Craddock & W. Joy, 1814.

Lane, Mills (ed.). *The Rambler in Georgia.* Savannah: The Beehive Press, 1973.

Levasseur, Auguste. *Lafayette in America 1824-1825.* 2 vols. Philadelphia: J. B. Nolan, 1829.

Lyell, Charles (Sir). *Travels in North America.* 2 vols. London: John Murray, 1845.

Martineau, Harriet. *Society in America.* 2 vols. New York: Saunders and Otley, 1837.

Melish, John. *Travels Through the United States of America in the Years 1806 & 1807, 1809, 1810 & 1811.* 2 vols. Philadelphia: By the author, 1815.

Mohl, Raymond A. (ed.). "A Scotsman Visits Georgia, 1811." *Georgia Historical Quarterly*: LV (Summer 1971), 259-294.

Moore, Francis. "Voyage to Georgia Begun in the Year 1735" in George White's (ed.) *Georgia Historical Collection.* New York: Putney & Russell, 1854.

Oliphant, J. Orme. *Through the South and the West with Jeremiah Sevarts*. Lewisberg, Pennsylvania: Bucknell University Press, 1956.

Power, Tyrone. *Impressions of America During the Years 1833-34-35*. 2 vols. London: Richard Bentley, 1836.

Sibbald, George. *Notes and Observations on the Pine Lands of Georgia*. Augusta: William J. Bunce, 1801.

Local and Special Histories

Chapter III

Baker, Pearl. *The Story of Wrightsboro 1768-1964*. Thomson, Georgia: By the Author, 1964.

Cate, Margaret Davis. *Our Todays and Yesterdays*. Brunswick, Georgia: Glover Bros., Inc., 1930.

Childs, Curtis W. "History of Brunswick, Georgia." M.A. Thesis, University of Alabama, 1960.

Corry, John P. "The Houses of Colonial Georgia." *Georgia Historical Quarterly*: XIV (September 1930), 181-201.

Flippin, Percy Scott. "The Royal Government in Georgia 1752-1776: The Judicial System and Administration." *Georgia Historical Quarterly*: X (December 1926), 251-276.

Gordon, Arthur G. "The Arrival of the Scotch Highlanders at Darien." *Georgia Historical Quarterly*: XX (September 1936), 199-210.

Historic Savannah Foundation, Inc. *Historic Savannah*. Savannah: The Foundation, 1968.

Hitz, Alex M. "The Wrightsborough Quaker Town and Township in Georgia." *The Bulletin of Friends Historical Association*: XLVI (Spring 1957), 10.

Hofer, J. M. "The Georgia Salzbergers." *Georgia Historical Quarterly*: XVIII (June 1934), 99-117.

Jones, Charles Colcock. "Dead Towns of Georgia." *Georgia Historical Collections*: IV (1878), 141-225.

———, O. F. Vedder, and Frank Weldon. *History of Savannah Georgia*. Syracuse, New York: D. Mason and Company, 1890.

Lee, F. D. and S. L. Agnew. *Historical Record of the City of Savannah*. Savannah: J. H. Estile, 1869.

McIlwain, Paul. *The Dead Town of Sunbury*. Hendersonville, North Carolina: By the Author, 1971.

Park, Orville A. "The Puritan in Georgia." *Georgia Historical Quarterly*: XIII (December 1929), 343-372.

Reps, John W. "Town Planning in Colonial Georgia." *Town Planning Review*: Jan. 1966, 272-278.

Smith, Joseph W. *Visits to Brunswick Georgia and Travels South*. Boston: Addison C. Getchell & Son, 1907.

Steele, Edward M. "Flush Times in Brunswick, Georgia in the 1830's." *Georgia Historical Quarterly*: XXVIII (September 1955), 221-229.

Strobel, Philip A., Rev. *The Salzburgers and Their Descendents*. Baltimore: T. Newton Kurtz, 1855.

Tankersley, Allen P. "A Study of Puritanism in Colonial Georgia." *Georgia Historical Quarterly*: XXXII (September 1948), 149-158.

Voight, G. P. "Ebenezer Georgia." *Georgia Review*: 9 (Summer 1965), 209-215.

Wylly, Charles Spalding. *The Seed That Was Sown in the Colony of Georgia 1740-1840*. New York: The Neale Publishing Co., 1910.

Chapter IV

Bowen, Eliza A. *The Story of Wilkes County, Georgia*. Marietta, Georgia: Continental Book Co., 1950.

Clark, Elmer T. (ed.). *The Journal and Letters of Francis Asbury.* 3 vols. Nashville: Abingdon Press, 1958. Vol. I: *The Journal 1771-1793.*

Coleman, Liodel (ed.). *Statesborough 1866-1960, a Century of Progress.* Statesborough, Georgia: Bulloch Herald Publishing Co., 1969.

Coulter, E. Merton. *Old Petersburg and the Broad River Valley of Georgia.* Athens, Georgia: University of Georgia Press, 1965.

——. "Francis Meson, An Early Georgia Merchant and Philanthropist." *Georgia Historical Quarterly:* XLII (March 1958), 26-44.

——. "Meson Academy, Lexington, Georgia." *Georgia Historical Quarterly:* XLII (June 1958), 125-162.

——. "William E. Martin and the School He Endowed: Martin Institute." *Georgia Historical Quarterly:* L (June 1966), 126-152.

Elrod, Frank. *Historical Notes on Jackson County, Georgia.* Jefferson, Georgia: Privately printed, 1967.

Hollingworth, Clyde. *A History of the Early Years of Screven County.* Screven County, Georgia: Privately printed, no date.

Lanceford, Alvin Mill, Jr. *Early Records of Taliaferro County, Georgia.* Crawfordville, Georgia: Privately printed, 1956.

McIntosh, John H. *Official History of Elbert County.* Atlanta: Atlanta Cherokee Publishing Co., 1968.

Mitchell, Ella. *History of Washington County.* Atlanta: Byrd Printing Co., 1924.

Moore, Virginia H. "Historic Sparta and Hancock County." *Georgia Magazine:* (October-November 1965), 16.

Reddick, J. H. "Lets Gather Screven's History." *Scriven County News:* 1 (February 1963), p. 8.

Smith, Flourie Carter. *History of Oglethorpe County, Georgia.* Washington, Georgia: Wilkes Publishing Co., 1970.

Vocelle, James T. *History of Camden County*. Jacksonville, Florida: Kenedy Brown-Hale Co., 1914.

———. *Reminiscenes of Old St. Mary's*. St. Marys, Georgia: St. Marys Publishing Co., 1913.

W.P.A. *Story of Washington, Wilkes*. Athens, Georgia: University Georgia Press, 1941.

Williams, Carolyn White and Rice, Thaddeus B., *History of Greene County, Georgia*. Macon, Georgia: J. W. Burke Co., 1961.

Chapter V

"As It Was." *Americus Times-Recorder*, September 4, 1894.

Battey, George McGruder, Jr. *A History of Rome and Floyd County*. Atlanta: The Webb and Vary Co., 1922.

Bonner, James C. *A Short History of Heard County*. 1958. (Typescript) Available, Department of Georgia Archives and History, Atlanta, Georgia.

———. *Georgia's Last Frontier, Carroll County*. Athens: University of Georgia Press, 1971.

Chalker, Fussell M. *Pioneer Days Along the Ocmulgee*. Carrollton, Georgia: By the Author, 1970.

Church, Mary L. *The Hills of Habersham*. Clarkesville, Georgia: By the Author, 1962.

Coulter, E. Merton. *Auraria: The Story of a Georgia Gold-Mining Town*. Athens: University of Georgia Press, 1956.

Cunyus, Lucy Josephine. *History of Bartow (Cass) County*. Cartersville, Georgia: "Tribune" Pub. Co., 1933.

Cuthbert Centennial Committee. *Cuthbert Centennial Booklet*. Cuthbert, Georgia, 1928.

Cuthbert Garden Clubs. "Cuthbert, Georgia, Tour of Homes." Cuthbert, Georgia, ca. 1974.

D.A.R. Hawkinsville Chapter (comp.). *History of Pulaski County, Ga. 1808-1935*. Atlanta: Walter W. Brown. No date.

DeKalb Chamber of Commerce. *Early DeKalb County History*. Decatur, Georgia, 1970.

Fayetteville Chamber of Commerce. *Fayetteville County Sesqui-Centennial Week June 26-July 3, 1971, Official Program*. Fayetteville, Georgia, 1970.

Flanigan, James C. *History of Gwinnett County, Georgia, 1818-1943*. Vol. 1. Hapeville, Georgia: Tupper & Co., 1959.

Hart, Bertha Sheppard. *History of Laurens County, Georgia, 1807-1941*. Dublin, Georgia, 1941.

Jones, Mary G. and Lilly Reynolds (eds.). *History of Coweta Co., Ga*. Atlanta: Stein Publishing Co., 1928.

Jordan, Robert H. *There Was a Land. History of Talbot County, Georgia*. Columbus, Georgia: Columbus Office Supply Co., 1971.

Lindsay, Mark C. "Ghost Town Close to Atlanta." *Atlanta Journal and Constitution Magazine*: XXIII (February 11, 1973), 28-34.

Marlin, Lloyd G., Rev. *History of Cherokee County*. Atlanta: Walter M. Brown, 1932.

Norwood, Thomas M. *The Story of Culloden: A Famous Village in Middle Georgia*. Savannah: Brain & Hutton, 1909.

Sams, Anita G. *Wayfarers in Walton. History of Walton County, Georgia, 1819-1967*. Monroe, Georgia: The General Charitable Foundation of Monroe, Georgia, Inc., 1967.

Sartain, James Alfred. *History of Walker County, Georgia*. Vol. 1. Dalton, Georgia: A. J. Showalter Co., 1932.

Smith, Clifford L. *History of Troup County*. Atlanta: Foote and Davies Co., 1953.

W.P.A. "Historical Sketch of Forsyth." Atlanta, no date. (Typescript). Available, Georgia Department of Archives and History, Atlanta, Georgia.

Ward, George Gordon. *Annals of Upper Georgia*. Carrollton, Georgia: Thomasson Printing Co., 1965.

Williams, Carolyn White. *History of Jones County, Georgia, From 1807-1907*. Macon: J. W. Burke, 1957.

Williford, William Bailey. *Americus Through the Years*. Atlanta: By the Author, 1960.

———. *The Glory of Covington*. Atlanta: Cherokee Publishing Company, 1973.

Zebulon Historical Society. *Sesquicentennial 1822-1972, Pike County, Georgia*. Zebulon, Georgia, 1970.

Yates, Bowling C. *Historic Highlights in Cobb County*. Marietta, Georgia: Cobb Exchange Bank, 1973.

Chapter VI

Besson, Leola S. *The 100 Years of the Old Governor's Mansion, 1838-1939*. Macon, Georgia: J. W. Burke and Co., 1938.

———. *Historical Stories of Milledgeville and Baldwin County*. Macon, Georgia: J. W. Burke and Co., 1943.

Butler, John C. *Historical Record of Macon and Central Georgia*. Macon, Georgia: J. W. Burke and Co., 1958. (Original printed in 1879.)

Cook, Anna Maria Green. *History of Baldwin County*. Anderson, South Carolina: Keys-Hecom Printing Co., 1925.

Corley, Florence Fleming. *Augusta, Confederate City*. Columbia, South Carolina: University of South Carolina Press, 1960.

Cumming, Mary Smith. *Two Centuries of Augusta*. Augusta: Privately printed, 1926.

Federal Writers Project. *Augusta*. Augusta, Georgia, 1938.

Ferguson, E. G. and V. Satterfield. *A Guidebook for Milledgeville*. Milledgeville: Library of the Georgia State College for Women, 1949.

Fleming, Berry. *Autobiography of a Colony: The First Half-Century of Augusta, Georgia*. Athens. Georgia: University of Georgia Press, 1957.

Hines, Nelle Womack. *A Treasure Album of Milledgeville and Baldwin County*. Milledgeville: J. W. Burke and Co., 1936.

Jones, Charles C. and Salem Dutcher. *Memorial History of Augusta, Georgia*. Syracuse, New York: S. Mason & Co., 1890.

The Macon Guide and Ocmulgee National Monument. Macon, Georgia: J. W. Burke and Co., 1939.

Martin, John C. *Columbus, Georgia*. Columbus, Georgia: Thomas Gilbert, 1874.

Mitchell, Louis. "City's Original Survey." *Columbus Sunday Ledger Enquirer*, December 16, 1945.

Myrick, Susan. "Macon." *Georgia Review*: II (Winter 1949), 413-423.

Phillips, Ulrich B. "Historical Notes on Milledgeville Georgia." *The Gulf States Historical Magazine*: 2 (November 1903), 161-171.

Salley, Harriet M. (ed.). *Correspondence of John Milledge, Governor of Georgia 1802-1806*. Columbia, South Carolina: State Commercial Printing Co., 1949.

Standard, Diffee W. *Columbus, Georgia in the Confederacy*. New York: Wm. Frederick Press, 1954.

Telfair, Nancy. *History of Columbus Georgia, 1828-1928*. Columbus, Georgia: The Historical Publishing Co., 1929.

Thomas, Edward Lloyd. *Field Book for Survey of Columbus and Commons*. Original in the State Archives, Atlanta, Georgia, 1828. (Handwritten.)

Thomas, Mrs. Z. V. *History of Jefferson County*. Macon, Georgia: J. W. Burke Co., 1927.

Woodall, W. C. *Hometown and Other Sketches*. Columbus, Georgia: Columbus Office Supply Co., 1935.

Worsley, Etta G. "Columbus." *Georgia Review*: I (Fall 1947), 166–177.

———. *Columbus on the Chattachoochee*. Columbus, Georgia: 1951.

Young, Ida, J. Gholson, and C. N. Hargrove. *History of Macon, Georgia*. Macon, Georgia: J. W. Burke and Co., 1950.

Index

—A—

Academy and college towns: 24; how founded, 27-29. *See also individual academy and college towns.*

"A Scotsman Visits Georgia": 92(n23)

Acts and Resolutions of the General Assembly: 156(n75, 77, 78, 79)

Albany, Ga.: 136

Alleys: in Greensborough, 168; in Sandersville, 74; in Monroe, 111; in Bainbridge, 137; in Newton, 138; problematic use of, 160, 181(n2); in Louisville, 166; in Milledgeville, 168; in Columbus, 180.

Americus, Ga.: 124; description of, 131-132

Anderson, James: 151, 152

Appalachicola River: 2, 137

Abercrombie, Charles: 75, 77

Altamaha River: 2, 33, 41, 42

Appalachian Mountains: 2

Appling, Ga : 66, 81; description of, 78-80

Appling, William: 78, 80

Asbury, Francis: 62, 93 (n17)

Athens: 27-29, 62, 78, 186

Atlanta: 29

Augusta: 2, 13, 24, 52, 55, 58, 59, 60, 67, 72, 82, 91(n1), 159, 160, 171, 181(n4, 6), 182(n8), 186; as example of "Augusta"-type plan, variation "A", 16, 101; laid out under Oglethorpe's direction, 34; and legislative acts of 1783 and 1784, 56; successful state-planned town, 157; description of, 160, 162-165, 53(n2, 8)

"Augusta" plan: genesis, 14; and town typology, 14-23; in headright towns, 60, 64, 65, 67, 69, 70, 71, 80, 82, 90; in lottery lands, 94, 95, 98, 101, 104, 105, 108, 111, 135, 141, 152-153

—B—

Bainbridge: 2, 24, 64, 134, 136; description of, 136-137

Baker County: 135, 136, 138

Baker, John: 67

Baker, Pearl, *The Story of Wrightsborough*: 54(n18)

Baldwin County: 95, 96, 169

Bartram, William: 49, 163-164

Battey, George M., *A History of Rome and Floyd County*: 156(n82)

Battle of Bloody Marsh: 41

Berrien, Ga.: 114, 116; description of, 122-123

Bibb County: 115, 174

Blairsville, Ga.: 142, 146-147

Blakely, Ga.: 132, 134, 136; description of, 139, 140, 141

Blue Ridge Mountains: 2

Bonner, James C., *Georgia's Last Frontier*: 130-131, 155(n61)

Broad River: 24
Broad River Valley: 27, 72
Brunswick: 13, 44, 53, 55, 88, 90, 186; planned under Crown rule, 46-48
Bryon, Ga.: 136
Bryan County: 45, 57
Buckingham, James Silk: 121, 126, 171
Bull, Colonel William: 35
Bulloch County: 16, 81, 83, 91(n12)
Burke County: 61
Butler, John C., *Historical Record of Macon and Central Georgia*: 175, 182(n24)
Butts County: 26, 115

—C—

Calhoun, John C.: 107
Campbell County: 129, 237
Campbellton, Ga.: 124, 129, 134
Cambridge, Mass.: 175
Camden, S.C.: 122
Camden County: 64, 95
Candler, Allen D.: *The Colonial Records of the State of Georgia*: 31(n1), 53(n12), 53(n16), 54(n18).
Canton, Ga.: 142, 145, 146, 147; description of, 147-148
Carnesville, Ga.: 65 78; sited at trading post, 67 description of, 70-71
Carroll County: 124, 125, 130
Carrollton, Ga.: 124, 125, 128, 186; description of, 130-131
Cass County: 145, 148
Cassville, Ga.: 142; became ghost town, 148
Cates, Margaret Davis, *Our Todays and Yesterdays*: 54(n17)

Chalker, Fussell M., *Pioneer Days Along the Ocmulgee*: 155(n50)
Charleston, S.C.: 34, 35
Chatham County: 37, 39
Chattahoochee River: and Georgia geography, 1, 2; and land acquisitions, 6; 1826 cession, 124, 125, 131; and Flint River, 136-137; Cherokee cession, 142; reliable for shipping, 157; and Columbus, 177, 180
Cherokee County: 145, 156(n81)
Cherokee Indians: 33, 67; land acquired from, 4, 6; changing culture of, 143; Cherokee cession, 142-153. See also treaties.
Chestatee River: 142
Clarke County: 28, 78
Clarkesville, Ga.: 105, 108; and "Sparta" plan, 16, 108; description of, 111, 112
Clayton, Augustin Smith, *A Compilation of the Laws of the State of Georgia, 1800-1810*: 92(n27), 153(n2-6, 8-9), 132(n9, 15, 17)
Clayton, Ga.: 105, 108; and "Sparta" plan, 108; description of, 111-113
Clinton, Ga.: 94; description of, 99-101
Coastal Plain: and geography, 1, 2; and land acquisition, 4.
Cobb County: 145, 152
Collier, Benjamin: 140
Colonial towns: 13, 35-36, 47, 99, 116; wide streets and open squares, 36; prosperity and siting, 51 large size, 59, 90; as a state legacy, 55, 184-185; and state towns, 89-90 Marion, 104; Augusta, 162 See also Brunswick, Darien, Ebenezer, Hard-

INDEX 211

wick, Savannah, Sunbury and Wrightsborough.
Columbia County: 49, 78
Columbus, Ga.: 2, 13, 24, 27, 29, 120, 124, 131, 149, 158, 159, 160, 164, 171-172, 174, 183 (n29, 30, 33) 184-185, 186; and stage route, 121, 126; successful state-planned town, 157; description of, 177-181
Correspondence of John Milledge, Governor of Georgia 1800-1806: 182(n16)
Coulter, E. Merton: 24; *Old Petersburg and the Broad River Valley of Georgia*, 32(n5), 91(n1); *Georgia, A Short History*, 53(n1, 13), 154(n29) 156(n66)
County organization: 13, 29; in headright period, 56-57, 70-71, 73, 92(n24); in lottery lands, 95-97, 106-108, 115-116, 118, 125-126, 135-136, 266-269. *See also individual counties.*
Courthouse towns: 1, 185; and state, 11-13, 29; and town typology, 13-22, 24; and land allotments, 57, 58, 60, 89-90, 91-92 (n12), 96-98, 108, 109-111, 155-116, 146, 154(n33), 158; procedure for town founding, 56-57, 66. compared with colonial towns, 90-91; and incorporation, 116-117; in lottery lands, 152-153. *See also individual courthouse towns.*
Covington, Ga.: 29. 113; description of, 118
Coweta County: 125, 155(n57)
Coweta Falls, Ga.: 125
Crawford County: 115
Crawfordville, Ga.: *Frontispiece*, 65, 71, 72; as "Washington"-type plans, variation "A", 16; description of, 74-75
Creek Indians: 67, 87, 144; land acquisitions summary, 4-6; burned Greensborough, 62; and Wilkinson and Baldwin counties, 95; and Pulaski County, 101; 1821 cession, 114; 1826 cession, 124, 125. *See also treaties.*
Culloden, Ga.: 29, 32(n7)
Cumberland Island: 64
Cumberland Mountains: 2
Cumming, Ga.: 142, 143, 145; description of, 147
Cuthbert, Ga.: 124, 125, 127, 131, 140; as "Sparta"-type plan, 22-23; description of, 132-133

—D—

Dahlonega, Ga.: 142, 149, 146; as "Sparta"-type plan, 16; description of, 147
Dallas, Ga.: 148
Danielsville, Ga.: 66, 75, 186; description of, 78
Darien, Ga.: 33, 48, 51, 52, 55, 90; laid out under Oglethorpe's direction, 34, 41; as protection against Spanish, 34, 35, 42; follows Savannah plan, 39; description of, 41-53
Dawson, William C., *A Compilation of the Laws of the State of Georgia 1819-1829*: 32(n5), 154(n20-21, 30-31, 34-37), 155(n38-41, 44, 46, 52, 54-56), 156(n67-70, 72), 132(n23, 28)
DeBrahm, J. G. William: 36, 53(n5)
Decatur County: 135, 137
Decatur, Ga.: 113; description of, 118, 119

DeKalb County: 115, 118, 119, 155(n45)
DeVorsey, Louis, *DeBrahm's Report of the General Survey in the Southern Districts of North America*: 53(n5)
Diamond, James: 118, 119
Dooley County: 115
Drayton, Ga.: 123. *See also Berrien, Georgia.*
Dublin, Ga.: 94; as "Sparta"-type plan, 20–22; site of, 24; library, 76; and Irish, 95; and Laurens County, 97 description of, 53 (n8) 101, 102

—E—

Early County: 106, 135, 139, 140
Easley's Cowpen, Ga.: 111
Eatonton, Ga.: 94, 108, 131; successful Piedmont town, 98; description of, 99
Ebenezer, Ga.: 13, 33, 48, 55; laid out under Oglethorpe's direction, 34, 41; poor location, 35; description of, 39–41; courthouse town, 84
Effingham County: 40, 84, 85
Effingham, Ga.: 56
Elbert County: 25, 57, 67, 68, 91 (n12), 92(n25)
Elberton, Ga.: 65, 186; site, 24, 67; description of, 67–68
Ellijay, Ga.: 142, 146; description of, 147–148
Emanuel County: 82
Emory Univeristy, first located in Oxford: 29
Etowah River: 3 149
Ettinger, Ames Aschback, *James Edward Oglethorpe, Imperial Idealist*: 53(n3)

Everitt, Josiah: 83, 93(n34)

—F—

Fall Line: 1–2, 51, 97, 115, 125, 157, 172
Fayette County: 115
Fayetteville, Ga.: 113, 186; description of, 118
Findley, James: 64, 65
Flanigan, James C., *History of Gwinnett County, Ga.*: 109, 154 (n22)
Flint River: 136, 137, 139; geography, 2, 3; Treaty of Indian Springs, 6; 1821 treaty, 114, 172; Berrien, 122; 1826 cession, 124, 125, 177; and Newton, 139
Floyd County: 14, 145, 146, 149, 156(n82)
Forsyth County: 145, 155(n49)
Forsyth, Ga.: 114; description of, 120–121
Fort Hawkins (East Macon): 172, 173
Fort Hughes: 137
Franklin College: *See University of Georgia.*
Franklin County: 5, 70, 73, 151
Franklin, Ga.: 124; description of, 131
Frederica, Ga.: 34, 53(n2)

—G—

Gainesville, Ga.: 43(n40) 127, 139, 147; as "Washington"-type plan, 16, 105, 108; description of, 109–111; land speculation, 109
Galphin Oldtown, Ga.: 167
Gardner, Sterling: 70
Georgia Historical Collections: 53 (n6), 53(n13), 54(n19), 91(n1), 92(n23)

INDEX

Georgia Historical Commission: 78
Georgia State Capitals: Augusta, Louisville, Milledgeville, 160–171. *See also individual towns.*
Georgia Trustees: 7, 10(n1). 31, 33, 34, 41, 44 45, 50, 51, 184–185; benevolent social policy, 11; utopian land use and land grant system, 36–38, 52(n1)
Geography: as a factor in Georgia town planning, 1–4; lottery lands, 95; 1817-1818, 1819 cession, 107–108; 1821 cession, 114; 1826 cession, 125, 131; 1814 cession, 135; Cherokee cession, 142–143; state-planned towns, 157–158. *See also descriptions of siting of individual towns.*
Gilmer County: 145, 153
Glover, John Hayward: 150
Glynn County: 48, 88, 95
Gold: discovered in North Georgia, 143–146
Greek Revival buildings: Sandersville, 74, Cuthbert, 133; Macon, 174
Greene County: 5, 56, 63
Greensborough, Ga.: 27, 58, 59, 76, 91(n11), 168; burned in Indian raid, 5; description of, 62–64
Greenville, Ga.: 124; description of, 128–129
Greer, William: 63
Gresham, Lemuel: 120, 121
Grey, Edmond: 48
Guillion, Clement: 148
Gwinnett County: 107, 154(n22)

—H—

Habersham County: 106, 107, 112, 154(n28)
Habersham, James: 47
Hall, Basil, *Travels in the United States*: 172, 178, 182(n22)
Hall, Basil, Mrs.: 178
Hall County: 106, 107, 110
Hamilton, Ga.: 124, 126
Hancock County: 21, 75, 77, 92 (n31)
Hartford, Ga.: 96; original site of Pulaski County, 101
Hardwick, Ga.: 13, 47, 51, 55; description of, 44–46
Hart, Bertha S., *History of Laurens County, Georgia*: 153(n12)
Hawkinsville, Ga.: 94; description of, 101, 104
Headright system: 7–10, 89–90, 96
Heath, Milton S., *Constructive Liberalism*, 10(n2)
Henderson, Archibald, *Washington's Southern Tour*. 53(n9), 92(n18)
Henry County: 115
"Historic Sparta and Hancock County": 92(n31)
Hitz, Alex M.: 54(n18)
Houston County: 14, 115, 117, 121, 122
Hollingsworth, Clyde, *A History of the Early Years of Screven County*: 93(n39)
Horry, Ga.: 124, 134, 155(n64)

—I—

Indian cessions: 5; and land lotteries, 9. *See Creek cessions and Cherokee cessions.*
Indian Springs: 26–27, 115
Indians and land acquisitions: 4–6. *See also Creek Indians and Cherokee Indians.*

Indianapolis, Ind.: 130
Industrial development: first decades after Independence, 24; North Georgia, 143; Rome, 149; Marietta, 151; state-planned towns, 157-158; Milledgeville, 171; Macon, 177; Columbus, 180-181
Irwin County: 106, 135, 140
Irwinton, Ga.: 94, 97; description of, 101
Irwinville, Ga.: 135, 136; description of, 141, 156(n74)

—J—

Jackson, Ga.: 113, 186; "Washington"-type plan, 120, 121
Jackson, Andrew: 144
Jackson, Governor James: 8
Jacksonborough, Ga.: 80; description of, 88-89
Jacksonville, Ga.: 95, 96, 141; sited on Ocmulgee River, 97; description of, 104-105
James River, Va.: 251
Jasper County: 20
Jefferson County: 167, 182(n13)
Jefferson, Ga.: 66, 75, 186; description of, 76, 78
Johnson, Thomas: 100
Jones, Charles C.: 54(n19)
Jones, Charles C and Dutcher, S., *Memorial History of Augusta, Georgia*: 181(n4) 182(n8)
Jones County: 96, 153(n11)
Journal and Letters of Francis Asbury, The: 92(n17)

—K—

Kennedy, R.: 68
Knight, Lucian Lamar, *Georgia's Landmarks, Memories and Legends*: 155(n48)
Knoxville, Ga.: 114; on route from Milledgeville to Columbus, 120; description of, 121

—L—

LaGrange, Ga.: 123, 126, 139; description of, 127-128
Lafayette, Ga.: 142, 146; as "Sparta"-type plan, 29; description of, 151-152
Lafayette, General: 172, 182(n19, 21)
Lamar, Lucius Q. C., *A Compilation of the Laws of the State of Georgia, 1810-1819*: 93(n32, 35) 153(n13), 154(n15, 17-19)
Land reserves: and the government, 7-10, 53(n7) 55-56, 114-115, 125-126, 158-159; and town founding, 11-13, 96; and the British, 10, 11-12, 35-36, 60. *See also individual courthouse and state-planned towns.*
Land speculation: 24, 31, 185-186; summary of, 7-8; beginnings, 32(n4), 46; headright period, 75, 90-91; lottery lands, 109-110; Campbell County, 129, 154(n25); Milledgeville, 170
Lane, Mills, *The Rambler in Georgia*: 53(n10), 182(n10, 14, 20)
Laurens County: 22, 96, 97, 102, 153(n12)
Lawrenceville, Ga.: 105; "Washington" plan, 108; description of, 108-109
Lee County: 125, 134
Leesburg, Ga.: 134
Legislative acts: 1803 land act, 8; and town planning, 11-14; Indian Springs, 27; in headright

INDEX 215

period, 56-57, 58-60, 62, 65, 70, 72, 78, 80, 82, 84, 88-89, 91 (n12), 92(n20); during lottery period, 96-98, 106-108, 114-117, 118, 125-126, 135-136, 144-146; and state-planned towns, 158-163, 165, 167-168, 170-171, 173, 177-178; summary of town planning acts, 185-186. *See also Compilations and Acts.*

Levasseur, A , *Lafayette in America in 1824 and 1825*: 182(n19, 21)

Lewis, Ulysses: 130

Lexington, Ga.: 65, 71; description of, 72-73; and Meson Academy, 72

Liberty County: 42, 84, 86

Lincoln County: 79

Lincolnton, Ga.: 66, 75, 79, 186; description of, 76

Lindsey, Mark C : 155(n60)

Little River: 44

Livingston, Ga.: 146, 149

Lottery system: 9-10, 95-98, 144-145

Louisville, Ga.: 13, 66, 157, 158, 159, 160, 171, 182(n12); problems, 157-158, 167, 168; and First State house, 166; description of, 165-167

Lumpkin County: 145, 147

Lumpkin, Ga : 124; description of, 131

Lumpkin, John: 72

—M—

MacIntosh, George: 47, 48

Macon, Ga.: 2, 13, 24, 27, 100, 114, 120, 122, 149, 157, 158, 159, 160, 171, 177, 180, 184, 186; and stage route, 121, 126; reduced importance of square, 159; description of, 172-177

Maddock, Joseph: 48, 49, 50

Madison, Ga.: 94, 97, 108; successful Piedmont town, 98; description of, 99-100

Marbury, Henry and Crawford, William H., *Digest of the Laws of the State of Georgia, From 1755-1800*: 91(n2-3, 5-10), 92 (n14, 16, 22, 26), 93(n36-38) 181(n3, 6)

Marion County: 134

Marion, Ga.: 95; as "Savannah"-type plan, 18; description of, 103, 104

Marietta, Ga.: 142, 146; as "Savannah"-type plan, 18; description of, 150-151, 152

Marlin, Lloyd G., *History of Cherokee County*, 156(n81)

Martineau, Harriet, *Society in America*: 178, 183(n32)

Marshall's Ferry, Ga.: 125

Martyn, Benjamin: 53(n6)

McAllister, Matthew: 84, 86

McDonough, Ga.: 113, 116; as 'Washington"-type plan, 118

McDuffie County: 49

McIlwaine, Paul, *Dead Town of Sunbury*: 54(n19)

McIntosh County: 57

McIntosh, John H., *Official History of Elbert County*: 92(n25)

McIntosh Reserve: 115

McIntosh's Ferry, Ga.: 125

Medway River: 50

Melish, John: 167

Mercer, Hermon: Frontispiece, 75, 90

Mercer Institute: 27

Mercer, Jesse: 27

Meriwether County: 129
Meson Academy: 72
Meson, Francis: 72
Mezzle, Jesse: 82
Milledge, Governor John: 27, 168, 182(n16)
Milledgeville, Ga.: 2, 13, 94, 99, 120, 121, 157, 158, 159, 184; sited, 95, 97; description of, 167-172; compared with Macon, 174; exception in town planning, 185
Mitchell, Daniel R.: 149
Mitchell, Margaret: 118
Monroe County: 115, 120
Monroe, Ga.: 64, 105, 108; description of, 111
Montgomery, Robert: 33
Montgomery County: 57, 86, 87
Monticello, Ga.: 94, 108; as "Washington"-type plan, 20-21; successful Piedmont town, 98; description of, 99
Moore, Francis: 53(n6)
Morgan County: 96, 97, 100
Mount Vernon, Ga.: 80; description of, 86-87
Murray County: 145, 148
Muscogee County: 125, 178, 179

—N—

New Orleans: 136
Newnan, Ga.: 123; description of, 126
Newton, Ga.: 64, 134, 136; description of, 138-139
Newton County: 30, 115
North Newport, Ga.: 84. *See Riceborough.*
Norwood, Thomas M., *The Story of Culloden*: 32(n7)

—O—

Ocmulgee River: 2-3, 6, 42, 95, 141, 155(n50), 157; Jacksonville and Hartford located on, 96; siting for Jacksonville, 97, 104; Hartford, 101; 1821 Treaty, 114, 115; towns west of, 117; and Macon, 172, 173
Oconee River: 2-3; 42, 55, 97, 157, 172; and site for Dublin, 24, 95; site of Milledgeville, 170, 171
Ogeechee River: 2-3, 4, 44-45, 55, 167; unreliable for transport, 157; and Louisville, 167
Oglethorpe County: 57, 72, 73, 92 (n30)
Oglethorpe, General James: founding of the Georgia colony, 34-36, 37, 40, 42, 51, 53(n1, 3), 185; built fort which was to become Augusta, 160
Oostanaula River: 3, 149
Orr, Dorothy, *A History of Education in Georgia*: 153(n10)
Oxford, Ga.: 29

—P—

Parishes: 12; changed to counties, 55
Paulding County: 145, 148-149
Paulding Courthouse, Ga.: 142
Penfield, Ga. and Mercer College: 27, 29
Penn, William: 53(n4)
Perry, Ga.: 114; an exception in Georgia court town plans, 14; incorporation, 117; description of, 121-122
Petersburg, Ga.: 24-25
Philadelphia, Pa.: 38, 53(n4)
Phillips, Dr. George: 73

INDEX 217

Piedmont: 11, 20, 24, 44, 55, 58, 72, 78, 94. 95, 93–101, 105, 108, 113, 114, 118, 119, 121, 123, 124, 125, 126, 127, 129, 131, 133, 136, 143, 147, 150, 152, 160; boundaries, 1, 2; and land acquisitions, 6; and "Washington" plan, 58, 152
Pike County: 115, 118, 155(n47)
Pine Barren-Wire Grass: 52, 55, 81, 84, 95, 106, 111, 114, 125, 135; boundaries, 1; and land acquisition, 6; Jacksonville, 104
Pine Mountains: 120, 121
Power, Tyrone, *Impressions of America*: 126, 183(n31)
Powers, Lara: 85
Priber, Christian: 33
Price, Edward: 31(n2)
Prince, Oliver H., *A Digest of the Laws of the State of Georgia Enacted Previous to 1820*: 155 (n53)
Public Towns, 13, 31(n1)
Pulaski County: 96, 101
Purry, Jean Pierre: 33
Putnam County: 96

—R—

Rabun County: 106, 107
Raleigh, N C.: 122
Randolph County: 23, 96, 133
Red Hills: 2, 94, 95, 114, 152; towns in 1802-1805 cession, 101-108; in the 1821 cession, 114, 121-123; in the 1826 cession, 125, 152
Reed, Bailey: 128
Reed, Stephen: 110
Reps, John W., *The Making of Urban America*: 155(n62)

Resort towns: 24-27, 182(n25)
Reynolds, John, and the founding of Hardwick: 45-46
Riceborough, Ga.: 80, 87; description of, 84, 86
Richmond Academy: 72, 181(n7)
Richmond County: 49, 164
Ried, Baily: 128
Rivers: 2-3. *See also individual Georgia rivers.*
Roberta, Ga.: 121
Rome, Ga.: 3, 14, 24, 142, 146, 153, 156(n82); as exception in town planning, 14; description of, 53(n8), 149-150
Rose, Simri: 175

—S—

St. Marys, Ga.: 4, 58, 59, 92(n21); description of, 64-65
St. Marys River: 2, 44
Sams, Anita B., *Wayfarers in Walton*: 154(n27)
Sand Bar, Ga.: 97
Sand Hills: 2
Sandersville, Ga.: 64, 65, 71, 138-139; description of, 73-74
Savannah, Ga.: 2, 12, 13, 31, 40, 41, 42, 45, 46, 47, 50, 51, 52 (n1), 55, 59, 65, 81, 82, 90, 157, 158, 160, 163, 170, 184, 186; laid out under Oglethorpe, 33-39; and 1784 act, 56
"Savannah" plan: genesis, 14; and town typology, 14-23; in colonial towns, 36, 38, 46, 51; in headright towns, 78, 162; in lottery lands, 95, 98, 104, 124, 132, 142, 150, 152-153; in state-planned towns, 184
Savannah River: 1, 2, 24, 33, 34,

44, 45, 55 reliable for shipping, 157; Augusta, 160, 164
Schreiter, H. A.: 155(n42)
Screven County: 88, 91(n12), 93 (n39)
Sea Island, Ga : 136
Sears, Joan N.: 154(n28)
Settlers: 1, 2, 4-6; and Georgia Trustees, 7; and town founding, 12; and town typology, 14; Salzburgers 39-41; Darien, 41; Wrightsborough Quakers, 48-51; Sunbury Puritans, 48, 50-51; 1790-1800, 55; St. Marys, 64; Broad River Valley, 72; Columbia County, 80; in lottery lands, 91 (n1), 95, 98; Eatonton, 99; Irwinton, 101; Twiggs County, 104; 1817-1818, 1819 cession, 107-108; 1821 cession, 118, 122 1826 cession, 125; 1814 cession, southern section of 1818 cession, 136; Newton, 138-139; Cherokee cession, 143; Marietta, 150; Lafayette, 151; and courthouse town plans, 185
Sherwood, Adiel, *A Gazeteer of the State of Georgia*: 117, 155(n43), 156(n73), 169
Sibbald, George: 81
Smith, Clifford L., *History of Troup County*: 155(n58-59)
Smith, F. C., *History of Oglethorpe County, Georgia*, 92(n30)
Smith, George G., *Story of Georgia and the Georgia People*: 148, 155(n51), 156(n71)
Soque River: 111
Sparta, Ga.: 66, 75, 92(n31); as example of "Sparta"-type plan, variation "A", 16, 21; description of, 75-76, 77

Sparta, Ohio: 130
"Sparta" plan: genesis, 14; and town typology, 14-23; in headright towns, 66, 70, 71, 75, 76, 78, 90; in lottery lands, 94, 98, 101, 104, 105, 108, 111, 113, 114, 118, 121, 124, 128, 134, 142, 146, 147, 151, 152-153
Spring Place, Ga.: 142, 146, 148
Springfield, Ga.: 80; description of, 82, 84
Stage routes and prosperity: 100
Starkville, Ga.: 124, 134, 155(n64)
State land surveys: before 1803, 7; 1803 land act, 8-9; 1802 cession, 95; 1818 cession, 106; 1821 cession, 114-115; 1826 cession, 124-125; Cherokee land, 144-145. *See also individual state-planned towns.*
State-planned towns: 13, 153(n7), 157-181 (Chapter VI); *See also individual towns.*
Statesborough 1866-1966, A Century of Progress: 93(n33)
Statesborough, Ga.: 80, 93 (n33-34); as example of "Augusta" plan, variation "C", 16; description of, 81-82, 83
Stephens, Alexander H.: 135
Story of Washington Wilkes: 92 (n15)
Strobel, P. A.: 40; *The Salzburgers and Their Decendents*, 53(n11)
Stuart, James (surveyor): Frontispiece
Stuart, James (traveler): 121
Sumter County: 132
Sunbury, Ga.: 13, 44, 54(n19), 55, 56, 84; description of, 48-51
Surveyors and state policy: headright period, 7, 8-10, 92(n13);

INDEX

regulations for, 9-10, 95, 125
Swainsborough, Ga.: 80; description of, 82, 83
Sylvania, Ga : 89

—T—

Talbot County: 125, 127
Talbotton, Ga : 123; description of, 126-127
Taliaferro County: *Frontispiece*, 74
Telfair County: 96, 97
Telfair, Nancy, *History of Columbus Georgia*, 183(n29)
Terrell, Timothy IV: 109, 110
Thackeray, William Makepeace: 38, 163
Thomas County: 135
Thomas, Edward Lloyd: town planner, 29, 32(n6); surveyor of Columbus, 179-180; *Field Book of Columbus Survey* 183(n33)
Thomas, Z. V., *History of Jefferson County*: 182(n13)
Thomaston, Ga : 114, 121; "Washington"-type plan, 120
Thomasville, Ga.: 134, 136; description of, 139-140
Tidewater: 1, 12, 84
Towers, William: 109
Town planning: for prototypes, 14-23; changes in, 14, 38, 89-90, 83(n40); influence of state, 29-31; and state-planned towns, 158-160; and county seats, 184-185. *See also individual towns.*
Travels of William Bartram, The: 182(n11)
Treaties: and land acquisitions, 4-6; under crown, 4, 44; 1763 treaty, 48, 49, 61; "New Purchase," 49, 55, 59, 68. 73, 79, 83; 1790 Treaty, 70, 92(n24); Fort Jackson Treaty, 105, 106, 135; 1817 Cherokee Agency, 1817 Creek Agency, 106; 1819 Treaty, 107; 1821 Treaty of Indian Springs, 114, 124; Treaty of 1825, 1826, 124, 177
Troup County: 125, 126, 128, 155 (n58, 59)
Turtle River: 47
Twiggs County: 18, 96, 103, 104

—U—

Union County: 145
University of Georgia (Franklin College): 27, 62
Upson County: 115
Utopian communities: 33-34, 44

—V—

Van Wert, Ga.: 149
Vernon, Ga.: 126
Vienna, Ga.: 123
Vocelle, James T.: 64; *Reminiscences of Old St. Marys*, 92(n21)

—W—

Walker County: 151
Walker, Joel: 121, 122
Walton County: 106, 107, 111, 154 (n27)
Ward, George G., *Annals of Upper Georgia*, 156(n80)
Warren County: 16, 57, 69, 92 (n12)
Warrenton, Ga.: 65, 67, 81; as an example of "Augusta"-type plan, variation "D", 16; description of, 68-70
Warthen, Ga.: 73
Washington County: 5, 73, 74
Washington, George: 38, 62, 92(n18)

Washington, Ga.: 59, 91(n) 92(n15), 107, 186; as an example of "Washington"-type plan, variation "A" 14–16; legislative act of 1783 and 1784, 56; description of, 58–60

"Washington" plan: genesis, 14; and town typology, 14–23; in headright towns, 65, 67, 70, 71, 72, 75, 78, 80, 84, 86, 90; in lottery lands, 94, 98, 99, 101, 104, 105, 108, 109, 113, 114, 118, 120, 123, 124, 125, 126, 129, 131, 134, 135, 137, 138, 139, 141, 142, 146, 152–153; in state-planned towns, 158

Watkins, Robert and Watkins, George, *A Digest of the Laws of the State of Georgia from Its Establishment to 1798*: 92(n19)

Watkinsville, Ga : 66, 78

Watts, John and McCord, Daniel: 74

Wayne County: 95

Waynesborough, Ga.: 58, 59, 91 (n11); as example of "Augusta"-type plan, variation "B", 16; 1783 and 1784 acts, 56; description of, 60–62

Webb, James: 172

Weed, Jacob: 64

Whatley, James: 118

White, George, *Historical Collections of Georgia*: 182(n26–27)

Wilkes County: 4, 14, 59, 72, 92 (n15)

Wilkinson County: 95, 96

Williams, Carolyn White, *History of Jones County, Georgia From 1807-1941*: 100, 153(n11)

Williams, Duke: 109

Williams, Farr (surveyor, along with Will Limbert and Roswell King):88

Williamsburg, Ga.: 57, 80, 91(n12); description of, 87–88

Worsley, Etta B., *Columbus on the Chattahoochee*: 183(n30)

Wright, Governor James: 44, 46, 49, 55

Wrightsborough, Ga.: 44, 51, 54(n18); description of, 48–50

—Y—

Yates, B.C., *Historic Highlights in Cobb County*: 156(n83)

Younger, Henry: 45

—Z—

Zebulon, Ga.: 113, 118, 186

The Author

Joan Niles Sears is a landscape architect in Ithaca, New York who has a wide and varied background in her profession and in the area of art history.

She holds the B.A. degree in the history of art from the University of Michigan (1939), the M.A. in the same discipline from Harvard University (1948), a bachelor's degree in landscape architecture from the University of Georgia (1963), and the Ph.D. in American Studies from Emory University (1977). She has studied also at Cornell University and the University of Dijon (France).

Early in her career Ms. Sears was a cataloguer at Parke-Bernet Galleries in New York and a lecturer at the Boston Museum of Fine Arts and at the Montreal Museum of Art. Later she was an assistant professor of art history at Sir George Williams College and at Georgia State University and a lecturer on landscape architecture at Emory and Cornell universities. Since 1965 she has been a registered landscape architect, practicing first in Atlanta and since 1973 in Ithaca.

Ms. Sears has traveled widely throughout the world. She holds membership in numerous professional and historical organizations and has written articles for architectural and historical publications. *The First One Hundred Years of Town Planning In Georgia*, her first book, evolved from her doctoral dissertation on that subject at Emory University.

www.ingramcontent.com/pod-product-compliance
Lightning Source LLC
Chambersburg PA
CBHW032040150426
43194CB00006B/367